ENTREPRENEURIAL SELVES

NEXT WAVE

New Directions in Women's Studies

A SERIES EDITED BY
Inderpal Grewal, Caren Kaplan,
and Robyn Wiegman

CARLA FREEMAN

ENTREPRENEURIAL SELVES

NEOLIBERAL RESPECTABILITY AND THE MAKING OF A CARIBBEAN MIDDLE CLASS

Duke University Press | Durham and London | 2014

© 2014 Duke University Press
All rights reserved
Printed in the United States of America on acid-free paper ∞
Designed by Heather Hensley
Typeset in Scala by Graphic Composition, Inc., Bogart, Georgia

Library of Congress Cataloging-in-Publication Data
Freeman, Carla.
Entrepreneurial selves : neoliberal respectability and the mak-
ing of a Caribbean middle class / Carla Freeman.
pages cm—(Next wave : new directions in women's studies)
Includes bibliographical references and index.
ISBN 978-0-8223-5792-6 (cloth : alk. paper)
ISBN 978-0-8223-5803-9 (pbk : alk. paper)
1. Middle class—Barbados. 2. Entrepreneurship—Barbados.
3. Businesspeople—Barbados. 4. Neoliberalism—Barbados.
I. Title. II. Series: Next wave.
HT690.B35F74 2014
305.5'50972981—dc23
2014007352

ISBN 978-0-8223-7600-2 (e-book)

Cover art: Tara Keens-Douglas, *Sublimation Costume*, paper;
Photography: Tyler Walker

Duke University Press gratefully acknowledges the support
of Emory College of Arts and Sciences, and Laney Graduate
School, which provided funds toward the publication of this
book.

for Rob, Isabel, and Alice

CONTENTS

ACKNOWLEDGMENTS

Ethnographic research and writing are often long and lonely processes. When we are lucky these pursuits can also foster intimate and collaborative engagements. I have been fortunate to experience both the creative intensity of isolated concentration and the benefit of diverse interlocutors with whom I have shared and debated the observations and ideas that fill these pages: colleagues, friends, family, and my entrepreneurial "informants" themselves.

The seeds of this project were planted in 1999 when Kate Browne invited me to study entrepreneurship through a comparative lens. We gathered parallel data about Barbados, Martinique, and Puerto Rico, with the hopes of understanding how the growing rise of entrepreneurship would unfold differently given the distinct colonial histories of these three Caribbean islands. Generous grants from the National Science Foundation supported this ambitious fieldwork. Although distance and life events intervened and our original plan for a three island comparison was not realized, I am indebted to Kate for her vision, scholarship, and friendship. Diane Cummins assisted in the identification of new Barbadian entrepreneurs, and Eudine Barriteau and Christine Barrow at the University of the West Indies, Cave Hill campus, have provided intellectual camaraderie for more than twenty years. Thanks to Serena Jones, Kim Goddard, Vicki Goddard, Lulu Martin, and Arthur and Siddy Streetly, who added to my roster of entrepreneurs.

At Emory University, I have received extraordinary support for this project in every possible form. The Institute of Comparative and International

Studies provided resources for transcription, the Alfred P. Sloan Foundation's Center for Myth and Ritual in American Life (MARIAL) provided not only research support for several summers of ongoing fieldwork but also a weekly venue in which I presented pieces of this project over many years. I thank Bradd Shore, Marshall Duke, and Robyn Fivush for a stimulating interdisciplinary base from which to study middle-classness and the confounding 'balance' of work/life. Many thanks to Tina Brownley and the FCHI staff for a nourishing year as a senior fellow at the Fox Center for Humanistic Inquiry (FCHI), where I wrote the kernel of what would eventually become this book. Many other colleagues, students and friends at Emory have provided input and commentary along the way. Thank you Allison Adams, Liz Bounds, Irene Browne, Steve Everett, Hemangini Gupta, Lynne Huffer, Prakiti KC, Bruce Knauft, David Nugent, Michael Peletz, Holloway Sparks, Elizabeth Wilson, Rachel Weitzenkorn, and Shunyuan Zhang for reading and engaging pieces of this work. Sydney Silverstein provided superb copyediting and indexing support at lightning speed. A special thank you to Lynne Huffer for sharing Foucault's words with which I begin and end. Berky Abreu's tremendous spirit and curiosity about all things Caribbean sustained me through the many years of researching and writing of this book.

I have had the very good fortune to present segments of this work in many academic venues over the years and to benefit from critiques and commentary of generous colleagues. I thank the faculty and students at Aalborg University; the College of William and Mary; the University of California, Los Angeles; the University of Colorado, Boulder; Ewha Woman's University; the University of Florida; Georgia State University; Goethe University; the University of Toronto; the Norwegian University of Science and Technology (NTNU); the University of Virginia; Washington University, St. Louis; and my own institution, Emory University. Particular thanks to the School for Advanced Research in Santa Fe and especially to Rachel Heiman and Mark Liechty, with whom I edited the volume *Global Middle Classes*, a collaboration that enhanced my own thinking about the meanings of middle class in this era of neoliberalism. My sincere gratitude to Anne Allison, Yari Bonilla, Florence Babb, Joanna Davidson, Sherri Grasmuck, Akhil Gupta, Jennifer Hirsch, Carla Jones, Cindi Katz, Helma Lutz, Purnima Mankekar, Kiran Mirchandani, Viranjini Munasinghe, Evelyn O'Callaghan, Aihwa Ong, Jennifer Patico, and Peggy Tally. Jean and Roger Goddard provided a comfortable base from which much of this fieldwork was conducted. My parents, Elaine and Leo Freeman, siblings, Jan, Nancy and Rick, and my cousin Mindy Fortin have supported and encouraged me every step of the way. Priscilla Hall made it possible for me to juggle my research and two young children in the field and enjoy the confusion.

I thank the following editors and several anonymous reviewers for helping me shape preliminary pieces of this work in other venues. An early effort to analyze "The 'Reputation' of Neoliberalism" appeared in *American Ethnologist* 34, no. 2: 252–67; a discussion of entrepreneurial marriage and middle middle-classness that has become chapter 2 appeared as "Neoliberal Respectability: Entrepreneurial Marriage, Affective Labor, and a New Caribbean Middle Class," in *The Global Middle Classes: Ethnographic Particularities, Theoretical Convergences*, edited by Rachel Heiman, Carla Freeman, and Mark Liechty (SAR Press, 2012); and a brief introduction to the embodied expressions of entrepreneurial flexibility appeared in the chapter "Embodying and Affecting Neoliberalism" in *A Companion to the Anthropology of Bodies and /Embodiments*, edited by Frances E. Mascia-Lees (Wiley Blackwell, 2011).

At Duke University Press, I have been lucky to work with an extraordinary editor, Ken Wissoker. With each of my projects Ken seemed to grasp, even before I did, what was most powerful and far-reaching about the story I was trying to tell and patiently supported its gestation. I am grateful to Jade Brooks for her steady editorial hand and cheerful, prompt engagement at every stage; thanks to Katie Courtland, Susan Albury, and Heather Hensley who have ushered the manuscript through to its final form. Two anonymous reviewers provided detailed, eloquent, and generous readings. Their insightful commentary helped me shape the final manuscript and their enthusiasm emboldened my voice. I am delighted to feature the work of Tara Keens Douglas on the book's cover, and am grateful for Heather Hensley's bold design.

Ethnography depends upon the patience and generosity of the many people whose testimonies and lives come to fill its pages. This is a bumpy process involving persistence, pestering, false starts, unexpected encounters and exchanges. Over ten years I interviewed, casually visited, and no doubt imposed upon many of the people who gave their time to me. Their willingness to endure my probing queries, and the colorful, funny, sad, and richly intimate stories they recounted, allowed me to rethink and redirect the account of entrepreneurialism as it ultimately unfolded. The dialogic quality of this research experience reflected the keen interest among many of my "informants" in the nuances of neoliberalism, middle classness, and the project of "self-making." I hope I have done justice to their experiences and reflections.

In the long pursuit of ethnography, and in life more generally, we are lucky to find people with whom we can share both the quotidian and the abstract, the political, the personal, and their inextricable entanglements. Since I arrived in Barbados in 1989, Annalee Davis has been a vibrant interlocutor, rendering in her art many of the themes about gender, race, class, and culture I have tried to explore ethnographically. I am grateful for her friendship and her help navigating the complex social worlds of this small island. I thank Gul Ozyegin for almost thirty years of sustaining conversation, collaboration, and sisterhood. She has sharpened my thinking, shortened my sentences, and made the process of research and writing less lonely. She has nourished me with exquisite Turkish cuisine, and analytical insight. Robert Goddard has painstakingly read this work and patiently lived this project from start to finish. From the unpredictable logistics of many years of fieldwork to the theoretical conundrums he has helped me unravel, he has experienced firsthand many of the dramas I aim to capture, and encouraged me to tell the story. Isabel and Alice have come of age along with this book. I am grateful for their patience, humor, frankness, and wisdom beyond their years. Rob, Izzy, and Alice, you have helped me know that labor and love can be passionately knitted together. This intricate intertwining can be onerous but also deeply pleasurable; I dedicate this book to you.

Entrepreneurial Selves

AN INTRODUCTION

The main interest in life and work is to become someone else that you were not in the beginning. If you knew when you began a book what you would say at the end, do you think that you would have the courage to write it? What is true for writing and for a love relationship is true also for life. The game is worthwhile insofar as we don't know what will be the end.
—FOUCAULT, *THE BIRTH OF BIOPOLITICS*, 9

Entrepreneurial Selves is an ethnography of economy, labor, and affect in a time and place of neoliberalism. This is a story about what it means to be *respectable* and *middle class*, and the manner in which these concepts work in tandem, in ways that are simultaneously gendered and culturally particular. *Entrepreneurialism*, I will argue, is becoming not simply a mechanism of self-employment—a vehicle for income generation, an economic matter of business, that is, entrepreneurship in a narrow sense—but a subtler, generalized way of being and way of feeling in the world. This entrepreneurialism connects market practices with self-making and is predicated upon porous boundaries of public and private life. The self as an entrepreneurial "project" under constant renovation is a key signpost of neoliberalism and its perpetual quest for flexibility in the changing global marketplace (Bourdieu 1998; Rose 1992; Illouz 2007, 2008; Walkerdine 2003). Foucault described four types of technologies by which human beings make sense of themselves, each of which is integral to the entrepreneurial pursuit:

(1) technologies of production, which permit us to produce, transform or manipulate things; (2) technologies of sign systems, which permit us to use signs, meanings, symbols, or signification; (3) technologies of power, which determine the conduct of individuals and submit them to certain ends or domination . . . ; (4) technologies of the self, which permit individuals to effect by their own means or with the help of others a certain number of operations on their own bodies and souls, thoughts, conduct, and way of being, so as to transform themselves in order to attain a certain state of happiness, purity, wisdom, perfection, or immortality. (Foucault 1988, 18)

I am particularly concerned with the last of these: the manner in which technologies of self-making are integral to the entrepreneurial ethos under the precarity of neoliberalism (Hardt and Negri 2004).

In the contemporary neoliberal milieu every aspect of life is becoming subject to regimes of flexibility, quests, and commands for self-mastery and self-examination.[1] The entrepreneurial enterprise constitutes a primary site and central practice of neoliberal self-creation and labor in today's global economy, a dual project in which economic livelihoods and new subjectivities are being forged in tandem. Entrepreneurialism denotes action and imagination, an ongoing process of envisioning and becoming, as opposed to a given position, status, or state of being that is achieved and established through economic means alone. In this dynamic sense, entrepreneurial self-making is always work *in formation*—akin to the processual work of class, gender, race, and culture—and inextricably bound up with these dimensions of identity. Its subtle ontological dynamism is inextricably bound up in new modes of labor and affect, new social relations and ways of feeling. Derived from the early nineteenth-century French verb *entreprendre* (to undertake), an *entrepreneur* is formally defined as one who creates and manages a business enterprise, taking financial risks with the hope of making a profit; a visionary figure, in other words, hailed for executing an innovative idea and, importantly, willing to undertake considerable risk to put it into practice. The entrepreneurial trope—from Henry Ford and Walt Disney to Madame C. J. Walker, Oprah Winfrey, and Steve Jobs—often highlights a restless personality and capacity to anticipate and embrace change, whether technological or social, and, as one of my informants suggested to me, "the tendency toward self-sufficiency; in other words (the entrepreneur is) stubborn and rebellious."

In this study of contemporary entrepreneurs and the wider esprit of neoliberal entrepreneurialism, I turn the focus beyond the *business* of economic independence and self-sufficiency (self-employment) to explore the self as entrepreneurial project inextricable from the enterprise and market sphere. This self is, Rose says, "a subjective being, it is to aspire to autonomy, it is to strive for personal fulfillment in its earthly life, it is to interpret its reality and destiny as matters of individual responsibility, it is to find meaning in existence by shaping its life through acts of choice" (1992, 142). The process of subjectification, as I see it, is *both* individual and social, animated in realms of the imagination and through quotidian practices in private and public life. Importantly, the means by which selfhood is contemplated, crafted, and judged, are not solely *private* or *personal* matters, in the narrow sense that they are simply up to the individual or made possible by sheer grit or "choice." Rather, new concepts of the self are vital to the broader workings—and power—of the political-economic and social order. At the heart of the entrepreneurial ethos is a vigorous entanglement of *selfhood* and *labor* for envisioning and making one's self entails particular forms (and a particular intensity) of work. Not only do entrepreneurial labors increasingly exceed the formal boundaries of productive enterprise to include every facet of social reproduction (i.e. work 'at home' and work 'at work' bleed into one another), they seem to permeate every crevice of conscious (and even unconscious)[2] life.

One element that marks these fluid and intensifying labors is a growing emphasis on *affects*—the embodied expressions of emotions and feelings. Indeed, the means by which affects of care, interest, and joy, for example, are conjured up, repressed, desired, and unleashed, are critical dimensions of entrepreneurial labor and subjective meaning-making. They also constitute a growing medium through which economic, political, and social transactions are made. Citing Berlant's (2011) *Cruel Optimism*, Sian Ngai (2013) suggests that "unlike the past or the future, the present is what is always affectively *felt* before it can be conceptually *known*." I suggest that a neoliberal "structure of feeling" (Williams 1961) is not simply a present awash in emotions through which the subject then makes sense of herself and her world, but a present and imagined future that are increasingly entangled in and through an emotional register. For Raymond Williams, the *"felt sense* of the quality of life" constitutes "the most difficult thing to get hold of in studying any past period" (1961, 63). This seems especially true in a period in which an emphasis on affects and affective exchange—the demand that people not only be emotional but that they show their emotions in identifiable and commodifiable ways—seemingly subsumes life from every angle.

It is easy to see that capitalism reproduces itself by virtue of our increasing willingness and subjugation to the entrepreneurial mandate. And it is hard not to notice the dynamic means by which capitalism morphs and seeps into even those recesses of life we might imagine impenetrable to market forces: intimate and family relationships, religious and spiritual lives, etc. However, what is most critical is not merely the inextricability of subjective understandings of the self and the means by which subjectivity and a new affective register become integral to modes of exchange within a larger political economic frame. Harder to decipher are the cultural differences within which these processes unevenly unfold. What are the implications for social, political, intimate, and interior life when this entrepreneurial imperative and its emphasis on self-examination, intimacy, psychological reflection, and cultivation unfold in places without prior investments in such self-enterprise? Michel-Rolph Trouillot (2003) warned us against the malaise of the déjà vu in such globalizing times, a caution that bears particular merit here. It is easy to lose sight of this particularity when the manner by which a neoliberal esprit is announced, cajoled, and regulated seems to take such familiar forms. For if there is little doubt that neoliberal discourses of entrepreneurialism reverberate across the world in the interest of global capitalism, the kind of subject being mobilized, the nature of the labor they are performing, the feelings rallied and produced within this supple and unstable system, and the meanings these affects hold cannot be assumed to be consistent. This ethnography explores the meanings and expressions of "entrepreneurial selves" in a part of the world well trodden by many of the relevant tropes of contemporary neoliberalism (economy, enterprise, flexibility, and power) but less inclined toward thinking reflexively about selves, much less about feelings or affective life.

The setting for this unfolding drama is the tiny and beautiful island of Barbados in the eastern Caribbean Sea. If a small and densely populated tropical island seems a surprising place to unearth the nuances of neoliberalism, it bears reminding that the Caribbean region, whose very existence is founded on colonial conquest, has provided a powerful lens for some of the most critical questions of our times: What is it to be modern (Mintz 1985; Williams 1944), and what cultural and economic complexities are bound up in systems of "globalization" (Trouillot 2003)? A former sugar-producing colony once more valuable to the British Crown than its large North American territories combined, today Barbados is known to the rest of the world for its pristine beaches, exclusive hotels, and upscale golf courses; a Mecca for British royals, prime ministers, and pop stars. Green fields of sugar cane still evoke the island's three-hundred-year plantation history and symbols of British tradition echo through tourism and everyday life, from tea and "rock buns" to cricket fever and even a ritualized changing of the guards in the crimson regalia of Queen Victoria's day.[3]

The only Caribbean territory to have remained squarely in British hands throughout the colonial period, Barbados's Anglophile tradition and nickname "little England" evoke both pride and mockery. Barbados's history of a stable parliamentary democracy and top ranking in the region's Human Development Index, along with its notably conservative national sensibility, have led to its gloss as a "middle-class" society. Today suburban subdivisions, gated communities, traffic-choked highways and American-style shopping malls increasingly define the island's landscape, while hotels and restaurants encroach ever rapidly upon the once expansive "windows to the sea." In addition to these striking visual transformations, other dimensions of Barbadian life and culture that are more subtle and easily overlooked in efforts to chart "development" and twenty-first-century modernity are also in flux. Along with the bold visual markers of middle-class society—the neon signs of new businesses and restaurants, the record number of cars on the road, and the rapidly changing face of mass consumption—what is less visible but equally dramatic are the changes to be found in the hidden recesses of people's hearts and in their subtly shifting understandings and expressions of selfhood. The questions—who am I in the world? how do I wish to live and feel?—are being articulated in new ways that I see as subtly intertwined with a general entrepreneurial ethic and neoliberal esprit. The significance of these questions, as familiar as they sound, can only be grasped with an understanding of Barbadian history and culture and with questions and modes of analysis that transcend traditional economic measures of development, entrepreneurship, or neoliberalism. Many of these changes in activity, sensibility, and desires appear deceptively common in an era of global capitalism: the rapid growth of fast food and retail chains, yoga studios and gyms, expanding public venues for leisure, extracurricular activities and camps for enriching childhood, and services offering conveniences and interventions for managing the stresses of middle-class working life, to name just a few.

More than ten years ago, I began this project with a focus very different than the one I have written. In collaboration with Katherine Browne, an anthropologist of Martinique, we aimed to capture what appeared to be a growing emphasis on entrepreneurship as a means for economic development across the Caribbean region (2004). Our goal was to examine how the growing international agenda of entrepreneurship would unfold in this balkanized region of different colonial histories (French,

Spanish, Dutch, and English), different linguistic and cultural traditions, and different state structures and political economies. In particular, we were interested in questions about gender and the ways in which women and men would be drawn into and participate in this economic niche in a time of global economic flux. Taking our cue from regional authorities and international development agencies alike, we aimed to track the growth of entrepreneurship and its gendered permutations for a region known for high rates of female labor force participation and feminine prowess more generally, and increasingly dependent upon tourism as local sugar production waned.

The longer I pursued this research the more its footing shifted. One of the most confounding but creative aspects of ethnographic fieldwork is the process by which seemingly peripheral sidenotes to the main research can become central preoccupations. They haunt and intrigue us to the point that they demand closer scrutiny. These captivating distractions and competing narratives sometimes worm their way into, and occasionally overtake, the central plotline. In this case the very premise of entrepreneurship as fundamentally an economic enterprise began to shift toward a broader concept about *entrepreneurialism*, related but not limited to the fact of owning and running a business. In other words, being entrepreneurial, I came to see, was being expressed as much in relation to new forms and fantasies of self-understanding, intimacy, parenting, spirituality, and so on, as it was in terms of "running the shop." These forms of entrepreneurialism reflect and call upon a rapidly changing cultural milieu in which affective relations—the expression and exchange of emotions—and affective labor are central. Where social relations, labor relations, kinship, conjugality, and other human relationships have been described and analyzed extensively in the region's social science literature, they are examined predominantly through the lens of economy and through the prism of the Caribbean's specific history of plantation slavery. The kinds of narratives and concerns I heard expressed in this fieldwork—sentiments and sensibilities surrounding middle-classness, entrepreneurialism, and contemporary life more generally—could not be captured within these familiar structural economic frameworks.

In addition to common markers of DIY culture, I found subtle but resounding referents to new, or at least newly articulated, desires and feelings integrally bound up with this project of flexible self-making. Others have written about the rise of "therapeutic culture" (Illouz 2007, 2008) as part of today's "regime of the self" (Rose 1990) in which therapy "is not just an adjustment device but an expression of generalized reflexivity" (Giddens

1991, 180). This marks a distinctive shift in late capitalism away from the scientific management of the body and toward an inward emphasis upon feelings and desires. Throughout entrepreneurs' testimonies about their businesses and about their lives, I was as struck by the emotional tenor of their accounts and stories as by the formal content about their paths to becoming an entrepreneur. Accounts of "stress" and emotional longings, efforts to juggle work and family life, and desires for greater inner peace and a sense of "balance" more generally are likely so familiar to a European or North American ear that they would hardly bear comment. However, their emergence holds distinctive meanings in the Caribbean.

These somewhat uneasy fieldwork observations converged several years ago with an invitation I received to participate in an interdisciplinary workshop on the theme of "Love and Globalization."[4] I found myself in a serious quandary as I attempted to bring into dialog the rising economic tide of Barbadian entrepreneurialism with the question of *love*. For after mining thousands of pages of interview transcripts with over a hundred entrepreneurs, life histories, field notes and observations of a growing culture of neoliberalism at large, I found not a single explicit mention of love. Despite the Caribbean's Nobel Prize–winning authors, a rich musical tradition of calypso, reggae, socca, etc., and the romantic lure of the region for honeymooning tourists, the love poem and romantic ballad are few and far between. The popularity of American soap operas and television dramas, and the ubiquitous presence of Hollywood movies, makes these genres of romance ever present in the popular sphere, and yet one is harder pressed to find "talk of love" (Swidler 2001) in what is immediately recognized Barbadian cultural expression or, for that matter, in academic analyses of Caribbean life and culture (Barriteau 2013). Of course the presence or absence of an explicit lexicon cannot be held alone as a barometer of emotion; the fact that little is *said* about love, for example, doesn't imply its absence in people's lives. As Foucault said, "silence itself—the things one declines to say, or is forbidden to name, the discretion that is required between different speakers—is less the absolute limit of discourse, the other side from which it is separated by a strict boundary, than an element that functions alongside the things said, with them and in relation to them within over-all strategies. . . . There is not one but many silences, and they are an integral part of the strategies that underlie and permeate discourses" (1980, 27).

As I discuss in chapter 2, my search for "love" in entrepreneurs' narratives and life histories revealed a different set of idioms of "support" that hark back to a long tradition by which a language of economy has overshadowed and subsumed that of affect. That excavation prompted my deeper consideration of emotions more generally, and their emerging prominence within the entrepreneurial spirit today. Indeed, what began as a seemingly puzzling silence/absence ultimately alerted me to the proliferation of new emotional discourses, themselves bound up in shifting axes of cultural tradition from one of social hierarchy, propriety and affective reserve to one in which longings and desires could be more readily imagined and expressed. My search for entrepreneurial discourses of "love" forced me to question not just the culturally specific meanings of love but the culturally specific manner in which feelings are being animated by neoliberalism. Changing desires for affective experience and new modes of emotional expression, as I see them, become ever more supple tools by which public and private, market and heart are mobilized by, and in turn expressive of, neoliberal entrepreneurial life.

It is precisely to these convergences that I shall return. For I see one of the most interesting and vexing aspects of my field research as a paradox between a globalizing culture of neoliberalism with its emphasis upon flexible self making, introspection, *feeling*, or what Illouz (2007) calls "emotional capitalism," and a culture historically grounded in the plantation system in which life and self have been solidly rooted in structural relations of kinship and economy and where, quite simply, the emotional register has been narrowly contained and seldom analyzed. One of my research informants expressed this observation boldly and succinctly: "*Feelings* in Barbados" are the preserve of "the priest or the bottle." That is to say, they can be expressed in church (for women) or in the rum shop (for men). The tension, therefore, between a current global climate that appears increasingly saturated in emotion (Reber 2012) and a place renowned for its rather severe, respectable and controlled conservatism offers an evocative locus to examine the affective nuances of neoliberalism. And it is within the middle classes, perhaps those groups most intensely invested within ideological, economic, and cultural articulations of neoliberal entrepreneurialism, that I see these tensions to be especially dramatic.

As I mined my narratives more closely, I came to see that while the explicit lexicon of love I was looking for was absent, the strong desire for a newly imagined intimacy, self-understanding, and new ways of feeling and expressing emotion figured throughout entrepreneurs' testimonies. I found an ever-increasing swirl of affects, whose display and exchange was demanded most visibly within the mushrooming service sector, but that resonated across all spheres of life. An awareness of these changes and their manifestations in the contexts of entrepreneurial work, leisure, religion, kinship, intimate relations, parenting, and virtually every domain of life gradually moved from the fringes to the center of my story. For it is in the combined longings and labors such affects entail, and the cultural specificity of these desires, feelings, and practices, that I see some of the most powerful and dramatic implications of neoliberalism today. Their increasing significance within the entrepreneurial milieu of Barbados in the early twenty-first century became at once unavoidable and dangerously seductive.

The changing landscapes of work and paths to middle-classness among the entrepreneurs I have been studying are both evidence of and active agents in the production of a new affective climate. I discovered not simply a growing array of new businesses offering services and goods that were brand new in the Barbadian context, but was led by my research subjects into whole new fields of leisure and therapeutic treatment, new-age and alternative churches, gyms, and holistic healing centers that signal radically new venues and domains of experience for this Caribbean island. The story of entrepreneurship, aspirational middle-classness, affect, and the powerful concept of respectability is a difficult one to narrate, for all of these elements are intertwined, mutually constitutive, permeable, and dynamically in flux. Entrepreneurship, it is true, constitutes a newly attractive means for livelihood, economic enterprise, and middle-class belonging. But it must be read simultaneously as a new way of being in the world that signifies not just a particular path of income generation and consumption but also a new way of living and feeling that is shaped by and simultaneously giving new expression to gendered, classed, and racialized subjectivities.

The unfolding entrepreneurial drama of neoliberal Barbados is complicated ironically because of the deceptively familiar, even mundane, quality these themes suggest to a North American or European reader. For here is a picture in which global economic forces and a local and national embrace of neoliberal flexibility set the stage on which entrepreneurship is presented as a new path, a new profile of possibility. This entrepreneurial impetus is emerging in part because the state and private sectors are shrinking and reconfiguring themselves such that long-standing expectations for stable, secure jobs with clear ladders of mobility are both less available and, according to many, less desired. We are well acquainted with this narrative of late capitalism. Equally familiar, it might seem, are the forms that many of the new entrepreneurial enterprises are taking—a growing array of services from event management and corporate consulting to personalized care and treatment of the home, body, and mind. In these new businesses, we witness a familiar centrality of electronic media, "immaterial" computer-generated work, and, for a small island, the critical importance of a global marketplace and supply chain made possible in part by the Internet and digital age.

The anthropologist is primed to observe and explain what is different, but she is less well trained to interpret phenomena that look and sound familiar. The challenge before us is to resist the numbness and unease that emerges from apparent similitude. I see the confluence of entrepreneurial elements of culture, economy, and selfhood as simultaneously expressive of the global marketplace and also means by which new social relations and ways of imagining and enacting personhood are being communicated in this small island in the Caribbean Sea. New desires for flexibility and self-mastery spoke of a globalizing neoliberal discourse and also evoked the Caribbean concept of reputation—those rebellious and creative modes of expressive "creole" culture that have long been mapped onto lower-class culture, masculinity, African-derived tradition, and, most importantly, an oppositional, anticolonial esprit—as I will discuss in detail in the next chapter. At the same time, other dimensions of flexibility, a flexibility of selfhood and relatedness, including interior exploration and the pursuit of intimate emotional connectedness and recognition, emerge without a similarly established cultural tradition on which to rest. The heart of my account lies in this convergence between global and local discourses of neoliberalism and reputation, entrepreneurship and respectability, spawned in very different historical moments but today intertwined and mutually transformative in the lives of new entrepreneurial middle-class actors.

This is an especially poignant story because Barbados, and the Caribbean more generally, represents a cultural sphere that is not new to forces of globalization and the penetration of cultural and economic agendas and imperatives brought from elsewhere. What has made the Caribbean of such great interest and importance in recent efforts to examine globalization is the fact of its formation some three hundred years ago precisely out of the force and combination of *other* nations and peoples. This is not a story of virgin lands or pristine cultures grappling with the recent penetration of foreign goods, ideologies, and modes of economic restructuring, but a place that has been created and developed precisely out of such mammoth processes centuries ago. This is a region largely without "natives" in the traditional sense. Its populations are immigrants and their descendants—enslaved, indentured, and free. What is "traditional" or "authentic" here, in other words, is best understood not as some set of practices and beliefs that stand in opposition to the "foreign" but as a supple capacity to incorporate influences, practices, structural forms, and institutions and give them relevance and meaning in a West Indian idiom steeped in the historical legacy of colonialism and plantation slavery and always in a process of dynamic change. Indeed, it is the tension between those cultural attributes and institutions derived from British colonial influences and those spawned in the New World that has fostered the region's most enduring conceptual frameworks (creole, hybridity, marronage, respectability, reputation, etc.), some of which have been widely borrowed and "globalized" with due attribution or not.

For the Barbadian case, I interpret these political and economic transformations as bound up in the process in which the local cultural model of *reputation*, long understood to stand in opposition to colonial order and capitalist interests, is becoming ascendant and intimately conjoined with the neoliberal capitalist agenda. Where a British colonial cultural model of respectability was encoded in bureaucratic hierarchy, order, and the propriety associated with institutions such as the Anglican Church, the civil service, and the "proper" feminine domestic sphere, a counterideology of reputation could be found in the lively domain of the public sphere in which Caribbean folk, especially those of the lower classes, have enacted a vibrant culture of *communitas* and an ethic of anticolonial social leveling through creative performance, wit, and guile (Wilson 1969).

Examining these processes offers not simply an opportunity to elucidate the "local" and the "global" as some might have it but also to highlight what is at stake in glossing *neoliberalism* or *globalization* too breezily, too all-encompassingly. While there has been a critical political impetus to see the familiar tracks of market-driven global economic flux as homogeneous and threatening, to limit our analyses to formal similitude risks losing the nuances and complexities of life and meaning that ethnography is especially well poised to unearth. In other words, in what may look to be merely tropical ripples in the tides of American or global trends, I see new cultures of enterprise, consumption, leisure, intimacy, and selfhood unfolding in the Barbadian context. And the importance of unearthing these developments is not only that they shed light on what is distinctive about this moment in time for a small and seemingly marginal Caribbean country but also that these distinctions invite us to ask how history and culture give specific meaning to some of our most potent concepts: capitalism, neoliberalism, middle-classness, respectability, and so on. My goal is not just to illustrate the manifestation of new modes of flexible labor and neoliberal self making and class making through entrepreneurship, but also to explore how specific dimensions of Barbadian culture and history reframe globalizing neoliberal techniques and affective culture and, in so doing, give them new meanings.

A NOTE ON METHODOLOGY AND THE RESEARCH PROCESS

Studying the middle classes not only suggests certain analytical ambivalences as I allude to above but also presents a different set of methodological conditions and challenges. For me, having conducted fieldwork in the island's informatics industry in the 1990s, studying middle-class entrepreneurs first meant an even more mobile undertaking. If the informatics sector implied a mode of ethnography that departed from the tradition of village-based anthropology of an earlier era, middle-class entrepreneurship took me even more dramatically into the rhythm of diffuse suburban living, shopping, leisure, and the tangle of traffic in an increasingly car-focused society. While concentrated in the most densely commercial parts of the country, such as the busy south coast, my "field site" was virtually the whole of the island, wherever these businesses were located and wherever these entrepreneurs lived and found recreational respite. These venues stretched from the airport to the countryside, beach and sea to urban and industrial sites. I conducted almost all of my interviews on the business premises generally after having toured the operation, and then retreating to a quiet (or not so quiet) and mostly air-conditioned office space. With some entrepreneurs, whom I got to know better over time, our conversations continued in their homes or other venues such as local cafés, beaches, cultural events, and social gatherings. In addition to my more purposeful follow-up meetings with entrepreneurs, frequent visits have allowed me to follow more informally the changing entrepreneurial landscape of the past decade. It bears reminding that Barbados is a small and densely populated island (fourteen miles wide and twenty-one miles long; population 260,000). Its size gives its social organization a particular complexity as well as intimacy. Almost daily, whether in the grocery store, walking, driving, going to the beach or the movies, attending public events, art shows, or university lectures, I encountered familiar faces, whether from my earlier fieldwork, the university community, networks of friends and family, and of course my many entrepreneurial informants. These encounters were a constant reminder of the complex social niches of this small society. I also became aware of new commercial sites, recreational venues, and public spaces that were bringing these groups increasingly into contact. During my first fieldwork from 1989 to 1992 I discovered the nuances of the Barbadian social landscape that do not map simply onto race or class boundaries. One might assume, as I did twenty-five years ago, that the small white community of less than 5 percent of the population represented a fairly homogeneous group who would likely know each other. The class and social diversity of this group were among my more surprising discoveries. In some senses Barbados has the feel of a small island where everyone seems to be "family" to everyone else. On the other hand, this is a society with intricate class, racial, kin-based and geographical complexities with linkages to many other parts of the world. And it is precisely the intensity of this simultaneously global and local dimension that makes it a fascinating place to live and study.

Over more than a decade I combined historical accounts and archival research on popular representations of business, entrepreneurship, and middle-classness, surveying newspapers, magazines, advertisements, and help columns, with interviews and life histories of contemporary Barbadian entrepreneurs of all ages. My ethnographic research included participant observation in shopping malls, restaurants, cafés, movie theaters, churches, the new south coast boardwalk, salons, galleries, beaches, and other popular venues for middle-class life. I listened to the island's ever-popular radio call-in programs, and attended cultural performances, lectures, and events featuring business promotion and youth entrepreneurship. I interviewed government officials and NGO representatives involved in supporting entrepreneurship on the island, as well as bank managers and consultants, about their views on the growth of the contemporary entrepreneurial landscape and the roles of gender and race in shaping the nation's entrepreneurial profile. I pored over census data about education, employment, and income to try to make sense of the meanings of *middle class* within this shifting arena of contemporary entrepreneurialism.

Between 1999 and 2009 I interviewed 107 entrepreneurs (seventy-two women and thirty-five men), some of whom I interviewed multiple times during those years. With the help of a university research assistant, I used a "snowball" sampling method whereby each of the entrepreneurs I met was asked to suggest others who might be interested in participating in the study. Identifying Barbadian-born owners of registered, midsized businesses (with at least one employee) was not difficult. Almost every interviewee gave me names of friends or acquaintances to interview. Indeed, their interest in the study and my findings was often so strong that our interview quickly became more of a collaborative discussion in which I both honed my questions and shared my initial impressions. My goal early on was to survey as wide a swath of entrepreneurs as possible, especially those entering "nontraditional" areas of enterprise—women in heavy construction or other physically demanding and more conventionally masculine arenas, men in fashion and food-related areas that have been commonly associated with women. I sought out entrepreneurs embarking in fields tied to brand new media and technology in the Barbadian context, and those offering new kinds of services and products suggestive of changing social mores (e.g., from yoga to personal fitness, nutrition counseling to holistic massage). I also deliberately included women and men in conventional fields: women running boutiques, flower shops, and food establishments, and men in plumbing, contracting, and business consulting. Roughly one quarter of the sample was in business partnerships, ten named their spouses as their partner, three others named other family members. With only one exception, a man who had taken over his mother's business, each of the entrepreneurs I interviewed was the primary (or co-)visionary and proprietor.

Each of these sources of data, especially my survey and interviews, led me to pursue the intersecting themes of middle-class self making and affective labor that constitute the heart of this book. I highlight in close detail selected entrepreneurial cases of individuals whose experiences and trajectories illustrate these most boldly and compellingly. These rich emotional narratives were often layered in longing, sadness, desire, joy and determination. When conversations continued over several years, they included retrospective reflection about structural as well as emotional changes over time—the reformulation of a business model, the birth of a child, an illness or divorce, feelings of optimism, hope, fear and anger. The individual biographies of these entrepreneurs and sometimes the unusual nature of their businesses are such that, on a small island, they could be easily recognizable. In attempting to protect their anonymity, I offered them the opportunity to "name themselves" with pseudonyms, and I have sometimes taken creative license in changing minor biographical elements or recasting a dimension of their enterprise that might make individuals less easily identifiable while preserving the central outlines of their lives, business trajectories, and sentiments. One woman entrepreneur with whom I discussed this conundrum and shared much of my analysis laughingly stated, "Well, the truth is, you could call me *George* and people on this island would still know me!"

Anthropologists have long been concerned with issues of representation and ethnographic positionality, and in some senses studying the middle classes might mask these concerns since even when studying "others" we may find ourselves among field subjects very much like ourselves. In my own case this project brought me into close ethnographic encounter with familiars. A large network of extended kin and friends I return to each year in Barbados permeated the research. I learned of many new businesses from these networks, and indeed everyone I know on the island shared their ideas and commentary about the research. Unlike the years in which I conducted my first project there, on a subject few knew much about, everyone had thoughts about entrepreneurial life. This made the boundaries separating when I was "working" (doing fieldwork) and not working always blurry. Perhaps this blurriness sharpened my own attunement to the work/life seepage in the entrepreneurial lives I examine.

With a central interest in the gender of entrepreneurship, and what Bruni, Gherardi, and Poggio (2005) see as the simultaneously entrepreneurial aspects of gender, I was intent on studying entrepreneurial femininity and masculinity broadly, and women and men in all stages of the life cycle—single, in conjugal unions of varied forms, married, separated, divorced, with and without children, young and middle aged—from all ethnic groups, and from all class origins. While sexuality was not an explicit dimension of recruitment, I was interested in the life stories of several non-heteronormative entrepreneurs. Although these individuals never explicitly identified their sexual orientation or described themselves as gay or lesbian, their lively interviews were illuminating of many of the general social patterns I explore.[5] The overwhelming majority of these 107 entrepreneurs are Afro-Barbadian (who represent 90 percent of the population at large): fifty-eight women and twenty-eight men described themselves as "black." I also interviewed ten women and five men who described themselves as "white," two men and four women who described themselves as "mixed" or "red" Barbadians, and one "Indian" man. Given the strong association of "business" with the local white population, I was also interested in interviewing middle-class entrepreneurs (i.e., not the big corporate conglomerates on the island, but small to midsized business owners) from this segment of the population. They offer a small window into the little-examined cultural world of white Barbadians, and in particular that of white women, a group long imagined to hold the reins of middle-class respectability but rarely if ever the focus of empirical study.

As a further point of comparison, I also interviewed a small subset of ten salaried professional women. These individuals shed light on aspects of middle-classness and the occupational hierarchies and trajectories today, as well as on the particularities of entrepreneurialism as a chosen path. I was curious as to why these women had chosen *not* to become entrepreneurs, opting for more conventional positions of respectable middle-classness: a bank manager, a permanent secretary in the government, an accountant, a government health professional, and so on. Were there particular aspects of entrepreneurship—risk, autonomy, innovation, flexibility—that these women shared or sought to avoid? Were there status differences or different claims to respectability marked by these choices? While these numbers are too small to bear the weight of statistical claims, they offer suggestive insights into convergences of gender, race, and middle-classness in this time of cultural and economic flux. Much of my discussion revolves around changing lifestyles, modes of work, and "class" identifications, though it bears noting that my informants did not generally use the language of class in their own discussion. They spoke about "improving," "doing better," "struggling" and "having it hard," "coming up," being "comfortable," or seeing others as "well-to-do," but seldom did anyone talk about being "middle class."

Ultimately, I found that entrepreneurialism and middle-classness today cannot be captured neatly by the measures with which I began (e.g., education, occupation, and income). All of the entrepreneurs I met embrace the label of entrepreneurship, though their "middle-class" profiles and the nature and size of their businesses varied. All employ at least one other person, though some have staffs of over twenty. Some left school in their teens, while others held advanced degrees, including several masters and one PhD degree. The vast majority of them left jobs in other sectors with two simply expressed desires: flexibility (especially for women) and creative autonomy—to be their "own boss." While my goal was not to track the success or failure rates of these businesses, the long period of my fieldwork led me to witness both growth and decline. Indeed, I saw business failures and successes, diversification, reconstitution, growth, contraction, illness, childbirth, marriage, and divorce among the many changes over time. I learned that entrepreneurialism is not about business per se; it has become a mode of labor and a way of life.

CHAPTER 1

Barbadian Neoliberalism and the Rise of a New Middle-Class Entrepreneurialism

Homo economicus is an entrepreneur, an entrepreneur of himself . . . being for himself his own capital . . . his own producer . . . the source of [his] earnings.
—FOUCAULT, *THE BIRTH OF BIOPOLITICS*, 266

The contemporary entrepreneur represents neoliberalism's heroic actor: supple, flexible, and keenly responsive to market fluctuations, always prepared to retool and retrain to advance in uncharted directions (Bourdieu 1998; Harvey 2005). Entrepreneurship and entrepreneurialism, however, carry neither generic shape nor historical tradition. Likewise, in its traffic between popular and academic settings, the concept of neoliberalism is fraught with conflicting, albeit mostly threatening, associations.[1] From the perspective of political economy, the neoliberal era of capitalism signifies the seemingly limitless advance of a global marketplace, a fully integrated apparatus serving the interests of a global corporate elite via new strategies of capital accumulation, while the protective arm of the state shrinks back from its commitments to regulation and social welfare. Under this agenda, the world market is envisioned as both engine and compass directing human action and new regimes of accumulation: privatization, deregulation, and "the commodification of everything" (Harvey 2005). Neoliberalism, in this sense, operates both as ideology and economic policy, producing unexpected and ironic effects (Comaroff and Comaroff 2000). Bourdieu refers to neoliberalism as "a mode of production that entails a mode of domination based on the institution of insecurity, domination through *precariousness*" (2003, 29; see also Clarke 2004).

For others, in particular those influenced by Foucault, neoliberalism marks the intensifying techniques of "governmentality" by which the logics of capitalism and the weight of economic rationality become so fully globalized (Hardt and Negri 2000) and so deeply engrained that people are compelled to become self-governing (Rose 1990, 1992). The concept of neoliberalism is most fruitfully conceived *not* as a specific set of structures or as Ong (2007, 5) aptly put it, an "economic tsunami . . . of market-driven forces" decimating all in its wake, or a single abstract "thing that acts in the world" (Kingfisher and Maskovsky 2008), but rather as a logic that can be adapted and melded within specific conditions, through specific cultural forms, in time and space.

I retain the concept of *neoliberalism*[2] not as a generic gloss for contemporary capitalism but with the hopes of adding greater cultural particularity and precision to its dynamic and multifaceted forms. As a concept, neoliberalism also signals a confounding "slippage" in my fieldwork where the term assumed both popular and analytical usage. In short, describing certain conditions and practices as "neoliberal" or as evidence of neoliberalism was not something confined to academic conference rooms or published papers. A critical discourse about neoliberalism also emanated from my informants in a way that seems to be an ever more common dimension of contemporary fieldwork. This is especially the case when studying the middle classes, whose life styles, modes of consumption, media worlds, and so on may resemble and overlap with those of the ethnographer. Every day I noticed not only convergences between the language and lives of my entrepreneurial informants and my own life and milieu in the United States, but the echoes of "official" neoliberal discourse were also unmistakable. Neoliberalism and its signature elements of *flexibility, entrepreneurship* and *entrepreneurialism* have entered the common parlance of state-level officials as well as many of my interlocutors, often with positive value attached. Among academics the concept has become an almost trite gloss for the ills of today's precarious global economy and cultural condition. Discursive blendings such as this one beg for conceptual excavation and close ethnographic exploration. For, familiar as these themes of flexibility and rationality sounded to my American ear, I was equally aware that they were steeped in a different set of cultural understandings and could not be interpreted through a single framework.

THE NEOLIBERAL LOGIC OF FLEXIBILITY

The clarion call for *flexibility* became a constant refrain resounding from all corners of society, from entrepreneurs' own testimonies and the programmatic charges of the Barbadian state, to the private sector, and NGO establishment. "The essence of neo-liberalism," as Bourdieu summed it up, is an "absolute reign of flexibility" (1998). From one vantage point, these bedfellows—neoliberalism and flexibility—connote the instability of labor and financial markets; ruptures, radical escalations, and the collapse of time and space; an erosion of state-sanctioned social welfare; and according to Lash and Urry (1987), "the end of organized (bureaucratic) capitalism." Across popular and academic discourses, neoliberal flexibility is variously portrayed as "slogan . . . ideology . . . dream and nightmare" (Marquand 1992, 61). In the terms of some of my Barbadian interviewees, flexibility is fundamentally about "insecurity and risk," while for others "flexibility is the name of the game," a de facto reality they not only embraced but also eagerly sought.[3] Whether a source of anxiety, an external command, a badge of honor, a chimera of promise, or a deeply internalized desire, if a single concept could capture the complex essence of the entrepreneurialism I will try to describe, it would be *flexibility*.

Few if any spheres of life are exempt from contemporary neoliberal demands for flexibility—from the structures of economic markets to the nuances of individuals' subjectivities as citizens, producers, consumers, migrants, tourists, members of families, and so on. Aihwa Ong (2006) has demonstrated the supple and sometimes unexpected maneuvers made by Asian states as they attempt to position themselves competitively under neoliberalism. She has also highlighted the degree to which flexibility and movement stand in direct challenge to the stability and solidity that were prized under earlier capitalist expansions. Emily Martin (1994) has described how the contemporary emphasis on flexible accumulation extends across domains of life from the immune system to the laboring and managing body within corporate enterprise. The tentacles of neoliberalism reach from on high—whether the corporation, the state, or agglomerations thereof, into the individual, the body, psyche, and cell.

The mandate for flexibility requires not only that individuals retrain for an ever-changing set of job requirements in the new economy but also that they foster a heightened sense of individualism in which, as many have noted, therapeutic culture has come to play a significant role in bolstering and soothing the self (Rieff 2006; Lasch 1991; Rose 1992). The directive to become an "entrepreneur of the self" implies an independence in which the individual is defined as a self-propelled, autonomous economic actor, ever responsive to a dynamic marketplace, and simultaneously encouraged to seek introspection, self-mastery, and personal fulfillment. This edict entails not only retraining and the procurement of new skills, networks, and the imagination and courage to break outside of the established channels of upward mobility but also an interior dimension of selfhood and flexible self making through enterprise in which capital accumulation is not an end in itself but a means to reinvent oneself. The reinvention at stake has many dimensions—that of producer, consumer, and citizen, a social being as well as an individual who cares for her own livelihood and her own body, mind, and soul.

North Americans and Europeans are intimately familiar with the flexibility discourse and the notion that in this era of late capitalism the onus is increasingly placed upon the individual to take charge of his own economic, social, and personal fate. Self-help manuals, life coaches, personal trainers, and counselors of all sorts are all part of an expanding network of services for adapting to the "precarity" of life (Hardt and Negri 2004). Workers are expected to respond quickly and with agility to labor market demands by constantly retraining; businesses are charged with developing special niche markets, customizable services and products, and to restructure, reorganize, and relocate in relation to the global marketplace; academics must anticipate and respond to market pressures by being more strategic and entrepreneurial in publication, utilize new media and digital technologies that expand public outreach, increase university revenues and justify costs; children are coaxed in their consumer habits, their extracurricular activities, and their schooling, to carefully craft their profiles in social media and for college applications. These are just a few illustrations of the ways in which middle-class life today is enmeshed within a culture and economy of neoliberalism and its messianic call for entrepreneurial flexibility.

CARIBBEAN LOGIC OF REPUTATIONAL FLEXIBILITY

The mantra of flexibility is not the sole preserve of neoliberal discourse, however, and its significance for Barbadian entrepreneurs cannot be interpreted as a simple echo of contemporary globalization. Flexibility has also been the keystone of a deeply rooted Caribbean cultural tradition, a value complex that for many analyses signifies what is most culturally authentic about these new world societies. Indeed, what I call the Caribbean logic of *reputational flexibility* recuperates conceptually one of the region's most powerful (and controversial) gatekeeping concepts—the reputation-respectability model. I argue that this regional idiom of reputation and respectability illustrates what Ong (2007, 5) evocatively describes as "the promiscuous entanglements of global and local logics" of neoliberalism. My larger goal is to highlight that even where landscapes and lives appear to imitate familiar signs of neoliberalism in the United States or Europe, we must not make the mistake of interpreting these forms as the same. This book recasts the reputation-respectability model as a tool with which to interrogate the nuances of global processes.

Polemically proposed by the anthropologist Peter Wilson in the 1960s, the model of reputation and respectability contends that Caribbean societies can be broadly understood as steeped in the structures and ideologies of two competing value systems. On one hand is *respectability*, the inescapable legacy of colonial dependence through which patterns of social hierarchy are upheld and reproduced, and on the other hand is *reputation*, a set of oppositional responses to colonial domination and the elusiveness of respectability through which people enact creative individualism and achieve a sort of social leveling or esprit of *communitas*. Respectability, for Wilson, encoded a set of British colonially defined institutions, values and mores endorsed and practiced largely by the middle class, by women in particular, and by old or married men. Steeped in Victorian tradition, respectability sanctioned the nuclear patriarchal family over the "matrifocal" household, the more fluid "visiting union," and more casual sexual relations. Respectability enshrined the white Christian church over other, syncretic denominations. Ideals of respectable social order, propriety, monogamy, and domesticity are enacted through formal patriarchal marriage, the Anglican Church, the pursuit of higher education, and a secure place in the hierarchy of the civil service or the professions of law or medicine. The essence of reputation, by contrast, is rooted in African culture and expressed through an improvisational adaptability associated primarily with a lower-class and masculine public sphere of performance and sociality. Reputation is performed in the public domain in such venues as street corners, the political platform, the rum shop, the market, and the musical stage, where people flaunt qualities such as sexual prowess, verbal wit, musical flair, and guile.

The qualities most central to reputation can be thought of as the embodiment of an entrepreneurial esprit—adaptive, self-defined, and resistant to the stiff, stultifying conventions of bureaucratic respectability. Whether performed by men or women, the culture of reputation has a distinctively masculine and lower-class aura. For Wilson, most importantly, reputation

TABLE 1.1 **Traditional Contours of Respectability/Reputation**

RESPECTABILITY	REPUTATION
European-derived	African-derived
Imitative-mimicry, colonial	Authentic, local
White	Black "Creole"
Elite, middle-class	Lower-class
Inside, yard	Outside, rum shop, political stage
Private	Public
Work, formal employment	Play
Formal/institutional/hierarchical	Informal/organic/*communitas*
Production	Consumption
Marriage, fidelity	Promiscuity
Church, home, work	Rum shop/street/stage
Stability, stasis	Mobility/flexibility
Women, older, married men/femininity	Men/masculinity
Family	Friends/crews/mates
Discipline, order, obedience	Chaos, bacchanal, "vexation"
Christmas	Carnival
Future-oriented	Present-oriented
Economy	Spending

Wilson 1973; Burton 1997; Miller 1994; Freeman 2000

embodied all that was creative, resilient, and anticolonial in the forging of an independent, creole, or New World Caribbean culture. Where respectability symbolized the false, imitative essence of colonial culture—its preoccupation with the codes of British decorum—reputation, by contrast, could be upheld as the model of authentic Caribbean-ness. If respectability upholds hierarchical order, reputation advances flexibility and communitas.

This emphasis on flexibility and adaptability as a paramount feature of Caribbean experience and culture is widely acknowledged within academic and popular realms. Movement, migration, and change, rather than insularity or stasis, have defined the Caribbean as a social and cultural field. And as Trouillot (2003, 42) reminds us, cultural practice in the Caribbean "takes firmer contours when we consider the provision grounds of slavery." When not under the whip in the cane fields, slaves carved both economic liberties and a robust internal marketing system out of the rigid structure of the plantation; the provisions they grew and traded became the diet of planter and slave alike, and their market acumen anchored a tradition of economic resilience and flexibility. Echoing Mintz (1978), Trouillot noted, "what started as an economic bonus for planters turned out to be a field of opportunities for individual slaves," critical not only materially but also as "symbolic fields for the production of *individual selves* by way of the production of material goods."[4] Indeed, a proclivity for "strategic flexibility" operates as a general cultural model with which West Indians approach most aspects of life.

This logic of flexibility at the core of Caribbean personhood is rooted in a history of movement and expressed structurally in numerous ways across the life course: in circuits of labor migration, the dispersed regional and transnational networks of kin and child fostering, shifting household constellations, the formally recognized "visiting union,"[5] the preponderance of female-headed households, and in the salience of "occupational multiplicity." The fisherman who keeps a rum shop that also rents pirated DVDs, office workers who spend weekends buying fashions and household wares in Miami for resale in their modest living-room markets, and even the successful Cambridge-educated medical doctor who keeps a kitchen garden and raises pigs and chickens in his yard are but a few examples of Barbadian resourcefulness I witnessed. They speak to the well-anchored culture of reputational flexibility that encompasses the wider Caribbean. As Trouillot (1992, 33) has said, "Caribbean peoples seem to have fewer problems than most in recognizing the fuzziness and overlap of categories, and *multiplicity is not confined to the economic realm or to the poor.*"

Historically the tension between cultures of reputation and respectability in the Caribbean fostered a dynamic that Wilson (1978, 58) called "crab antics"—an expression I continued to hear among entrepreneurs today. The saying connotes a barrel full of crabs. Each crab in pursuit of his own freedom yanks the one above back down. A newly defined struggle between reputation and respectability might be said to be especially pronounced today and to embody the entrepreneurial heart of Barbadian neoliberalism. For where entrepreneurship has historically been rooted in the tradition of reputation, it is the middle class—as a group and a set of ideals—that has constituted the axis of respectability. In short the tension between reputation and respectability today is unfolding in a direction that Wilson did not anticipate. Where once the values and practices of reputation stood in stark opposition to the ethic of bureaucratic, capitalist respectability, they now align perfectly within the neoliberal order. For Wilson, the reputation-respectability model offered not a mere academic heuristic but a political agenda. He saw the cultural values of reputation as the way to combat a neocolonial order and beckon a more culturally authentic future for the Caribbean region. This reputational propensity for flexibility, innovation, and self-invention—whether in realms of economy, conjugality, kinship or self-expression—constituted an adaptive, alternative set of economic and cultural responses to capitalist domination, and as such, reputation suggested an alternative, counterhegemonic esprit.[6] Today, however, these values and entrepreneurial practices are precisely the ticket to neoliberal orthodoxy. Entrepreneurial flexibility increasingly represents not simply a survival strategy but also an aspirational and officially mandated path, not only a means of a livelihood but also a *lifestyle* and way of being. And as reputation becomes upwardly mobile, its new relationship to respectability poses new opportunities as well as challenges along the lines of gender, class, and race. No longer the preserve of lower-class black masculinity, reputational flexibility is attractive to and hailed by more and more people, including and perhaps especially middle-class women, whom Wilson would have seen as the very anchor of traditional, intractable respectability.

THE PARADOX OF ENTREPRENEURSHIP AND MIDDLE-CLASS RESPECTABILITY

> I sold flowers. I didn't sell myself. Now you've made a lady of me I'm not fit to sell anything else.
> —ELIZA DOOLITTLE, *MY FAIR LADY*

If becoming a "lady" required Eliza Doolittle to relinquish her place in the hard-scrabble public market only to fashion her voice, manner, and self for the more respectable "marriage market," the conjoining of middle-class femininity and entrepreneurialism also poses a paradox in the Barbadian context. On one hand, the market higgler has long represented a figure of feminine strength and economic ingenuity. Throughout the historical record, and still today, one finds such strong women traveling the countryside and now abroad buying and selling produce and goods in town and throughout the island, trading gossip and news as well as basic food provisions and other items. From the back of a donkey cart to the wheel of a Suzuki minivan, these market women have represented the backbone of the region's internal marketing system (Mintz 1955; Katzin 1959). Images of their bountiful trays and colorfully wrapped heads form a staple of touristic tchotchkes from tea towels to key chains. By contrast, the middle-class businesswoman has been a more ambiguous and shadowy figure.

Rachel Pringle Polgreen is perhaps the most notable and exceptional example—a freed mulatto woman of the eighteenth century who became a highly successful hotelier, brothel owner, and master of thirty-seven slaves. Polgreen is boldly caricatured in a lithograph by the British artist Thomas Rowlandson, and she is thus perhaps the iconic if complex profile of middle-class entrepreneurial womanhood. Seated, self-assuredly, bejeweled in a low-cut frock before her busy establishment, she stares directly into the eyes of her observer. The sign above her head reads, in classic double entendre, "Pawpaw Sweet meats & Pickles of all Sorts," denoting both the sexual nature of her hotel's offerings as well as her likely participation in the informal market (Fuentes 2010). Everything about her bespeaks the uncomfortable position of women's middle-class entrepreneurship.[7] Freed slave and mulatto daughter of a Scotch schoolmaster and his African slave, she amassed a "small fortune" on par with the wealth of white urban-dwelling men of Bridgetown through the dubious sale of other women's bodies and labor. Like other freed mulatto women who became shopkeepers, Polgreen catered to white society, Royal Navy officers, and was known even to a royal prince. At the time of her death she owned at least ten properties, some thirty-seven slaves, and was proudly addressed as "Miss Rachel," a mark of honor not generally afforded black or mixed-race women (Handler 1981). However, motherhood and marriage, the true mark of feminine respectability, had eluded her.

Our knowledge of entrepreneurship in the Caribbean is, like most other aspects of West Indian society, framed by the legacy of plantation slavery. The domination of a white corporate elite, stemming from the old white plantocracy, is most often noted to have held back the expansion of black Barbadians in business. Cecilia A. Karch (1985) and Patricia Stafford (2002, 2006) have documented that by 1839, an emergent middle class made up of 'freed blacks and browns' owned 25 percent of the property in the expanding urban sphere of Bridgetown. This growing black and brown middle class between 1880 and 1937 included a tiny professional segment and "a substantial well-heeled group of artisans and shopkeepers" (Stafford 2005, 117). However, reflecting perfectly Wilson's portrait of respectability, Stafford (2005, 117) also notes that "these groups used the money earned from business . . . not to set up their children in similar careers, but to invest in education . . . to enable them to become schoolteachers (in the case of young women, nurses) or to enable them to join

RACHEL PRINGLE *of* BARBADOES

FIGURE 1.1. Rachel Pringle of Barbados, entrepreneur. Illustration by Thomas Rowland-
son, published by William Holland (London, 1796); engraving held by the Barbados
Museum. Slide of engraving, courtesy of the late Neville Connell, director of the Barbados
Museum, as shown on www.slaveryimages.org, compiled by Jerome Handler and Michael
Tuite and sponsored by the Virginia Foundation for the Humanities and the University of
Virginia Library.

the higher professions." Whereas Greenfield wrote in 1966 that post–
Second World War upward mobility in Barbados could be achieved by men
through occupation and by women through marriage, entrepreneurial
middle-class women today demonstrate dramatically new paths of change.
On one hand, education, the primary vehicle through which Barbadians,
since independence, have sought occupational upward mobility, now is reported to be overwhelmingly feminized. With women constituting roughly
70 percent of university students in the University of the West Indies

(UWI) system, Stafford (2005, 37) and others have noted that "many Barbadian women with a higher educational status than their partners now see themselves as household heads." Many women entrepreneurs today reveal that, in parallel to educational achievement en route to professional status, economic advancement and upward mobility through business also foster their comfortable claim on household headship, regardless of their conjugal status.

The expansion of the black middle class in Barbados is most widely attributed to the government's free-education policy, dating from the early 1960s, on the cusp of the island's independence from the British Crown, when "for the first time . . . in history, society seemed fluid, and working-class families were able to produce individuals who could be found within all social groups" (Beckles 1990, 207). Barbados ranks among the leaders in the region on the Human Development Index (47 out of 187 countries worldwide) and is especially touted for its established middle class.[8] Intriguingly, however, not a single ethnographic study has focused on the Barbadian middle class. Balanced between its poorer "developing" Caribbean neighbors and the postindustrial power brokers to the north, and given the ideological weight of its conservative respectability, Barbados is an especially powerful site for exploring ethnographically the dynamics of middle-classness.

At the time of Wilson's fieldwork, Caribbean economies were centered on commodity production for metropolitan consumption. Many of the commodities were agricultural goods such as bananas, sugar, rice, and cocoa, but there were also products of extractive industries, for example, bauxite and oil. These industries were oriented to an export market in the metropolis and controlled by multinational corporations, which often exercised quasi-governmental functions. Corresponding to these private-sector entities were large, well-organized labor unions with powerful political influence and state bureaucracies that directed the individual economies. What each of these sectors—the corporate, the state, and the union— shared was a pronounced bureaucratic form of organization. Highly integrated industries, they controlled each step of the productive process, from the growing of the crop or the extraction of the ore to its disposal on the international market, and they were able to count on powerful political support both in the metropolis and in the Caribbean region. Conforming to this model, the labor unions of the Caribbean grew vigorously after the Depression to the point at which they, likewise, assumed a monopoly control over the labor market and adopted a highly bureaucratic management structure. The civil service grew in much the same way, with robust establishments to manage the large industries and to deliver services on the basis of revenues derived from these industries. These bureaucratic state and corporate structures generated an "organizational man" of the Caribbean reminiscent of William H. Whyte's (1956) post–Second World War portrayal of bureaucratic conformity, with an emphasis on security over innovative, rugged individualism, a set of attitudes and values that prized hierarchical order and respectability.

Recent years, however, have seen the disintegration of the older imperial trade networks and the gradual displacement of traditional industries. Sugar, which once dominated the economic landscape, has shrunk to a small fraction of its former scale, and its relative importance as an earner of foreign exchange and an employer has diminished even more. Oil and bauxite in Trinidad and Tobago and Jamaica continue to be important, but their vulnerability to price fluctuations on the world market has made them erratic engines of economic growth. In the place of these traditional industries, the Caribbean, Barbados in particular, has become increasingly reliant on the service sector, most importantly tourism but also an expanding array of offshore banking, insurance, and information-processing. These newer service industries rely less on government bureaucracies for marketing and trade negotiation in the manner of the older industries and, instead, orchestrate these functions independently. Many are owned by or partnered with foreign companies and have also spurred the development of an array of locally owned ancillary services that privilege entrepreneurial flexibility in contrast to bureaucratic skills and structure. Adding even greater urgency to the entrepreneurial mandate has been a deep recession since the 2008 financial crisis. Today, according to Central Bank figures, the per capita GDP of Barbados is roughly $19,000, unemployment hovers just above 11 percent, and agriculture represents a mere 3.1 percent, industry 13.6 percent, and services 83.3 percent of the GDP. Government debt nears 70 percent of the GDP (from 60 percent in 2011), and Barbados spends more than 13 percent of its revenues to pay its debt (U.S. Central Intelligence Agency 2012). Not since independence has the public discourse of economic uncertainty been more pronounced, and the mantra of neoliberal flexibility resounds from all corners.

NEOLIBERALISM, OFFICIAL DISCOURSE, AND THE NATIONAL "STRATEGIC PLAN"

The Barbados government's recent strategic plan for 2005 to 2025, boldly titled *Global Excellence, Barbadian Traditions*, offers a rich portrait of Barbadian neoliberalism. The plan identifies the building of social capital as the heart of the development process, stating that its number one goal is "a cultural transformation that will reinforce Barbadian values and national identity and act as a catalyst for propelling Barbados into the 21st century as a fully developed society. This goal will seek to create greater equity and social justice, while building an inclusive society with opportunities for all" (Government of Barbados 2005, 2). Central to this mission is the expansion of entrepreneurship as a mechanism for enhancing "nation building" both symbolically and economically. In addition to symbolizing Barbadian nationhood via innovation, creativity and independent entrepreneurialism are familiar neoliberal positions toward retrenching social welfare and the state. Indeed, its authors articulate the converging models of local reputational flexibility and neoliberal flexibility, stating that "Barbadians are blessed with the gift of adaptability. It has served us well in the past. We must now build the future on the best of the past." The key, they state, lies in "high value services in the new global economy" (26). Two interconnected goals are emblematic of the neoliberal regime: the retrenchment of state supports, such as welfare, and the encouragement of self-employment and entrepreneurship as the engine of economic growth. The strategic initiative addresses not only ingredients for economic growth, security, law and order, and environmental protection but also for other more general dimensions of life in contemporary Barbadian society. The first three goals are telling, as each figured prominently in my own observations of change amid the entrepreneurial culture.

- Find creative ways of reconciling races, differences of class, culture and generation through social interaction, shared activities and a shared vision of Barbados.
- Create a dynamic, vibrant and extended public space where different races, groups, generations and classes can mingle in physical and social activities so as to create mutual respect, tolerance and build community.
- Break down the old paradigm of the black community functioning in the public sector and political life, and the white and other minorities in the private sector, and ensure that there is a welcoming and enabling social and economic environment that embraces diversity. (Government of Barbados 2005, 46)

The emphasis on creativity and innovation as integral to a vibrant society and entrepreneurship as the key to advancement of the nation as a whole are reflected in each and every section of the lengthy plan. Branding the nation is another of its main goals.

The old paradigm whereby the state "belonged to the black community while the white community and other minorities functioned exclusively in the private economy is now" according to its authors, "bankrupt." Equally in need of change is the tradition of "dependency on the State rather than on self." Instead, "independence, self-reliance and thrift must therefore be re-emphasized" (Government of Barbados 2005, 31). In virtually every domain of life—education, formal skills training, religion, and political life—independent thinking and entrepreneurial acumen are hailed. Central to this process, the plan says, in a global marketplace and a "knowledge-based services economy," is "the creation of appropriate family, community and societal values." Intriguingly, "the family" is pictorially represented in nuclear form, by a father, mother, and two children, smiling happily together. It would be easy to read this one image as the state's reassertion of the "respectability" complex of Wilson's paradigm. However, such a reading ignores a number of changes at work in the meanings and experiences of not only kinship but also of a new *self* as economic agent, citizen, and reflexive, feeling subject, which is being imagined through contemporary neoliberalism.

Within official discourse and policy, especially amid a persistent economic recession, *flexibility* is among the most frequent catch terms of the day. Certainly the most ambitious illustration of a region-wide effort to create economic flexibility is the recently ratified Caribbean Single Market and Economy (CSME) (Newstead 2009). Owen Arthur, the former prime minister of Barbados, outlined the CSME rationale in a speech during my fieldwork. Modeled directly on the European Union, the "CSME brings together 14 separate and distinct markets and economies, each governed by their own rules and divided from each other by formidable barriers, to be organized and to be made to operate in the future effectively as *one* market and *one* economy, free of restrictive barriers, and governed by common rules, policies and institutions."[9] Arthur's regional free-market mantra departs intriguingly from the Marxist-inspired dependency critiques of the postindependence era, which were often tied to the nationalization of major industries (e.g., bauxite, sugar). The creation of a regional market, Arthur argues, provides such little island nations as Barbados with a "larger market and a wider set of options." He adds that the "liberalizing of services especially offers . . . an opportunity for expanded productivity that can compensate for any loss in commodity production."[10] Arthur's referent here is the dramatic decline in manufacturing industries as well as in sugar production, the island's historical economic base. In recent years sugar has been taken over by foreign interests and yielded to tourism and offshore services as the island's economic linchpin. The language of neoliberalism encoded in the prime minister's speech—the reign of free-market flexibility—has become so mainstream in Barbados that the association of sugar and protectionism is with an old, outmoded model of globalization. This in turn has been replaced by an assumed equation of services and new entrepreneurial enterprises with the rationality and flexibility of a new global era. The rigid hierarchy of government offices, the slow rate of promotions, and the sense of "time-serving" jobs under the surveillance of controlling bosses were all aspects associated with the bureaucratic respectability of an older order that the contemporary Barbadians I have interviewed describe and aim to transcend.

The neoliberal vision, with its emphasis on flexibility, has given rise not only to regional free-trade initiatives but also, at the national level, to a host of both private-sector and government-sponsored programs, such as the Small Business Development Center and the Youth Entrepreneurial Scheme,[11] and to a subtly changing profile for upward mobility in contemporary Barbados. Lynette Eastmond, a former senator and minister of Commerce, Consumer Affairs, and Business Development, summarized the new emphasis on a postcolonial order of flexibility and self-invention in a speech launching the National Innovation Competition of the Enterprise Growth Fund Ltd.[12] Asserting innovation and creativity and bemoaning the rigid tradition of respectability and bureaucratic conservatism, Eastmond said,

> What I urge in this context is a maximum degree of *flexibility* . . . the strength of a new economy must be in a structure where there are more opportunities . . . and . . . more flexibility. . . . I often wonder if there is not a Bill Gates or Michael Dell in Gall Hill that does not have access to a computer, a Venus Williams somewhere in St. Patrick's that does not have access to a tennis court, a Tiger Woods somewhere in St. Martin's that does not have access to a golf course . . . an Oprah Winfrey in Baxter's Road or Bathsheba that never got the opportunity to dream just a little. . . . This initiative should signal . . . the liberation of a mindset that restricts us to a sameness and a dullness. . . . There must be a change in attitude. We must believe that we are an innovative people . . . a creative people. . . . We must show support for creativity—we must not stifle it. . . . And it starts in the home—it is still the wish of most parents that their children should get a job—and if they are lucky a Government job—no matter the ability of the child or the inclination—unless of course their child could become a lawyer or a doctor.

Whereas reputation has long been seen as a set of strategies with which the lower classes have managed the risks and precariousness of life, East-mond emphasizes many of its central qualities (individualism, creativity, and flexibility) as vehicles for individual achievement and success in the current neoliberal regime. But the reputational referent is not restricted only to the practice of flexibility and individualism. It resounds as well in the senator's selection of icons of U.S. success, heroes of the new economy, many of whom are African American performers and athletes known also for their public sociality and generosity. In her examples she signals a pointed shift away from a tradition of British colonial order to one of U.S.-led neoliberal ingenuity and self-invention.[13]

Then parliamentary secretary in the Ministry of Economic Affairs, Senator Jepter Ince offered suggestive kernels of advice during a free "Life Lessons Rebalancing" seminar: "In these recessionary times people are going to be bothered . . . from the sense [of] 'whether or not I will be working tomorrow' but there are also advantages in a recession. You have the capacity to build another house in a recession, to rebalance your portfolio." Rebalancing entails "making a list of your assets" and personal skills. He advocates "productive debt" and paring down on relationships that are draining key resources: "The reality is that when you are looking at your lifestyle and rebalancing, there are some people that you have to leave because they are like parasitic plants in your bosom. . . . So . . . sit down and ask yourself whether or not you are spending your money wisely by having this parasitic plant hanging on to you" (Gittens 2013).

The modern Barbadian citizen conjured in these official remarks is entreated to be individualistic and adaptable, creative as well as industrious, and keenly attuned to a growing and changing market. These official invocations of flexibility and balance through the encouragement of a neoliberal vision of regional trade, support for local entrepreneurship, and shedding "parasitic" relationships have several unspoken referents: a retrenchment in the nation's public sector, the decline of the islands once-dominant sugar industry, the flight of global industries in search of cheaper labor, and a gradual erosion of the power of trade unions, not to mention the stranglehold of traditional respectability that threatens to choke the creative imagination and drive of today's youth.[14]

Jimmy, a successful black Barbadian fashion entrepreneur in his mid-thirties, described the milieu of his upbringing as follows,

> in Barbados you tend to grow up believing that there is only one way to do things and that's the way that the society dictates umm, you know . . .

you finish school, you get a good job in their minds which is, like, you know . . . blah blah blah, whatever . . . and that you get married, you have kids you build a big house and you travel once a year and . . . that's like the glorious life. Having left Barbados and lived abroad, I am realizing that, oh my God, you know . . . you actually have choices and that's actually the biggest thing with me . . . I try whatever situation I'm in, to always have choice even if the choice means like just cutting everything loose, accepting the losses and just leaving or going somewhere else or moving on.

To me that's a choice . . . I don't believe in being stuck in situations . . . I have friends and family who are in relationships whether it be married relationships or whatever the case is they're just there and they're, like, 'okay, we have kids, so that we know there's nothing that I can do about it . . . umm you know, what am I supposed to do, leave this? I don't know what I can find out there, so you know I've got to stay here even though it's not the best for me. I've got to stay here . . . ' That's crap, I mean things like that drive me absolutely insane, you know, but people seem to settle for that . . . around here.

Jimmy highlights several key themes: changes to the conservative conventions of upward mobility and middle-classness in Barbados and the centrality of "choice," individualism, and flexibility as concepts within these neoliberal transformations (Gill 2008; Walkerdine 2003).

Sylvia, a middle-aged black Barbadian events planner, characterized the impetus for change and her sense of Barbadian traditional culture as follows,

Barbadians are not like people in the States. They feel you work some place for forty years and that's stability and so on. Whereas in the States, you know, you encourage people to go out and, you know, pursue other things, broaden your horizons. . . . But here people feel if you have a good job? Why not stay in it? I think . . . it might be a colonial type mentality . . . you know a kind of master-servant relationship, and if you look at basically, umm, the type of sectors, the main sectors here . . . like sugar, the distributive sector, it is always . . . kind of a master-servant relationship, and I don't think people have got out of that as yet, especially the older ones. . . . A lot of younger people now, through exposure to education, going overseas . . . see that there is a lot more to life than working for a company and then at the end of forty years getting a reclining chair or a gold watch . . . I really can do a lot more with my life and I think as you get older and you look at your parents' lives you realize that maybe they were not as happy as they pretended to be, but they wanted to put bread on the table, they wanted to improve the financial conditions for the family.

Sylvia's mention of the "master-servant" structure of the plantation system was echoed in numerous testimonies of both black and white entrepreneurs when asked about the history of entrepreneurship in Barbados. Black Barbadians spoke about the disadvantage they felt not having grown up in families where children are expected to take over a family enterprise and where business was the center of dinner conversation, as they perceived to be the case for the white establishment. White women, on the other hand, described the sense that few options were open to them apart from the back offices ("doing the books"), since the government sector and the professions as well as the "storefront" were all "off limits" to them. For middle-class black Barbadians like Queenie, a successful designer and architect in her thirties, getting access to a bank loan was "easy" because her family is "well connected" and she came with "a good degree." Without such credentials and contacts, she noted, "start-up support is near to impossible." Indeed, class and connection more than race overridingly shaped entrepreneurs' access to loans and formal networks, and as we will see, gender profoundly shapes the entrepreneurial course.

Entrepreneurs echo in their testimonies this changing aspirational ethic in which self-determination is increasingly prized over a long-standing official valuation of bureaucratic security, and entrepreneurship is seen as a path to be sought rather than a path of last resort.[15] As many have expressed the shift to me, business as either the nepotistic preserve of a small number of white elite families or the survival strategy for the poor is currently ceding to a new esprit of middle-class entrepreneurial aspiration. Like the government officials, the entrepreneurs I have interviewed quote familiar U.S. business gurus like the late Peter Drucker and the Microsoft giant Bill Gates; they make contact with U.S. firms to source materials and supplies, and they view U.S. business culture as a goal to be achieved. Nevertheless, they simultaneously employ social networks and cultural resources that must be understood within a national and regional frame. Entrepreneurship, for them, represents a new promise of upward mobility and social esteem once perceived to be the preserve of other more "respectable" occupations. Entrepreneurial pursuits are motivated frequently by the goal of creative self-invention, dispensing with hierarchy, bosses, and the "establishment" in ways that are reminiscent of reputation's long-standing oppositional qualities. Middle-class entrepreneurship is often taken up in ways deeply reminiscent of lower-class reputational ingenuity, whereby individuals create two or more businesses in an effort to manage risk, sometimes in consonant enterprises and sometimes in completely unconnected fields. Entrepreneurship also allows for middle-class women to enter fields (manufacturing, transportation, etc.) that would otherwise be viewed as unsuitable for "respectable ladies." For these entrepreneurs, increasingly, reputational flexibility is being decoupled from its lower-class associations and is being harnessed for the goals of class mobility, economic security, and middle-class self-invention in the context of the contemporary neoliberal economy. And this decoupling is fostered within a dynamic in which the two logics of flexibility are converging.

Following the paths of contemporary middle-class entrepreneurs over the past decade in Barbados has been a study in these two convergent but paradoxical logics of flexibility. The Caribbean logic of reputational flexibility is grounded in a set of cultural values of the subaltern, *in resistance* to bureaucratic hierarchy and (neo)colonial domination, while the logic of neoliberal flexibility sits firmly in the center of contemporary global capitalist orthodoxy. By examining the discourses of neoliberal flexibility and the broadly defined project of entrepreneurialism in the contemporary Barbadian context, my goal is not simply to "localize" an understanding of neoliberalism but also to examine how the convergence of these logics opens the lens on what Trouillot (2003, 126) has called "the particulars hidden by . . . sameness." The intertwining of these systems of flexibility suggests radically new middle-class ways of life. These new entrepreneurial practices and new subjectivities are both shaped by and actively reformulate the conventional parameters of reputation and respectability and in so doing crystallize new conditions of possibility under Barbadian neoliberalism.

MIDDLE-CLASS ENTREPRENEURIALISM

I see the emergent entrepreneurial middle class in contemporary Barbados as a new domain in which women and men from diverse class and racial origins are actively rearticulating class, gender, and race in ways that stand in uncomfortable juxtaposition to many of the persistent analytical binaries relating to class and capitalism—proletariat/bourgeoisie; blue/white collar; labor/leisure; production/consumption; market/domestic; public/private; masculine/feminine; Third/First Worlds; black or "other"/white. The story of neoliberal entrepreneurialism in Barbados offers an opportunity to recast our understandings of middle-classness not simply by shifting our gaze solely to realms and practices of consumption and lifestyles but also by bringing these into view through their relationship to labor in its broadest sense and its role in life more generally. Implicitly *class* analysis implied a *working*-class protagonist embroiled in struggle defined around labor and its extraction. *Middle class*, meanwhile, has been implicitly equated with classlessness, an empty category of labor nonetheless full of ideological meanings. By broadening the purview of class to include labor in all its guises, we will see that middle-classness is not reducible to consumption and lifestyle alone, and that lifestyle itself entails subtle forms of labor especially of an affective form. Put simply, middle-class entrepreneurialism entails a confluence of practices that meld production, consumption, symbolic meaning making, emotional engagement, and feeling that highlight some of the signatures of neoliberalism today. These contain the flexible labor of imagining, creating, and marketing goods, relationships, and selves, the expectations of having certain material things, enacting certain modes of leisure, and embodying certain ways of being in the world. Whether consumption-oriented, care-related, or self-directed, these practices are often inextricable from the work of entrepreneurship. The labor performed in many of these new realms is labor of a particular sort, often marked by its affective dimensions. And these affective elements are themselves *gendered*. To examine the rise of entrepreneurial middle classes, therefore, we must foreground their affective, gender, class, and cultural underpinnings.

These are especially anxious times for the middle class. The anxieties that blanket middle classes and what defines middle-classness today cut across political, cultural, academic, and popular spheres. While some are intent to argue that "class is dead" (Pakulski and Waters 1996), others are attempting to bring both sharper and more nuanced approaches to class analysis, especially in relation to the murky category of the middle class(es) (Wacquant 1991; Stewart 2010; Heiman, Freeman, and Liechty 2012). Aspirational longings to *become* middle class and nervous struggles to *retain* a middle-class foothold in a rapidly changing and insecure economy are common themes of the contemporary moment. The trumpeting defense of "middle-class families" and the sanctity of the middle class as the backbone of the nation and its democratic ethic, famously noted by de Tocqueville in the 1830s, resound in Barbados as it does in the United States. Increasingly such claims, worries, and dreams are echoed around the globe. For example, India has witnessed an exponential growth in its middle classes after its liberalization in 1990, growth embodied most evocatively in its dazzling IT sector of call centers and informatics zones and in the tremendous surge in new modes of consumption, leisure, and the refashioning of national culture, melding "global" with distinctively Indian elements (Baviskar and Ray 2011; Radhakrishnan 2011). In China, where the very concept of middle class was made controversial under socialism, the past two decades of a dual capitalist economy and an expanding middle class, a hunger for new modes of consumption and modern American-like lifestyles, will profoundly influence the country's cultural, political-economic, and environmental trajectory.[16]

Middle-class anxieties are also expressed within the academic terrain of social science, where efforts to define and measure who and what is middle class have been deeply contested. Indeed for the social analyst, the advertising and marketing industry, the political pundit and the voter today, middle-classness is a loaded and seductively vague concept. So capacious is the category of middle class that both the rich and the poor have been known to claim it, and so ill-defined are its analytical parameters that its utility has been questioned in the study of class. While classical social theories of Marx and Weber have been potent tools of class analysis of the bourgeoisie and proletariat, the particular place of the middle "strata" or class has been a notably murky terrain. Whereas historians have devoted careful study to the modern middle-class subject (Bledstein and Johnston 2001; Davidoff and Hall 1987; Frazier 1962; Hall 1992; Heinze 1992; Mills 1951; Peiss 1986; Smail 1994), and sociologists, political scientists, and psychologists have often assumed the middle class to be the ideal subject of research, middle classes have only relatively recently come under anthropology's "spy-glass" (Hurston 1990, 1). For a majority of anthropologists, poor, rural, and remote "non-Western" peoples have represented an almost sacred ethnographic subject. Indeed, until quite recently, one could say there existed a rough division of scholarly labor and analysis whereby anthropology, when not focused exclusively on exotic "others" in the Global South, turned its attention primarily to the poor (ethnic minorities, rural and urban lower classes) in the Global North, leaving the middle strata (most often equated with *white* middle class) to their sociologist, political scientist, or psychologist colleagues. Equally, albeit in different ways, the middle class has represented a problematic subject for feminist scholarship and for Caribbean studies. Together these ambivalences have created a notable silence I aim to begin to break with the stories of these emerging entrepreneurs.

ANTHROPOLOGY'S MIDDLE-CLASS ANXIETIES

The increasingly complex economic, political, and cultural dimensions of contemporary globalization have contributed to anthropology's growing interest in emergent "middling" groups. Questions about the restructuring of labor, the rise of mass consumption, and multidirectional flows of capital, commodities, information, and people, together with new articulations of "modernity," culture, and selfhood have drawn increasing ethnographic attention. The intensification of new global service industries and the inducement and attraction toward self-employment, new modes of leisure, and the project of self making now suggest new domains of study and reveal new complexities in the intersections of gender, class, race, and culture. Contemporary neoliberal emphases on market-driven economic growth and laissez-faire policies have brought about political-economic and cultural transformations that have compelled anthropology to broaden its traditional ethnographic frame. Today, especially with the dramatic growth of middle classes in China and India, a burgeoning new literature is beginning to address the particularities of culture and history in shaping middle-class sensibilities, practices, and politics (Baviskar and Ray 2011; Heiman, Freeman, and Leichty 2012; Jaffrelot and Van der Veer 2008; Liechty 2003; Patico 2008; Potrzeba 1998; Zhang 2010). I am not suggesting that middle classes have been wholly absent from anthropological accounts, but there has been a notable ethnographic ambivalence toward these groups, a distinctively suspect gaze and less "respectful recognition" (Kruks 2001, 160). In the extreme, middle-class subjects are portrayed as politically flaccid and economically corrupt, perhaps in part reflecting Marx's own characterization of the middle class as inherently unstable, destined for absorption into one of the "fundamental" classes, the bourgeoisie or the proletariat. At best the middle class offered potential allies to the working class, but their significance was subordinated to the legitimate protagonists or "universal class" of the proletariat. Laura Nader's (1972) suggestion several decades ago, that we "study up," urged anthropologists to take up "the colonizers rather than the colonized, the culture of power rather than the culture of powerless, the culture of affluence rather than the culture of poverty" (289). This call gained traction in the field, advancing ethnographies of corporations, bureaucracies, and state systems both in the United States and abroad. However, a preference for "the underdog," as Nader observed, has remained a powerful if generally unstated anthropological vow. Not surprisingly, the growing ethnographic interest in the global middle classes is lamented by some as a rejection of both a time-honored disciplinary tradition and righteous commitment. For Scheper-Hughes and Bourgois (2003), for instance, the recent thrust toward subjects whose lifestyles and lifeways seem to closely resemble our own represents too easy a path, a troublesome avoidance of the "thankless" and more difficult fieldwork constituting the center of anthropology's true mission: the study of the poor and the powerless. Wishing to reaffirm a disciplinary responsibility to the marginalized, they ask if anthropologists turn their backs on the dispossessed, who else will take up the charge (Scheper-Hughes and Bourgois 2003: xiv)?[17] Anthropology's privileged stance toward its traditional subjects has not only reflected a widespread political-economic identification with the disenfranchised but also an equally powerful sense that cultural authenticity and richness equally reside within the poor, the peasant, and the worker. The middle classes, by contrast, symbolized not only political and economic advantage (derived, by implication, at the expense of those lower on the social hierarchy) but also cultural mimicry and comparative *in*authenticity. In short, these groups have often been cast as too bland, too striving, and too familiar to warrant the ethnographic commitment of close and intimate examination. And if such middle-class ambivalences and avoidances have reflected the dominant tradition of anthropology, they are evident in somewhat different ways within the development of feminist social science, which one could argue has compounded the avoidance of middle-class women as worthy ethnographic subjects.

FEMINISM'S MIDDLE-CLASS ANXIETIES

For feminism, class analysis in general and the concept of middle-classness in particular have been fraught with dilemmas in other ways. On one hand, defining and placing women in class analysis (whether in relation to husbands or fathers as the true bearers of class by virtue of their relation to capital and labor) has long been a conundrum in many of the ways that "placing women" in development theory or classical theories of any kind have been problematic. Feminist scholars have questioned the persistent equation of class status and position with occupational brackets of "male breadwinners" or household heads, and they have drawn our attention to the complex dimensions of class as inextricably gendered and dynamic (Crompton 1989; Crompton and Mann 1986; Skeggs 1997; Steedman 1986). Second-wave socialist feminism helped to illuminate the gendered specificity of class by broadening the lens of analysis beyond the "shop floor" and the waged economy to include the family and private sphere as domains of labor and domestic relations as class relations (Sacks 1989). Ester Boserup (1970) inspired many feminist critics to attend to the particular position of women in relation to emergent capitalist development in the developing world. The underlying premise that "class structure" and "development" are neutral processes defined through structural economic relationships cast women's dual participation in reproductive and productive labor, a capitalist waged economy and an intimate domestic economy, as problematic, rather than the premise of gender neutrality within the models themselves. Arguments by U.S. feminists of color have been integral to this critique that the waged and unwaged distinction between public and private spheres failed to capture black, Latina, Asian, and white working-class women's active participation in waged *and* unwaged labor in the domestic realm. Brodkin (2000, 138) concluded that "one should not expect to find any generic worker or essential worker, or for that matter, working class consciousness . . . not only is class experienced in historically specific ways, but it is also experienced in racially specific, gender-specific and kinship-specific ways." Why then has it been so easy to assume a singular middle-class temperament and political sensibility? Whereas *difference* has been emphasized within the lower classes across axes of race and gender, sexuality, and religion, middle-classness is frequently understood in one-dimensional terms, often reduced to structural position (particular occupational or income categories) and/or cultural and political conservatism. Middle-class entrepreneurs push us to extend such historical and cultural specificity and the particular convergences of class, gender, and race as we have found critical to analyzing the working classes (Freeman 2000; Ong 1987).[18]

For some twenty-five years, black, Third World, and postcolonial feminists in particular have questioned an assumed white middle class as the unmarked subject of social analysis,[19] and they have defined themselves in contrast to "middle-class feminism" (i.e., second-wave liberal, white middle-class feminism). Emphasizing a "dialectics of black womanhood" and a rubric of "intersectionality," they have called for relational analyses of race, gender, and class (and sexuality). The concept of intersectionality (or multiracial or multicultural feminism) both deepened and reoriented feminist analysis, pointing to the ways in which the tripartite system of race, class, and gender work to mutually effect and constitute subjectivity and experience. In so doing, it has become clear, for instance, that motherhood and employment, reproductive and productive labor, private and public spheres must be engaged dialectically and not as discrete or oppositional domains of power and social practice.

So persuasive and strenuous have critiques been of second-wave liberal and white Western feminism that the very category of middle class has, in large part, been the putative baby thrown out with the analytical bathwater. Because middle-classness has often been collapsed as white and Western and the emphasis on axes of difference has been critical to newer feminist models of intersectionality, a logic has emerged in which lower-class women are implicitly understood to be nonwhite and, in turn, middle-class women (and middle-classness itself) as implicitly white. As Reynolds (1997, 10) notes, "'black' and 'working class' are used simultaneously, as if being a black person automatically equates with occupying a working-class position."[20] The middle, as such, becomes an empty and illegitimate category, place, and idea. Zora Neale Hurston (1950: 954) noted over a half century ago the importance of documenting the middle-class African American experience, arguing that while the upper class is "an interesting problem" to consider in contradistinction to poor black "folk," conspicuously absent was a "realistic story around a Negro insurance official, dentist, general practitioner, undertaker and the like."[21] So too did C. L. R. James (1962, 80) wonder "who and what are our middle classes? So shrouded in . . . ignorance, abstinence, shame, or fear . . . their situation is never analyzed in writing, or even mentioned in public discussion."

Intriguingly, while intersectionality has become mundane (or outmoded) as a prism of contemporary social science, little notice has been given to the invisibility of the middle class as anything but an empty category. When class is engaged, the binarisms of (white) middle-class femininity versus (black) lower-class femininity often reinforce an implicit elemental difference (Rollins 1985; Collins 1992). The mutual and lively interplay of gender and sexuality and race become hardened in reference to class, where the middle is often subject to analytical erasure.[22] Middle-classness becomes what Roland Barthes would call a myth, not in the sense of falsehood but in generating fixity or singularity of meaning and association: "Myth does not deny things, on the contrary, its function is to talk about them . . . it gives them a natural and eternal justification . . . it gives them the simplicity of essences" (Barthes 1972, 18).[23]

CARIBBEAN MIDDLE-CLASS ANXIETIES

All regions of the world have produced and been subject to certain powerful analytical preoccupations that attain enduring significance. These "gatekeeping concepts" can be said to reflect dominant social "facts" about these places and cultures as well as the particular theoretical and analytic interests of the scholars who generate them and the ferment or fashion of their times. If the value complex of honor and shame, for example, has served as a conceptual synecdoche for Mediterranean societies, *caste* has functioned as a keyword for India (Appadurai 1986; Fardon 1990). Whereas South and Southeast Asia spawned a large ethnographic corpus of symbolic and psychological analysis of culture (as well as political-economic and other traditions of ethnographic work), such analytical traditions are almost entirely absent in the anthropology of the Caribbean. I mention this to emphasize that gatekeeping concepts structure not only what kinds of knowledge get produced about a place and its people but also the kinds of questions that are *not* asked, and what spheres of life become off-limits. One of the ways in which the weight of the region's strong political economy tradition has been expressed is in a fundamental understanding of class. For Barbados, a country in which *both* major political parties are labor parties, the nation's history has been framed predominantly as one of struggle between a small elite and a large laboring majority (Beckles 1990; Lewis 1968). As I will explore throughout the chapters to follow, this fundamental relationship has fostered not only the marginality of the middle classes but also the avoidance of aspects of life that are especially pronounced within these middle strata.

For the Caribbean, no institution or idea has been more powerful in shaping social structure and our understanding of the region than the system of plantation slavery. The history of class in the Caribbean is mapped onto the pyramidal structure of the plantation economy, which is also framed in racial terms: a small tip of the pyramid occupied by the white plantation owners and later business elite, a thin middle layer occupied by professionals and civil servants (who, in some parts of the region are also classified as racially mixed, "brown," or lighter-skinned blacks), and a vast majority of poor blacks at the base of the pyramid. Caribbean ethnography has been framed in reference to the plantation, whether the focus has been that of agriculture and economic development or kinship, religion, and social organization. Of course, as a region literally formed out of the colonial quest for expansion and riches, there are good historical reasons to root any analysis of Caribbean societies and cultures in the historical fact of the plantation. Added to this fact has been a robust scholarly tradition of Marxist political economy and structural functionalism that have anchored the region's anthropological tradition (Freeman and Murdock 2001). The notion that "ethnicity is the cultural artifact and class stratification is the social artifact of the particular economic system of colonial and neo-colonial capitalism" encapsulates the dominant tradition (Lewis 1974, 124).[24]

The particularly ambivalent relationship between middle-classness and entrepreneurialism is widely rooted in the enduring legacy of the plantation. Knowles (1956) describes the predicament of post-emancipation Jamaica, where opportunities were few beyond the "quasi-feudal conditions of the estate" or scratching out a meager peasant life in the hills. What existed of a so-called middle class consisted of a small "brown strata,"

> the progeny of white settlers and the more comely slave girls. These people, given freedom, given the education and the minor posts in government which apologetic paternity bestowed, became a buffer between the whites and blacks at a very early date. Emulating the patterns of their white superiors, they were apathetic to business, industry, and capital accumulation. Membership in one of the professions, usually law (and never engineering), was a major goal, with the civil-service treadmill a second alternative. If unable to enter these fields, the last alternative was a clerkship in a large mercantile or warehousing firm. Their precious though precarious social status prevented them from indulging in the hard work and parsimony which business pioneering entailed and forbade entrepreneurship as a way of life. (Knowles 1956, 134–35)

This structure of the plantation established the social pyramid of Caribbean societies at large, while several factors distinguished Barbados from other sugar islands by the eighteenth century, including a female majority of slaves and the growing predominance of Creole or island-born slaves. After Emancipation, unlike Jamaica, for example, Barbados retained most of its resident planter class and had no peasantry to speak of. Some have argued that the presence of large numbers of both black and white women fostered the island's stability as well as its social conservatism. According to William Dickson in the late eighteenth century, "the white female majority tempered the brutish frontier mentality of planters and integrated white men into developed family structures" (Beckles 1990), ameliorating the slaves' condition as well as producing a smaller mulatto segment of the population and limiting opportunities for "free coloured" women to enter into the orbit of respectability through marriage (Beckles 1990:42). By the start of the eighteenth century, generations of slaves were born and raised on Barbadian plantations, establishing strong female figures of morality and familial support in the slave yards. Two elements of this history are especially significant for my discussion: if this presence of a large number of white women effectively curtailed the racial mixture, and subsequently the upward mobility of "coloured" women and men that characterized much of the rest of the region, so too did the tradition of matrifocality and the emphasis on labor and motherhood become central to the island's culture and economy.

For the social science of the Caribbean, Marx's premise that the middle and unproductive petit-bourgeoisie class would ultimately become absorbed either by the capitalist class or the proletariat has fit well within a similar dominant social structure between the planter elite and the former-slave majority. A strong trade-union history together with this long-standing Marxist scholarly tradition oriented much of the historical and ethnographic research in the region to the primacy of class conflict between the two extremes of the pyramid, leaving the middle stratum less well examined. Given the emphasis by most scholars of "Third World development" on the importance of a local middle class for the establishment of social and political stability and economic growth, this lacuna is striking. As within much of anthropology at large, the middle class(es) have largely eluded Caribbean anthropology, and social analysis more generally, as C. L. R. James's quote at the outset of the chapter suggests. Eager to describe the complex and distinctive expressions of the creole (new world) culture of people who defied the discipline's definition of *native* population by virtue of tracing their roots from elsewhere (Africa, Europe, and Asia), the anthropological focus turned on two main themes. First was the plantation economy and its poor and proletarianized inhabitants, whose suffering and marginal economic position under plantation slavery and its aftermath pitted them logically against their planter and capitalist counterparts. Second was the anomaly of Caribbean kinship, primarily that of matrifocality and its articulation, again, with the region's generalized economic impoverishment or, as some argued, as an expression of notable African cultural survivals. Both strands of argument, when put together with the powerful reputation-respectability paradigm, help to explain the analytic erasure of the region's middle-class subject.

Many of the region's most famous writers and scholars are known for their open antipathy toward the Caribbean middle class. George Lamming, a novelist and essayist and one of Barbados's most important native sons, pronounced that "there is no island in the Caribbean quite like my island. . . . We are, in Barbados, what you could call the colonizers. We are to be found everywhere in the Caribbean and when we arrived . . . we arrived in the role of organizers of other people's lives. We are either the policemen or the schoolmasters or the overseers on plantations" (2011, 36). Lamming's characterization of the middle-class Barbadian as fundamentally conservative and "colonial" pours forth in a speech he delivered to the Barbados Workers' Union titled "The Honourable Member." His naked hostility echoes the reputation-respectability complex, where cultural authenticity is securely anchored in the working class and the middle classes are repositories of colonial or neocolonial mimicry and a habitus mired in false consciousness.

> A man . . . you may have some reason to admire. He was born . . . in an urban village with a local primary school. Later he attended two secondary schools before going on a Government scholarship to a university abroad. He qualified as a lawyer, felt a passing interest in the study of economics, but was persuaded by his godfather, a senior public figure, to return to Barbados where his chances of a political career looked very promising. He had a moderate success at the bar, before he successfully contested an election. He has served as a Minister of Government and represented his country in various international negotiations. Today he owns three houses and a chicken farm. There is also substantial rumor of investments in an auxiliary transport service locally known as the mini-bus, and shares in various tourist resorts. . . . He occupies a large four-bedroom house in the rural suburbs with an ample view of six parishes. . . . His tastes have been influenced by foreign travel. The furniture is modern Scandinavian. . . . The walls, on all sides, are disfigured by juvenile souvenirs of illuminated nights in New York. . . . There are no books anywhere. . . . The family has two cars . . . his cultural preference in magazine reading and film is irreversibly American. . . . Many of his contemporaries had a privilege of schooling similar to his. Some have been chairmen of corporations, junior functionaries in development banks of one kind or another. A few are in general medical practice. No one of his acquaintance went into business. (Lamming 2011, 36)

While this "honourable member" is entrepreneurial in the old ways of reputation (in raising chickens, investing in mini-bus ownership, and diversifying economic investments), his middle-classness is secured within the civil service and that of his friends' in medicine or law. "No one . . . went into business," this antipathy to and avoidance of the middle-class subject and middle-class business in particular is noted by C. L. R. James as early as the 1940s, Jack Alexander in the 1970s, and more recently by Trouillot in the 1990s.[25] I suggest that analyzing middle-classness as a social category and subjective identity, both aspirational and "real," not only fills a critical gap in our understanding of Caribbean social and economic life today but also such an analysis challenges familiar understandings of some of the sacred concepts of contemporary social thought within and beyond the region: respectability, matrifocality, mobility, neoliberalism, and class.

In the Barbadian context the new entrepreneurial ventures and livelihoods I observed are evidence of shifting ideological and structural expectations about class mobility that move away from those entrenched in colonial and early postcolonial Barbados. Whereas petty traders and higglers are well-established historical icons of the lower classes, and the professional educated middle class marks a proud illustration of the fruits of free and universal education, the business sector has been a resilient symbol of white economic domination within Barbadian society (Beckles 1989). Today, the stigma long associated with business as a "nonrespectable" path for the Afro-Barbadian majority and the privileging of higher education as the route to upward mobility through the professions and civil service are gradually changing. Where business has been viewed as the privileged preserve of a small, nepotistic white elite or, as some point out to me, the path for "dummies" who couldn't advance at school, today these are increasingly aspirational paths for Barbadians of all backgrounds (Barrow and Greene 1979; Beckles 1990; Karch 1981; Ryan and Barclay 1992).

Some of the most striking new trajectories are being charted by women. Female autonomy and visibility in the labor force among Afro-Barbadian women is rooted in a history of plantation slavery, where women worked shoulder to shoulder with men, often in the most arduous field labor. Many scholars have claimed that greater egalitarianism was fostered amid women's long history of combined employment and motherhood. The place of white women's relationship to economic life and social mores are more shadowy in the historical record. Economic enterprise and "occupational multiplicity" are well known and prized qualities associated with Caribbean men and women of all races and social classes, and Caribbean women are especially hailed for their capacity to "cut and contrive." However, in light of this history, and the remarkable fact of women's equal representation in public- and private-sector employment today, current census figures are all the more surprising in revealing the number of self-employed males as more than twice that of females (Government of Barbados 2010:212). I contend that despite the proud feminine traditions of the resourceful and independent laborer, market higgler, and employed women in the respectable domains of teaching, nursing, and "pink collar" civil service or private sectors, middle-class entrepreneurship poses a risky terrain for women. Deeply rooted ideologies of gender and respectability that are inextricably bound up with class and race continue to challenge those who attempt to enter this niche of middle-classness, and white and black women alike shared stories of their challenges that cut across private, domestic, market, and public arenas. At the same time, popular rhetoric (and frequent resentment) about women's growing primacy in the economy, their increased rate of home and car ownership, and their numerical dominance in the university rosters was repeated to me over and over by men and women alike. One local official was outraged when I requested a "gender breakdown" of the numerical data on entrepreneurship, claiming there was no difference and why did "people keep harping on the hardships of women, when they're buying up all the houses and cars on the island?!"

Indeed, this new entrepreneurial fraction of society occupies a space of increasing political optimism and some degree of social anxiety as Barbados renews its vows to a neoliberal political economy. These entrepreneurs show us that understanding class in Barbados today cannot be reduced to a fundamental struggle between the planter and corporate elite and the laboring poor majority. They also illustrate gaps and erasures in the traditional gendered and racialized mapping of reputation and respectability. The draw toward middle-class entrepreneurship and its enactment by such a wide array of social actors provides a new lens through which to view class and mobility and the ways in which these are inflected within parameters of gender and race. In so doing, they illustrate a dramatic reconstitution of reputation and respectability. And they also support others' observations that far from disappearing, the middle classes and the set of desires and aspirations associated with middle-classness appear to be expanding, albeit in various and contested guises.

MIDDLE-CLASS TRAJECTORIES: UPWARD AND SIDEWAYS MOBILITY AND THE CONUNDRUM OF ENTREPRENEURSHIP

When one considers an emergent group such as middle-class entrepreneurs in Barbados and highlights rather than simplifies the complexities, multiplicities, and transformations marked by historical and cultural specificity, then the need for a new analytics of class is clear. I am interested in emphasizing not just the dynamic element of class as a process (Rapp 1978) but also simultaneously, and inextricably, the multiple dimensions of class, the economic and affective, material and subjective elements and expressions that lie at the core of the entrepreneurial story. In this sense the entrepreneurialism today encompasses not only efforts to craft new forms of middle-class livelihood and sensibilities but also new modes of labor integrally related to these transformations bringing materiality and subjectivity together as co-constitutive of class. Entrepreneurialism today represents simultaneously greater pressure placed upon the individual

TABLE 1.2 **Neoliberal realignments of respectability and reputation**

BUREAUCRATIC RESPECTABILITY	NEOLIBERAL ENTREPRENEURIAL RESPECTABILITY
Formal (higher) education	Practical experience
Corporate sector, civil service, professions	Self-employment
Hierarchy	Individualism, team building
Anglican, Methodist, mainline churches	Pentecostal/new age spirituality
Future-oriented	Present-oriented
Risk-averse	Risk-taker
Rigid structure	Flexibility
Security, stasis	Adventure, change
Patriarchal marriage	Intimate "partnership" marriage
Material-economic support	Emotional support
"Grin and bear"	Introspection, emotional expressiveness
Family duty	"Quality time"

to create her or his own livelihood in the absence or changing face of formal sector employment and opportunities to break out of traditional confines of gender, race, and class. In so doing, these practices and ways of being suggest radical transformations in some of the familiar institutions and cultural models that have long characterized Barbadian life. These are at once creative and onerous, spaces of aspiration and precarity, engaging and reconstituting both reputation and respectability.

Here, by way of introduction, I have selected three cases of entrepreneurs whose stories open up some of the intriguing ways in which Barbadians of all backgrounds, men and women, black and white, young and middle-aged, negotiate the path of entrepreneurship and, more broadly, give new meanings to the contours of reputation, respectability, and middle-classness. For some, this involves dramatic upward mobility; for others it means a more "horizontal" course that entails equally remarkable navigation of gender, conjugality, kinship, sexuality, and business ownership. In all cases, this points to both the need to read middle-classness through the lens of class and to the impossibility of reading these entrepreneurial endeavors as class acts or projects alone. Many of the most striking contradictions and new forms of life and livelihood emerging under the new entrepreneurialism are especially pronounced among women entrepreneurs. On an individual basis, Colleen, Sheila, and Suzanne each navigate the rough seas of middle-class respectability in ways that specifically relate to their different class origins, race, and efforts to forge new definitions of middle-class entrepreneurial femininity. These portraits, and those woven through the rest of the book, offer a small window into some of the trajectories being undertaken in the name of entrepreneurship that are illustrative of new ways of being and new ways of defining the self in a culture of neoliberalism.

Colleen (her pseudonym of choice) is the youngest of three sisters raised alone by their mother, a domestic worker. Her father had abandoned the family by the time of her birth. Raised to value education, go to church, and strive for a secure job, all central markers of Barbadian respectability, Colleen achieved her mother's dream by landing a position in a bank on completion of secondary school. Like many of the entrepreneurs I have studied, however, Colleen left the security of her respectable job at the bank in favor of other dreams. Disheartened and bored by her bank job, and inspired by experiences she had traveling in the United States, at nineteen she started the island's first motivational Outward Bound–like operation—offering "wellness weekends" and "team-building" expeditions on the island's undeveloped and rugged east coast for companies and government divisions as well as tourists. She describes her business as a way of combating the "conservative and homebodyish" Barbadian sensibility, which she says has never generated "much of a culture for exploration of the outdoors." Trading "skirt suits" for climbing gear, shorts, and head wrap and the interior air-conditioned office domain of the bank for the hot sun and rugged outdoors, she honed new skills of physical fitness and turned her energies to converting twenty-six acres of rab (uncultivated) land into an operating wellness retreat and to growing herbs and vegetables "on the side" for sale to local groceries and supermarkets. She rejects some of the most prized signs of middle-class livelihood and status in favor of some of the most fraught markers of plantation labor (toil and sweat under a blazing sun)—but in so doing she moves from waged employee to owner, from service worker to entrepreneur.

A reorientation of middle-class ideologies of the colonial past is exemplified as well by Colleen's move away from the Anglican Church of her husband's solidly middle-class family to seek more individualized spirituality. Like many of the entrepreneurs I encountered (men, women, black, white, young, and old), she invokes God and the sense of divine guidance as central to her life and her entrepreneurial quest. But her faith and commitment to God are enacted personally, through individual discussions with a new pastor, and on and in her own spiritual terms, which often involve nature and rigorous physical exercise. Combining a love of sport, adventure, nature, and what David Brooks (2005) has recently called "aspirational capital"—the "fire in the belly" determination to prove herself to her absent father and to the highly stratified society in which she was raised—together with $12,000 in personal savings, a $5,000 loan from a government program to spur youth entrepreneurship, six employees, and the help of a supportive husband, she had grossed $200,000 the year I met her (2001), a figure that has increased substantially since.

Barbadian entrepreneurs like Colleen vigorously embrace the neoliberal mantra of *flexibility* and *autonomy*, using these terms often as well as highlighting their various meanings. They articulate a passionate desire to break out of and move beyond the limits set for them by bosses and by bureaucratic institutional frameworks, seeking self-realization, greater economic rewards, and, in the case of women, the pressing goal of managing competing demands of work and family life. For Colleen, the decision to marry, and the kind of intimate "partnership" she works to build with her husband, depart dramatically from both the matrifocal household of her upbringing and from the patriarchal norms of "traditional" Barbadian middle-class respectability. Her rejection of the respectability of her bank job and her adventurous cultivation (both literally and symbolically) of new landscapes and economic vistas through her business are met with both wonder as well as pointed barbs by those around her. As she recalled: "Recently this guy came up the gap and he said to me, 'What are you . . . what are you *doing* up there?! Don't you know . . . you women . . . you always got a problem . . . you don't know *your place*. . . . You should be on the ground, you should be wearing a skirt!!' I mean, he was livid, he was mad! And I said, 'Don't you think those days are gone!?'"

Unlike Colleen and the many other black Barbadian women and men who have propelled themselves upward into the middle class and embrace entrepreneurship as a new path of self-definition, creativity, and livelihood, the case of Sheila charts another trajectory. Sheila's middle-class upbringing offered her opportunities that she acknowledges as integral to her entrepreneurial success—even as it also registers her failures in the conventionally valued realm of academic achievement. The twenty-five-year-old owner of Red Carpet Express, a small company she started in 1999 after having worked as a marketing manager of a business software company, Sheila describes her mother's reaction to her leaving a "good"—that is, secure—job in a private, foreign-owned marketing firm in favor of self-employment as one of bemusement and chagrin. Her family is steeped in some of the most valued signs of middle-class respectability, especially education—her father is a doctor, her mother a secretary in the Ministry of Education; one aunt is a university professor, another a secretary in the prime minister's office. Nevertheless, reputation lurks around the edges of this middle-class respectability, as Sheila's father left the family when she was young and has maintained only tenuous ties and intermittent support. Sheila is the only entrepreneur in her family. While traveling across the region marketing software for hotels, she came to realize how the vagaries of travel and poor service can deter repeat tourism, and she turned this observation into the basis for a thriving new business.

Unlike the numerous registered tour operators in Barbados, required by airport regulations to abide by certain rules and regulations, Sheila's company has a special arrangement that exempts VIP guests from some of the red tape related to arrival and departure. Having secured contracts with all of the island's most exclusive hotels, utilizing excellent self-promotion skills, she has cracked a normally dense and notoriously rigid bureaucracy. She is also grossing $10,000 a month (more than a well-paid doctor would earn). Her overhead is $1,500 a month for her two full-time employees and her cell-phone bills.

Sheila is an attractive and vivacious Afro-Barbadian woman. She admits to using her good looks and flirting acumen to her advantage, saying, "I didn't have a hard time getting myself through the door when it came to men but I had a very hard time keeping it above board." Her entry into entrepreneurial work and its relation to the rest of her life, family background, and modes of femininity are full of contradiction; at every turn, Sheila signals her negotiation of the boundaries of middle-class respectability and the more risky, public aspects of her entrepreneurial life. Like many others I interviewed (men and women alike), she describes herself as a maverick—a rebel of sorts in the conservative Barbadian context.

Sheila started the business as a way of creating flexible hours to care for her young daughter and a nephew she is raising as her own. Now that the business has grown, she employs a nanny-housekeeper and enlists the occasional help of her mother to juggle her busy work schedule with school pickups, dinner, and other family responsibilities. Her active social life has helped her to gain the contacts she has needed to make her way, inventing from scratch a new entrepreneurial niche within the tourism sector. They, in turn, have earned her privileged access in this sector and speak to her entrepreneurial savvy—garnered during long nights in the public space of the airport.

Married young, the mother of two young children, and the employer of a full-time domestic worker, Sheila upholds some of the key indicators of respectability that were precarious in her own upbringing. Although, in the professional realm, education and occupational status conferred middle-class respectability upon the family, her absent father, like Colleen's, diminished their respectable status. Now separated from her own husband, Sheila enjoys a less formal "friendship" of an older man but is careful to keep this more flexible and intimate relationship "quiet," hidden.[26] She described, with tremendous emotion, the process of going to two banks to apply for a mortgage for a house, to be financed entirely by herself, another of the primary signs of middle-class respectability.

> We were still living under one roof but we knew we were going to separate so the plan was that when I bought the house, I would just move out and go into my new home. He signed the document saying he has no claim on the house . . . he has not contributed anything to the house, he doesn't want the house, whatever, and they [the banks] would not accept it [my mortgage application]. They would not accept it. . . . I gave them my contracts from my hotels . . . my hotels are *very* good hotels, *well-known* hotels, and the [female bank manager] says, "you know what . . . we will feel safer if your husband was guarantor." Fine, I said, all right. They went through. And then, to find out when the mortgage papers came through that they had on [only] . . . my husband's name. . . . My name was not even on the damn mortgage. I got my lawyer to write them . . . but up to this day when I go to pay my mortgage, it is not even in my name.

With her repeated attempt to claim respectability in her own name, Sheila embodies a struggle that is at once about changing configurations of gender, class, marriage, and local capitalist relations. Her story highlights the dialectical tussle between the gendered expectations of respectable femininity and the impetus toward self-invention and economic independence through entrepreneurship. It speaks to the lengths to which women entrepreneurs in particular must go to offset their participation in the realm of reputation with the signs and symbols of "proper" femininity. She has utilized her well-honed reputation to generate contacts, enhance her business, and secure her own economic base with the respectable goals of home ownership and both economic and emotional security for her children. Her encounters with not one but two female bank managers—themselves iconic gatekeepers of respectability—are reminders, however, of the complex ways in which the moral codes and boundaries of respectability can be enforced to serve the interest of an older patriarchal order. Her struggle over her marriage was fraught with tension over maternal duty and a model of intimate partnership that eluded her. When her marriage no longer conformed to the partnership she desired, she described in emotionless terms, as she would a business deal gone bad, that divorce and shared custody was the logical solution. That she was not beholden to her husband as a primary breadwinner gave her the flexibility to end her marriage and pursue other romantic and business relations while continuing to rely on the paid services of nannies and maids and on her extended family to sustain her single-household headship and business.

For Sheila and for several other divorced or single entrepreneurial mothers whose stories will be explored more closely in chapter 3, and like the lower-class women described by Olive Senior (1991) and Y. T. Moses (1981), a "traditional" or patriarchal husband may offer financial support but still be seen as an impediment to the flexible livelihood, sentiment, and partnered relationship they seek. For middle-class entrepreneurial women, risk taking, innovation, travel, adapting to changing market niche specializations, and other aspects of neoliberal flexibility become integrally connected to those practices more frequently associated with conventional middle-class respectability (saving, reinvesting in the company, relying on family networks and support, and, in the household realm, assuming responsibility for all of the domestic and child-care duties). They negotiate the masculine public sphere to gain economic resources with which to procure some of the key markers of middle-classness, but, as both Sheila and Colleen demonstrate, this can require a delicate balancing act. To leave the secure and respectable worlds of conventional employment and marriage and embrace the public domain of entrepreneurship entails a new model of upward mobility and self-definition. These paths are neither seamless nor predictable.

The story of Suzanne encapsulates a different middle-class story and trajectory into entrepreneurship. The daughter of a white Barbadian family, her upbringing has the appearance of quintessential upper-middle-class respectability—her father a businessman and her mother active in her parish church, available to her grandchildren, and behind the scenes of her husband's company. Suzanne was educated at the same top public secondary school as Sheila and many of the entrepreneurs from all social backgrounds (an interesting story in itself, and like Sheila and other Afro-Barbadian Queens grads, Suzanne noted that she too had "failed her deportment badge").[27] She went to university in Canada, where she earned a degree in art and business, returned home, and worked in a popular tourist restaurant. As she put it, to be a white woman in Barbados, the usual areas of work were off-limits: the civil service, the professions—"how many white women do you see in government jobs or as doctors and lawyers? No way. We could never make it there, so if we want to stay at home in Barbados, business is the only way."

After marrying the white Barbadian son of a small local hotelier, she had a baby and quit her job. Restless and lonely in their modest middle-class subdivision—a pink "wall house" surrounded by chain-link fence—she began a small clothing design company from her living room sewing machine. What began as a combined effort to "pay for nappies" and other growing expenses related to their new family life, and a diversion from the isolation of suburban motherhood, grew into a hugely successful enterprise in which she currently employs six people full time and exported a large delivery recently valued at half a million U.S. dollars. On one hand, Suzanne has benefitted from financial and other forms of support of her extended family—her father served to back the bank loan for $20,000 she needed for equipment and machinery. His friendship with the bank's manager, no doubt, helped her application go through. Meanwhile, Suzanne's mother and sister regularly help out with child care and school runs when meetings and travel keep her away from home. And perhaps most significant of all, her reliance upon a full-time nanny-housekeeper, an ubiquitous ingredient in black and white middle-class life, was, as she put it, "her life-line": "I couldn't do all this without her." When we commiserated about finding good daycare and juggling our work and children, she, like many of the mothers I got to know, added that she could never live like I do in the States working and raising kids "without a full-time 'helper.'" I return to the question of "work and life" and the central role of paid domestic labor in middle-class entrepreneurial life in chapter 4.

Suzanne's remark, however, was more than a throwaway line. With her business's success, and nomination for the island's Entrepreneur of the Year Award, however, her marriage progressively faltered: "He just couldn't handle the fact that I earned more and didn't need him in the same way." The story of her marital demise is poignantly echoed in the narratives of a striking number of women entrepreneurs I interviewed, both white and black.[28] In addition to the growth of women's economic independence through entrepreneurship, mounting tensions revolved around two other "traditionally" gendered dimensions of Barbadian life, a remarkably sex-segregated social sphere and the expectations for women to assume full responsibility for the domestic arena (themes I develop in chapters 4 and 5). Four years after our first meeting, I returned to interview Suzanne again to find that she had "had an affair" and had ended her ten-year marriage. She described with visible affection the ways in which her boyfriend had challenged some of the "frustrating and selfish" qualities of her husband, whom she described as "your typical Bajan man." Meanwhile, her economic circumstances were now more precarious, and her story circulated wildly through the island's rumor mill. As Jamaica Kincaid (1982, 52) has noted of neighboring Antigua, "in a small place . . . [t]he small event is isolated, blown up, turned over and over, and then absorbed into the everyday so that at any moment it can and will roll off the inhabitants of the small place's tongues." Suzanne's transgression of expected gender and race norms for proper middle-class womanhood had further ramifications beyond the well-honed gossip and social awkwardness among friends and family. So threatening to the social norm was her extramarital affair that her husband had managed to get immigration officials to revoke her boyfriend's work permit and "kick him off the island."

Read together, these three very different stories of young women's entrée into entrepreneurship and their social and intimate webs of kinship, conjugality, and work elucidate just how impossible it is to interpret middle-class entrepreneurship outside an analytical framework that simultaneously engages race, gender, kinship, and class. For each of these individuals, the pursuit of entrepreneurship is framed both by a system of neoliberal economic demands and restraints and within a cultural context in which economic conditions of possibility are themselves mapped onto particular racial, gendered, and classed expectations of respectability and reputation. Their delicate negotiations to pursue economic independence, distinction, and new modes of self making reveal striking convergences along gender and race lines and speak simultaneously to the remaking of the middle class and the slippery capacity for respectability to reassert old patriarchal norms.

Increasing numbers of Barbadian women and men are drawn to entrepreneurship in ways that depart from previous generations' notions about business, "respectable" femininity, and middle-classness. Of the 107 entrepreneurs I interviewed and surveyed, their backgrounds are as varied as their businesses. One set of questions I raised in my interviews with entrepreneurs related to class mobility and the manner in which their entrepreneurial path and life-style departed from their familial roots. I found cases of dramatic upward mobility, cases of sideways mobility (from civil service or other realms of employment to entrepreneurship but maintaining similar economic and social relations), and a few cases of downward mobility among women and men from both black and white households in which the lifestyles and economic circumstances of their upbringing were more tenuous and limited currently. Barbados offers a rich site in which to examine the subtle meanings of middle-classness, with a stable parliamentary democracy, and a culture both praised and caricatured in the region for its staid, middle-class conservatism. Perched atop the international list of "developing" countries, Barbados boasts a 99 percent literacy rate (among the top five nations in the world),[29] an excellent free education system through secondary school, and a heavily subsidized university system modeled on the British system. Not surprisingly all but four of the entrepreneurs had at least a high school education. Some had pursued associates degrees, university, a few held masters degrees and one had earned her PhD. Most of those I interviewed had traveled outside of Barbados on at least one occasion if not more frequently to visit family, on holiday, or to pursue education. Every one of them lived in a home that they (and I) would describe as a comfortable "wall" house in distinction from a traditional lower-class "chattel house" made of wood—whether a middle-class house in a suburban subdivision, in a more densely populated part of town, or in a rural part of the island.

As I will examine more closely in the next chapter, an overwhelming majority of these entrepreneurs are married in a national context in which a majority of adults are not. Their religious profiles, like their business trajectories, show signs of flux: more than a third described migrating from the religious traditions of their upbringing (Anglican, Methodist, Catholic) to other churches or alternative spheres of spiritual life. All told, these social actors are poised to change the entrepreneurial profile and, simultaneously, the contours of what it means to be middle class and respectable today. But the path they navigate is not uniform or smooth, and the pitfalls are often uniquely gendered. The opportunities for new self-definition as well as the traps and curtailments signal fertile terrain on which to analyze how gender, race, and class are intimately intertwined in specific cultural terms via familiar tropes of neoliberalism.

CHAPTER 2

Entrepreneurial Affects

"PARTNERSHIP" MARRIAGE AND THE NEW INTIMACY

Marriage is regarded with a certain amount of reverence . . . yet many prefer to admire it from afar. To Caribbean women, in particular, its benefits seem dubious.
—HODGE 2002, 481

The contemporary esprit of Barbadian neoliberalism, with its emphasis on flexibility, economic self-sufficiency, and supple responsiveness to an ever-changing marketplace, has unleashed a groundswell of entrepreneurship that is not contained within the sphere of business enterprise and the pursuit of economic livelihood alone. In this and the following chapter, I turn to life outside (but not unconnected to) the immediate sphere of "work" to illustrate how this neoliberal spirit permeates many other dimensions of life, including those we might be inclined to see as part of the "private" domains of the intimate and personal. This chapter highlights both the porous boundaries of public and private, "work" and "life," and the permeability of these relations within an emerging neoliberal culture or what I will describe as a neoliberal structure of feeling (Williams 1977, 131). Entrepreneurialism becomes a manner of life not restricted to the running of a "business" but the enactment of selfhood more generally. As the spirit of flexibility and desires to craft entrepreneurial lives seep across the market and nonmarket realms, we also will see new permutations of gender that give new meanings to both the Caribbean formulation of reputation and respectability and, I will argue, challenge some of the arguments about the gendered qualities of neoliberalism at large. And while the rise of neoliberal entrepreneurship, as outlined earlier, highlights global resonances of these trends, it is especially in these less public, explicitly economic spheres of life—in realms of kinship, conjugality, and parenting, for example—that we see some of the most profound locally significant dimensions of these transformations.

I will suggest that the multiple reformulations of marriage, matrifocality, parenting, leisure, therapeutic and spiritual life can be interpreted as dimensions of contemporary political-economic and sociocultural restructuring of middle-class life. They articulate new affective and economic desires under neoliberalism (Rofel 2007). In the project of entrepreneurial self making, individual benchmarks of success and the compartmentalization of leisure, work, the social, the family, the child, the couple, and the self are all subject to regimes of flexibility such that they can be defined and reordered. In short, marriage, intimate relationships, parenthood, and selfhood, like businesses, become projects that demand similar adaptability, innovation, sensitivity to external demands, creativity, and responsiveness. I will take each of these examples in turn to illustrate the intricate processes and affective labors involved in these respective and interconnected projects.

Scholars and the popular media across the world have noted two intriguing trends about marriage today. On one hand are high rates of divorce and a growing number of households that defy the nuclear profile of a married couple and their dependent children.[1] On the other hand, romantic love and a modern formulation of "companionate marriage" or marriage founded upon intimacy and emotional compatibility appear to be "going global" (Hirsch and Wardlow 2006, 2). In this and the following chapters, I interpret what were surprising findings about marriage, desires for intimacy, and the domestic lives of many of the entrepreneurs I have studied for the past ten years in Barbados. In a country well known for the independence and active roles played by women across all levels of the economy, and the predominance of the "matrifocal" (woman or mother-centered) family, one dimension of entrepreneurs' lives I had not anticipated was the salience of marriage. When I first surveyed them, a striking majority (67 percent) of the entrepreneurs in my study (107) were married, when according to the latest census, less than a quarter of the adult Barbadian population is married (Government of Barbados 2000). According to recent statistics, the patterns I observed early on and transformations I have witnessed subsequently reflect two general trends on the island: a rise in marriage and a simultaneous rise in divorce.[2]

TABLE 2.1 **Entrepreneurs vs. national marriage rates**

MARITAL STATUS	NEVER MARRIED	MARRIED	LEGALLY SEPARATED/ DIVORCED
General Population (226,193)	66.60%	23%	1.30%
Entrepreneurs (n = 107)	22%	67%	11%

Source: Tabulable Population, Barbados Census (May 2010)

I see the simultaneous growth in marriage and divorce as an indication of a subtle sea change in gender ideologies and a growing affective culture in which desires for intimacy and emotional life more generally are on the rise. In Barbados the conjoining of flexibility and marriage has an ironic ring, as elaborated in chapter 3, because adaptability and flexibility are qualities long associated with matrifocal, nonmarried, lower-class families precisely in contradistinction to the rigid, orderly, and hierarchical values of patriarchy imbued by British colonial tradition (Smith 1988; Alexander 1977; Barrow 1988; Senior 1991; Wilson 1973). However, the reconceptualization of marriage as a *partnership* involves notions of flexibility, mutual support, and shared responsibility that challenge some of the rigidities and hierarchies of a more traditional patriarchal marriage form. Indeed, the convergence of entrepreneurial livelihoods with a reconfiguration of marriage as a romantic and economic partnership demonstrates precisely the manner by which technologies of subjectivity become most marked under neoliberalism.

Especially striking, however, was not just the prominence of marriage among these entrepreneurs but also the manner in which marriage was being envisioned and evaluated in their musings about life, business, and the fashioning of themselves. Along with a new emphasis on and formulation of marriage, powerful illustrations emerged of entrepreneurial women enacting what can best be described as matrifocal kinship and households, where they are self-described heads of their families and homes. Both processes—the emergence of a new vision of marriage and of matrifocality within the entrepreneurial middle class—suggest new articulations of neoliberal kinship and selfhood, a new cultural matrix of respectability and reputation that is being forged across economic and affective domains of life. Marriage has long been portrayed as integral to the value complex of respectability established by British colonial tradition, enacted within the elite and middle classes, and the aspiration of all people, especially women.[3] At the same time, no institution has been more suggestive of the heart of lower-class Afro-Caribbean culture than the matrifocal woman- or mother-centered family, associated with the flexible survival skills and generalized strength of lower-class women and the creole cultural complex of reputation more generally.[4]

The articulation of these new partnership marriages with an upward mobility of the tradition of matrifocality demonstrates complex interconnections between broad economic trends and the most intimate facets of people's lives. By 1979 the concept of illegitimacy was eliminated under the law, and since 1975 inheritance has been protected for all children regardless of the marital status of their parents. Roughly three quarters of children born on the island are born outside of formal wedlock (Epstein and Limage 2008, 57). The Barbados Family Law Act of 1981 changed the basis for divorce from "fault to mutual consent by stipulating 'irretrievable breakdown' as the sole grounds." Intriguingly, just as marriage rates and divorce rates climb in tandem in Latin America and the Caribbean region at large, moderate increases in divorce rates occur alongside substantial increases in female headship, especially among women with higher levels of education (World Bank 2011, 21). Today Barbados has the tenth highest divorce rate in the world, which is especially notable in light of its historically low rates of marriage.[5] Some have speculated that the steady increase in divorce reflects "a cultural redefinition of conjugality from the previous emphasis on individual autonomy, a division of labor and place between spouses, and attachment to one's own kin group, to new and more intense expectations of intimacy, romantic love, togetherness, fidelity and commitment for the future" (Epstein and Limage 2008, 57). Meanwhile higher expectations for marital satisfaction as promoted by a growing neoliberal culture of free-market choice as well as entrepreneurial self-mastery, self-improvement, and self-actualization can be understood to prompt heightened awareness of gaps, flaws, and unsatisfying marital projects, hence their dissolution. In order to interpret these observations and relate them to the often sensationalized global, modern trends of romantic love, divorce, and alternative definitions of *family*, it is critical that we situate the particulars of contemporary neoliberal Barbados within the cultural legacy of *reputation* and *respectability* that has framed its history (Trouillot 1989).[6]

Three adages about women are well known in the Afro-Caribbean community and are explored richly in the region's social science literature: *Caribbean women have always worked; work has never precluded motherhood in the Caribbean; motherhood often precedes marriage and surpasses it in im-*

portance. It is difficult to emphasize strongly enough how important these are to understanding contemporary women's lives and the more general transformations at work in gendered social relations and subjectivities today. Knowing the history of women's work and kinship formation in Barbados, I had anticipated that the upward mobility of petty trade and entrepreneurship into the ranks of midsized businesses and middle-class status would provide a logical extension of the creative economic ingenuity and independence that Barbadian women have long been known for. However, it quickly became apparent that these new middle-class "adventurers," operating within a domain historically associated with either the white (masculine) corporate elite and/or the less respectable public domain of the market higgler or petty entrepreneur, simultaneously and unexpectedly also prioritized new visions of selfhood and a continuum of intimate relationships, including marriage. In addition to the three precepts, it is also well understood that while marriage has constituted one dimension of a set of respectable *ideals,* its historical practice has been imbued with ambivalence and trepidation. Though idealized, marriage has never been a necessary part of family life or of the life-course more generally in Barbados.

Part and parcel of these historical traditions of gender and kinship is the institution of matrifocality, particularly within lower-class Afro-Caribbean households. With these understandings in mind, I had every expectation of finding dynamic entrepreneurial Barbadian women shouldering the double burdens (and pleasures) of family obligations, child rearing, and their new businesses. My explorations led unexpectedly into the domain of marriage and what appears to be a new discourse of intimate partnership. I frame these new articulations of partnership and matrifocality in the light of a robust and enduring legacy of Caribbean kinship studies and amid the national cultural milieu in which popular music, romance novels, and political discourse signpost the kinds of social, economic, and affective changes coursing through the testimonies of contemporary middle-class entrepreneurs.

IDEALIZING PARTNERSHIP

New goals for partnership marriages are described most often by entrepreneurs as individual quests for fulfilling mutual emotional and financial relationships. They also embody, at the community level, changing social and economic configurations of social ties and support and historical arrangements of kin and the extended family network. These intimate partnerships and their emphasis on self-determination, mutual support, and nuclear containment emerge in concert with mechanisms by which the state is gradually shrinking back from public service and support, and defining an integrated, flexible, modern nation of adaptable entrepreneurial citizens. Finally, this notion of marriage as a partnership, whether idealized, attempted, or realized, both reflects and gives specific, local meaning to the rapid global circulation of "love marriage" or "companionate marriage" as an integral dimension of modernity itself. Not only was the sheer proportion of married entrepreneurs in my sample (64 percent of the women, 71 percent of the men, and 67 percent overall) a striking inverse of the national profile (23 percent married), as depicted in table 2.1, but also the particular manner of describing this new marital ideal was especially evocative, as I have said, in the testimonies of women entrepreneurs.

Significantly, in light of the strong emphasis on the economic underpinnings of kinship forms in the Caribbean, no neat mapping exists between class origins or race and the sway of the new marital partnership ideal. Equally, as the next chapter explores in detail, matrifocality is increasingly a form of kinship and household organization that is being enacted by black and white middle-class women as well as those in the lower classes. Women who described themselves as "black," "mixed," "brown," or "white," whether they were raised in modest chattel houses, suburban "wall" houses, or in the stately homes of established corporate or plantation families, articulate a remarkably shared vision for the marital partnership they desire.

The cases I highlight in this chapter have been selected to illustrate several dimensions of the new conceptualization of marriage as a partnership across and among a diverse group of middle-class entrepreneurs. For some, the crafting of a partnership marriage represents a radical departure from individuals' upbringing and family of origin, where either patriarchal marriage or various formulations of matrifocality predominated. Women are often intent to forge loving and supportive egalitarian relationships that they distinguish from their parents' relationships in a variety of ways. In some cases these trajectories might appear to be part of broader paths of upward mobility entrepreneurs are blazing, moving into comfortable middle-class livelihoods and lifestyles from childhoods of struggle and economic vulnerability. One might read a parallelism in the courageous embrace by such women, emboldened by the historical legacy of matrifocality and women's economic ingenuity, to face the uncharted territories of both business and marriage. Other cases reveal middle-class individuals raised in what they themselves describe as conventionally respectable middle-class homes—married parents, a strong emphasis on education and formal religion, and so on—who are now articulating desires for a new form of marriage that departs in both structural as well as emotional ways from the patriarchal relations of their parents' generation. Many of my interviews contained what Hochschild (2003, 128) refers to as "cautionary tales" or elements drawn from personal experience that fuel individuals' later ideological stances (toward marriage, work, household arrangements, and one could say life in general) as well as the paths they have followed in life. These tales were laden with feeling rules, suggesting the emotional weight and direction behind the ideological stances and rationales they were able and inclined to voice. As in Hochschild's study, the underlying feelings that came through in the interviews worked in several ways, sometimes reinforcing the surface ideology, sometimes subverting it. Among the Barbadian entrepreneurs, men and women alike glanced back upon "days gone by" and their parents' and grandparents' generations, the struggles they had faced, and often the emotional coldness that characterized both conjugal and parental relationships.

"THE WIND BENEATH MY WINGS": WOMEN'S NARRATIVES

Although the voice may be individual, and differs from one to another, the form memory assumes, the ways in which it is collated and expressed, is collective, is culturally and socially constructed.
—CHAMBERLAIN 1998, 95

Heather is a busy public figure whose work life includes not only a vibrant consultancy business but also leadership on a number of prominent boards. She describes her marriage and its relationship to her thriving business and active political life through the use of a telling stage metaphor: "it's kind of like a singer, and a manager. It's . . . that type of relationship. He cannot sing, but he can do all the other things that help me and allow *me* to sing. . . . I am good at what I do . . . it was only obvious that I would be playing this particular front role within the business . . . and my husband . . . he not only does the support in terms of the administrative, financial management . . . I really could not have done it without him." The music metaphor resurfaced: "I think it is Bette Midler that sang 'The Wind beneath My Wings'? Nobody really sees the wind, they see the bird flying . . . but really that is what he is. I realized that if ever I was going to succeed at what I was doing, I would need that wind beneath my wings." According to Heather, her relationship is an example of recent changes in marriage and the nature of intimate relationships in Barbados.

For example, your grandparents would have tolerated . . . outside women . . . would have tolerated the occasional lash (beating), would have tolerated drinking, would have tolerated non-participation in the upbringing of children. They tolerated a lot of things . . . because they didn't have any economic alternative. Then, the generation of my mother and father, their generation tolerated outside women. That generation did not tolerate the beating. But . . . eventually the marriage would turn sour from this outside woman business, because they wanted more . . . the women wanted more fidelity. And gradually they would grow apart but they would just keep the shell going because they don't want anybody to know and *hell no*, they're *not* getting divorced. . . . Many, many children of my generation grew up in that type of home, and the women in *my* age group (mid-forties) said *nobody* is doing that to me. I'm not tolerating it and *if marriage is not producing for me what I feel it should, I am prepared to destroy it, I will break it and I will move on* because *I am not tolerating that kind of thing.* . . . Those were the types of things that I said to myself . . . that as girls coming along, we discussed . . . *we're not doing what our mothers did.* . . . If I have to get divorced and find somebody else, I will do that, but I am not prepared to tolerate someone who is not putting an effort into this marriage and that this marriage isn't producing emotional satisfaction that I am looking for.

Heather's delineation of the generational changes in what women have "tolerated" in the past suggests the pragmatic changes such as the general advancements in standards of living, the availability and the successful utilization of family planning, and the increase in divorce. But the change cannot be captured solely in structural terms. The change includes new social conventions of respectability as well as new desires, new imagined possibilities for self-understanding, expressing emotion, and hence, new modes of feeling itself. These changes are at once affectively embodied as well as signaled and communicated through new social practices. It is, therefore, the generational shifts and the feelingness of structure that deserves highlighting:

One generation may train its successor, with reasonable success, in the social character or the general cultural pattern, but the new generation will have its own structure of feeling, which will not appear to have come "from" anywhere. For here, most distinctly, the changing organization is enacted in the organism: the new generation responds in its own ways to the unique world it is inheriting, taking up many continuities, that can be traced, and reproducing many aspects of the organization, which can be separately described, yet feeling its whole life in certain ways differently, and shaping its creative response into a new structure of feeling. (Williams 1961, 65)

Heather's testimony reveals changes in the structure of feeling of her generation, what I interpret to be a call for a new affective order, *a new emotional relatedness or intimacy*. This desire for intimacy was expressed as a longing for deep empathy, the capacity to *be oneself* with another and feel supported and in synch with that person, *sympatico*, understood, and upheld as a person.

When Colleen, in chapter 1, talks about the degree to which her fiancée encouraged her to find her path both spiritually and in her business, she signaled her pleasure and appreciation for his empathic understanding, his emotional capacity to relate to her and allow her to find meaning, which in turn made her feel connected to him. The "shell" of an empty marriage that women of her grandparents' generation frequently endured is neither a requirement of social convention nor of economic survival for women like Heather. The partnership she and her husband have built is something she and others describe as something new and valuable: "It's one of the things I would always be grateful for in my life . . . that I was able to love and be loved . . . I bless God every day for him." Interestingly, she and her husband have remained childless after more than eleven years of marriage. *Barren* is the word she used to describe herself. Although there were clear and painful elements of regret in her recounting of the absence of children, now, she says, "My life is full. It would have been nice if [a child] came but the fact that it didn't . . . I could not squeeze that into my life now." The emotional bond and explicit description of the love she and her husband share is striking, especially in a context in which motherhood, as I have said, is prized above marriage, and where it is rare for women not to have or foster a child regardless of their marital status.[7] Where emotional support is almost always described as part of the wide range of female alliances of kinship and friendship in Caribbean social science, here these affective bonds are nurtured and valued between husband and wife. Love, for Heather, is illustrated by a deep empathy and understanding, being "in synch" with her husband to such a degree that he knew, without needing the specific events or explicit description, what she was feeling and also what might console and comfort her.

For Heather, however, whose own business success has insured the economic security of herself and her husband, love and emotional commitment, not the expectation of financial provision, constitutes the core of her marriage. What is striking in her testimony above is not just the characterization of generational changes in what women "tolerated," and her own generation's capacity to refuse what earlier generations of women had to endure, but also a tender intimacy and understanding that she says she shares with her own husband:

> The thing about (him) is that he is emotionally sensitive to anything that is happening to me and what that does, it means that if there is anything that is distressing me, he steps in and helps to bring me to a [new] perspective. He is not afraid of my emotions, which is unusual in men because most men feel overwhelmed by their women having emotions and they will abandon them in terms of . . . oh gosh, you're upset? Let me go out . . . or let me whatever. Or, they brush it off. . . . He never does that. It doesn't mean we don't have disagreements, or what have you, but they're never mean. We never say things to each other that afterward you know has stung anybody's skin. We've learned to be patient with each other . . . we are soul mates.

Heather recounts a recent experience that moved her visibly in her retelling, and encapsulates her partnership marriage and the ease with which her husband understands and responds to her. It also suggests some of the intimate connections between such partnership marriages and the particular needs of entrepreneurial women. On her first trip to Europe, Heather traveled to Paris for a series of business meetings. She was eager to do some shopping in between her formal appointments:

> It was the first time in my life I ever felt obese. I felt obese! To get anything above a size 10 you have to go to a specialty shop. You can't get a shoe size over a 7 or an 8. What is this? I was really frustrated . . . and it was more expensive. I had heard it was more expensive so I had planned! I wanted to get one or two things, . . . one or two really nice European suits, you know, but then the exchange rate with the United States was bad . . . so it meant that the money could not [stretch]. So, on Saturday, I'm walking and every time I find something . . . they don't have this size and they don't have the color. . . . And [my husband] had talked to me just before as I was going . . . shopping, we'd talked on the phone and I said, "look I'm just going" and he said "okay I'll call you tomorrow morning." But that frustration set in on me . . . and I felt so uhhhh. . . . He picked it up and my phone rang. "What's the problem?" Not hello . . . and then, he picked up my

distress . . . and I said I'm just . . . I'm just frustrated I can't . . . and he said [using an endearing diminutive of her name] "it's alright if you can't find anything, just relax, when you come back home later on you could send to the States or whatever, but don't . . . instead of focusing on suits, find a couple of blouses . . . or get a handbag, you know, any of those little things you know, but don't let yourself get stressed over it." I said, "oh honey, thanks," and I put down the phone and I was ohhhhhhhhhh you know. You know, it's *amazing* how he does it . . . so, partnering for me, and that emotional satisfaction, is somebody who is willing to do that for me, and somebody for whom I can do this.

The combined stress and excitement of traveling to Europe on her own for a business trip was somewhat overwhelming for Heather. Far from belittling her tears and upset over the shopping disappointment, her husband reassured her and offered her the kind of sage and tangible advice he often provides on matters of finance and accounting. His calm voice and comforting suggestion soothed her and allowed her to enjoy herself as well as to feel bolstered and confident again. Freud (1966, 13) noted, "By words one person can make another blissfully happy or drive him to despair. . . . Words provoke effects and are in general the means of mutual influence." While Freud has had little footing in the cultural tradition of Barbados, his observation aptly marks a growing emphasis on and desire for expressive communication.

Ashanti similarly reflected upon her childhood and women's experiences across the generations, as she announced boldly and early in our first interview that she had never planned on getting married. Quite unexpectedly, however, she found a man with whom she has built something different than the kinds of relationships she had witnessed in growing up. She recounted with vivid detail a frantic and frightening rush to the police station with her mother's friend, who had been branded with an iron on her face by her abusive husband,

We looked at all these things. I must only have been about six at the time, and my mum was herself in an abusive relationship until she got the courage to get out of it. . . . So, growing up I made the decision . . . I wasn't getting married. I might have a relationship with somebody but I'm gonna live right next door to them. . . . I want to have my own house and he'll have his own house and then if we split up it won't matter cause I'll still be in my own house. I grew up with this thing where couples broke up and then the mum and children had to go and find somewhere else to live . . . brothers and sisters got scattered all over the place, I decided there and then I'm not having that.

Ashanti is one of nine children; her father left the family when she was five. Raised by a single mother with the support of her siblings, she has actively sought a different path in all dimensions of her life: marriage, family life, and work. The bond she found with her husband grew in part from their mutual desires for self-invention and from a shared experience of difficult childhoods, hers in Barbados and his in a Barbadian migrant family in America: "We were in synch, we'd had the same kind of experience of life and the hurt and disappointment and all, and we connected over the next couple years we got to know each other. His attitude was not to be coy and macho, and all these things. Growing up had left him with an outlook on life that I hadn't heard before." Both were searching for a part of themselves, Ashanti said, after a rocky childhood, years of partying, and a very intense work life in a corporate setting. Their marriage and their separate entrepreneurial ventures represented decidedly new paths in which to forge new selves:[8] "He's very open, he's actually a very sensitive person, open with his feelings, which is not something I'm used to . . . not your average Bajan man." Ashanti attributes his unusual qualities to growing up in the United States and watching his parents' struggle: "My husband is very special because he doesn't think like most Bajan men. Every single achievement I have, my husband is right there in my cheering section. I can hear his voice right there with me." From Ashanti's perspective, her husband is different from other Bajan men because he is sensitive, emotional, and caring toward her as a supportive life partner, sharing her desire to break from conventional patterns of gender roles, family, and work trajectories and chart their own course in life as a couple.

The desire for a balanced, supportive partnership was echoed by two entrepreneurs I interviewed who alluded to their same sex relationships.[9] Each described her respective household as comprised of herself and a female partner. In a culture steeped in homophobia,[10] Pat and Sophie have each achieved remarkable and very public entrepreneurial success, one in the food industry, and the other running a popular children's sports and recreational program. Their businesses reside, in one sense, in conventionally female-oriented niches: food and children. In many ways their descriptions of juggling work and home life resounded with themes raised by other women entrepreneurs managing domestic divisions of labor with the often unpredictable pace and demands of business ownership. Their household divisions of labor and the role of their partners in their businesses echoed many of the dimensions discussed by heterosexual entrepreneurs. They did not discuss their sexuality per se, or claim a lesbian identity, though the sentiments they expressed about care, intimacy, and sharing the burdens and pleasures of work and life more generally were similar.

The stresses of demanding schedules, managing employees, pleasing customers, and responding to a fluctuating market place stand in tension with the needs and desires associated with private, domestic life, leisure, and the quest for self-definition and meaning. However, in each case, in addition to their unspoken sexuality, there are dimensions of their lives and work that position them on the dangerous edges of reputation—one operating a busy restaurant in the center of Bridgetown, and the other a former and well-known athlete whose fame and popularity, in the spirit of island "crab antics," also made her the subject of gossip, innuendo, and even a well-known calypso. On a small island, their sexuality and partners are widely known and, generally, quietly respected. As De Caires Narain (2012, 198) suggests, the evasion of women's same-sex desire in the Caribbean (where violent homophobia toward men still prevails), both academically and in the popular milieu, is upheld in part by the ongoing investment in "an African-Creole maternal that by default consolidates heterosexual normativity." Notable in both cases was their childlessness. As I have said, in the historical logic of West Indian gender ideology, motherhood, more than marriage, remains the keystone of adult femininity. As we could see from Heather's testimony earlier in this chapter, in addition to the emotional sadness associated with her "barrenness" the social stigma and placelessness of the childless woman can highlight the reputational costs of women's entrepreneurial lives, which many salve through close involvement in extended networks of kin and their desires for intimate partnership and marriage. In Sophie's case working with children every day, and interacting with their families as a trusted and experienced teacher, helps to diminish the "costs" to her respectability that might be brought about by her sexuality and lifestyle of physical exertion and competition outdoors in the sun, much of which is associated with the masculine sphere of reputation.

The desires for emotional compatibility, comfort, and intimacy expressed by so many of the women entrepreneurs as they described their efforts to forge partnership marriages are echoed verbatim in Sophie's testimony. She seeks "a calm balance" in a life otherwise consumed by the hectic demands of work and handling accounts, scheduling, and the like: "It seems like if I'm having a day where the children (her students) are just getting to me it so happens that *she* (her partner) is having a great day or vice versa . . . and then if we're both having a bad day we just come home and grumble . . . and then end up laughing." Sharing the trials and tribulations of stressful workdays, relating the mishaps as well as triumphs, and counting on emotional support and understanding are at the core of the intimacy being sought. Although her same-sex relationship and some aspects of her entrepreneurial life might situate Sophie on the edges of feminine respectability, her narrative highlighted the common themes of emotional connection rather than financial support or stability as the elements most cherished in the intimate partnership.

Discourses of "flexibility" and "balance" so emblematic of the work-life rhetoric in North America today emerge from almost all of my interviews with women entrepreneurs. Not only are they searching for ways of combining their many responsibilities and desires, they are simultaneously, consciously or not, mitigating the symbolic cultural threats posed by their entrepreneurialism and its ties to reputation (navigating public spaces and enacting activities associated with lower-classness and/or masculinity). As others have noted, the expectations that women's homosexuality is private and hidden (relegated like all of respectable femininity to the private sphere) has made it less subject to homophobic assault than male homosexuality, frequently the focus of aggressive public commentary (dub, calypso, and otherwise) and even physical violence. On the other hand, as the desires for new modes of self-expression and intimacy among couples, families, friends, and individuals find outlets in a growing array of venues in public as well as traditional private spaces, the possible threats posed for homosexual couples may become more pronounced.[11]

IDIOMS OF "SUPPORT": MEN'S NARRATIVES

Entrepreneurial men also speak about the importance of family and marriage (in that order) in their lives. They were also overwhelmingly (71 percent, $n = 34$) married as a group. However, their testimonies about marriage are framed differently. Men's talk of marriage, like women's, is conveyed in a language of "support." However, the meanings of *support* are subtly but profoundly different. Men focus predominantly on divisions of labor and on the time management of their businesses vis-à-vis the demands of wives and family life, as opposed to the explicitly emotional contours of women's narratives. Men's descriptions of the kind of relationship they desire in marriage conform more to traditionally gendered norms of the patriarchal household than the egalitarian companionship increasingly prized by most of the women.[12] They often express the need or desire to retain their independent social lives with male friends, a reflection of a long tradition of sex-segregated social life and spheres of sociality (Greenfield 1966, 104; Freeman 2000) and an aspect to being "part of the old boys' club" that several of them conceded has made business an easier path for them than for women. Similarly, they are less likely to frame aspects of support and shared vision in the explicitly emotional terms used by women. This desire is often in tension with women's pursuit of intimate coupling and shared "quality time" as will be explored in chapter 4.

Andrew, for example, married five years and without children, said that being married has made his entrepreneurial venture easier in the sense that his wife provides moral support for the risks he is taking. She is employed in the tourism sector and earns a modest but steadier income than he does. Andrew qualifies his remarks by saying, "I think support is really the key element . . . but not support to a point where the person is nosey." For Andrew, the kind of intimate sharing of all aspects of business, including the management of the company's accounts that women tended to cite as evidence of their husband's demonstration of love and caring, was precisely crossing the bounds of appropriate support. Where women's tendency to describe their marital partnerships in ways that reference but emotionally transcend the simple divisions of labor, the married male entrepreneurs confined most of their discussions to these domestic and entrepreneurial balancing acts. And, like most of the other thirty-four men I interviewed, Andrew describes a fairly traditional gendered division of labor, stating that "there is a strong female presence in Barbados in terms of the home structure so naturally it's her who would bring it to the fore [take responsibility for the home]." Indeed, his wife takes primary responsibility for all of the domestic realm—the laundry, cooking, shopping, and he helps out with some of the cleaning. Unlike the majority of the entrepreneurs I interviewed, they do not employ a domestic worker: "Most of that [the domestic work] is handled by her, I lend my two cents worth . . . because women always feel, well, men can't do it . . . or they do it differently . . . messily."

Viewing the household and family as primarily an economic entity has not only been the dominant historical framework but characterized the tenor of most of my conversations with entrepreneurial men and with many of the older women, too. They focused upon marriage as an institution for ordering specific productive and reproductive roles, dividing up the tasks of earning and keeping up the household. When emphasizing their own desires and inclinations, however, women also highlighted an intimate relationship of trust, care, and mutual emotional attunement.

Lilliana, for example, described one of her male cousins and the kinds of ribbing and condemnation he received for not being a proper provider. Trained as an accountant, he had been unable to hold down a regular job, and his wife was providing the more steady income as well as the family's domestic management. In the case of a white Barbadian family, one might say these values express what Wilson would have described as mainstream mores of respectability.

> There was certainly no support for what he was doing . . . he just needed to *be a man* and have a job. . . . Generally people feel . . . in this society it's looked upon more favorably if it's primarily the man who supports the family . . . although I think a lot of women augment their . . . husband's income. I remember years ago [my son)] had to . . . write about what his parents did [at school] and he said his father had an important job at an office and his mother washed dishes, made dinner, and did something else . . . I . . . was, at that point, using one room as a studio and I was working for a big show in Washington and I was really [shocked]. I said *"but, what do I do?! Wash dishes? . . . what else do I do?!,"* you know . . . "I don't know, like take care of me? or whatever?" I said "but I *make things, I work, I am a designer!"* And when I told that to my brother, he said "Well? That is an enormous compliment that he has *not even noticed* your profession and that you are just . . . taking care of him. That is *such a compliment to you!"* You *know* that!? . . . What I do is not noticed.

For fathers, discussions of marriage tended to jump quickly to "the family" and away from the conjugal relationship itself. In hindsight, I regret not probing more persistently, retaining a focus on questions of emotional relatedness and intimacy when men shifted in their seats and turned the discussion otherwise. For some, their cues suggested not a discomfort but a generalized unfamiliarity with my questions that asked them to reflect upon the nature of their relationships. In short, the gendered differences in awareness and talk of emotional intimacy within partnerships demonstrate how new structures of affect, as they intertwine with neoliberal economic restructurings, are not totalizing or generic but rather manifested in gender-specific ways.

Antoinne was thirty-eight and married with four children between the ages of five and ten when we met. He described all aspects of his carpentry business and marriage together as a partnership in which "she is the boss . . . I take orders from her, you know, basically she takes care of all the admin." While his wife runs the office side of the business, Antoinne trains and manages staff and goes out on the job with his team. Meanwhile, like most wives, she also takes responsibility for the domestic sphere and most aspects of their four children's lives. For Antoinne, like most of the other married entrepreneurs, the structural emphasis on roles and divisions of labor, duty, and responsibility overshadowed the affective dimensions and intimacy of these relationships. The following excerpt from his narrative expresses his clear commitment to the traditional gendered norm that prescribes a male as breadwinner and protector. Most striking is his clear articulation of the relationship he sees between his family and his business, and his prioritization of family above and beyond all else:

> I think [being married and having a family] have made [the business] more challenging . . . because before I was married I used to offer twenty-four-hour service . . . I could just get up and go. . . . Now, not necessarily the spouse but the children, they want you there. They want to know that you are there. I am not one of these people that believe you could kill yourself in business seeing that you're working for the family and then you lose your family! I believe that the business should revolve around the family and not the other way around . . . people don't understand when I say this. I would rather lose business than to lose family because I believe that . . . if you lose the business and you have the family you can start over. What is the sense to losing the family who you're saying that you're trying to protect? So I don't agree that business should come before family, I am sorry I don't believe that, alright? I would rather lose a job . . . than to disappoint the family for a job. That is my belief.

There are marked gender differences in the ways in which expectations for marriage and other conjugal relations are portrayed by entrepreneurial men and by women. For the married men I interviewed, as well as those in other conjugal arrangements, when asked, most described their wives or partners as emotionally supportive of them and of their businesses, although emotional support was seldom a subject or concern they raised independently. Those who were less glowing about their marriages framed their discontent around the tendency for their wives to resent the risks involved in the entrepreneurial pursuit and their demands for more solid economic security. In both cases men's focus was fixed upon aspects of logistical and financial support, the degree to which their own travel or long working hours were tolerated by their spouses, how the ups and downs of their business profits were managed, schedules juggled and so on. While some described their wives and partners as integral to their businesses, again men most often conveyed their wives' support in conventional terms of gender roles and divisions of labor—maintaining the home front and therefore allowing them to concentrate on the growth and development of their businesses. For them, the affective dimensions of marriage were either negative (the irritating pressure wives exerted to be more available) or positive. Even when positive they were narrowly understood within the confines of conventional "support." Women, by contrast, expansively discussed their desires for, and sometimes their appreciation of, many facets of support, intimacy, and care. They portrayed partnership marriage as a relationship in which both tangible and material assistance (financial, labor, expertise, guidance) and emotional connection are intimately intertwined.

For entrepreneurial couples with children, the shift from inward expressions of love to practical expressions enacted in the social world (Alexander 1984) was especially pronounced, and dominated mothers' portrayals of their marriages. In other words divisions of labor and aspects of household power, when felt to be supportive and generous, were themselves the locus of emotion, love, and positive affective experience. For some women, like Ashanti, the shift from being a loving couple with her husband to a family with two active children, from "inward" love to "social" obligation, stood in such sharp contrast to her own father's desertion and the common domestic violence of her upbringing that it brings little tension or upheaval. For others, this transition, and the subsequent challenges of managing domestic, parental, and entrepreneurial duties and labor, constituted the greatest source of marital unraveling.

For Ashanti, like many others, the planning of outings and special shared time becomes one aspect of the generalized emotional labor she continues to perform in both her domestic life as well as among her employees in her company: "I have had to institute date by date just so that me and my husband can get out and go have dinner or see a movie or something like that." For most couples with young and school-aged children, the priority of their lives as a couple is often subsumed by the larger domain of "the family." Ashanti continues, "it's not worked out as well as I had intended, because the kids have always been with us and we have never shied away from having them . . . they're a very big part of what we do socially, to be honest, so it's the beach, that's really what we do. On occasion one of my sisters will come and stay with the kids at our house or take them to their house and we get out for a couple hours by ourselves." Again, the importance of extended kin networks to facilitate the combined labors

FIGURE 2.1. Quality time in the new public sphere. Photo by Dondré Trotman

and desires that encompass entrepreneurial life is a notable continuation of one of the region's most marked social form. The extended family is critical not solely for the survival of poor matrifocal households but also for these entrepreneurial middle-class couples. And the differential degrees to which married women in nuclear households versus woman-headed matrifocal households were able to tap into and depend upon these age-old support systems was a critical element in their capacity to manage the challenges of their businesses and their busy lives more generally.

FROM MATERIAL SUPPORT TO THE INTIMATE ECONOMY

In Caribbean kinship studies discussions of the continuum of conjugality and the domestic sphere have long centred upon *support* and the *economic* underpinnings and material benefits of marriage versus matrifocality. For instance, Greenfield (1966, 102; emphasis added) suggests that the status derived through marriage is that of an "easier life": "There is a general belief that a married woman should live better than a woman in another type of union. Her status of 'mistress' implies that her husband will be able to support her in the manner of a mistress of a home. The choice of working for wages or staying home is to be left to her discretion. *She expects life to be easier for her than it was before she married. Since these expectations are not always realized, marriage is frequently a great disappointment to women.*" In the same vein the female-headed household suggests the necessary economic struggle by which lower-class women "cut and contrive" to make ends meet, enlisting the support of extended kin networks and often serial partners or fathers to ensure survival. In both cases economic security and the idiom of *support* are paramount.

The affective dimensions of these relationships, by contrast, have been less often addressed or analyzed.[13] One might imagine that given the highly gendered (feminine) cast of Caribbean kinship and the emphasis in many parts of the world on gendered (feminine) caregiving and socialization, of all social spheres, this would be the locus of affective life and, hence, analysis. Indeed, one significance of the scholarly emphasis on matrifocality has been the premise that Caribbean people's primary affective ties are concentrated in the mother-child bond, in contrast to the conjugal bond, which has been depicted as casual and unstable. "Within the Caribbean family," as Barrow (1966, 3) relates, "a man's most intensive and enduring relationship is the one he has with his mother."[14] Surprisingly little scholarship in the region has attempted to examine the nature of emotional relationships across the conjugal continuum, and even within the parental bond most of the emphasis remains fixed on tangible, material forms of support and care, with little discussion of emotional experience, longings, or expression.

Women's active determination to achieve new modes of intimacy and new affective ideals more generally, and their admission of frustration when their dreams were not realized, were persistent and moving illustrations of the challenges of the new "partnerships." Whereas Greenfield noted as early as 1966 that marriage often brought disappointment to women whose dreams for greater economic security and comfort were not met, the tenor of the disappointment among these middle-class entrepreneurs is quite different. Their disappointments and desires are steeped in a language of affect: longing for closeness, empathy, emotional interest, excitement, connection. As business owners themselves, their expectations for their marriages highlighted noneconomic dimensions of partnership. I focus therefore on their formulation of what such a partnership entails, both practically and symbolically. In contrast to the "traditional" patriarchal marriage associated with Wilson's respectability, in which a male breadwinner was understood to be the authoritative "head" of the household, many women entrepreneurs describe their desires for and efforts to achieve a more egalitarian and more emotionally satisfying and dynamic marriage.[15]

Contemporary middle-class women's narratives often blend references to the emotional and practical support of their entrepreneurial mission as well as the juggling acts of work and domestic responsibilities, the care of children, and a more general sense of "understanding" of themselves as a person. These narratives often place a priority on sharing "quality" time, leisure, and romantic intimacy. In some cases, reference to support of a financial or otherwise tangible form of assistance in the realm of business (driving an order over to make a deadline, helping to navigate the port and ensure that a shipment of supplies got through, overseeing the accounts behind the scenes, etc.) melded with notable appreciation for a spouse's understanding of the stresses and worries associated with a busy entrepreneurial life. Further, the stresses of the job were frequently in delicate balance with personal or family responsibilities of raising children, managing an illness, or meeting expectations and obligations within the extended family.

A growing affective milieu of emotional intimacy and self-exploration is emerging amid a resounding preoccupation with marriage as "traditional" and "respectable" in the Barbadian public domain. For Dara, the co-owner of a thriving interior design company, her husband is both her marriage and business partner. She says of their relationship, "we're very yin-yang, opposites in many ways, but complementary." She is candid about her need for security, emotional as well as financial, and says, "women like pampering, knowing that they'll be taken care of, and . . . this is one of the main incentives toward marriage. . . . At the end of the day the idea of security, the idea of respectability is important." However, there is much more to her marriage than just the traditional forms of security or respectability: "We make sure to keep the spark in the marriage by having Friday nights together," going out for dinner, to a movie, an art opening, or just spending time alone together, while their twelve-year-old daughter goes to her grandparents' for the night. This closeness and the assertion of their needs as a couple are key to sustaining their partnership marriage, and their involvement in a growing sphere of middle-class forms of leisure, entertainment, and self-cultivation foster these new social forms.

For contemporary middle-class women whose own entrepreneurial ventures have often brought about or secured their middle-class status, marriage ideally encompasses practical and material demonstrations of support as well as a continued romantic and emotional intimacy. When these sources of support and intimacy are felt to be missing, their marriages show marked fissures. This was made painfully clear in the cases of at least five women entrepreneurs whose unraveling marriages and shift to matrifocal households I witnessed during the period of research. I suspect that there are many more. The next chapter explores some of the

FIGURE 2.2. Art gallery reception. Photo by Dondré Trotman

permutations of these tensions and the transformations they prompted, both structurally and affectively.

SOCIALITY AND NEOLIBERAL MASCULINITY

It is not enough to characterize the growing interest in these intimate partnerships without noting specifically how gendered identities for women and men are equally in flux. Much of this book focuses upon the various contradictions and challenges entailed in women's efforts to craft a new entrepreneurial femininity that combines economic independence, professional creativity, emotional intimacy, self-exploration, and respectability. The challenges for men are also significant and integrally bound up in these economic, social, and affective changes. The caricature of the "traditional Barbadian man" is well understood throughout the country and was referenced in many of my interviews and conversations. Graham Dann (1987, 71) paints it rather crudely but effectively, "The commonly held stereotype of the Barbadian male is that of a roaming wolf seeking whom he may sexually devour, with conquests in every parish adding notch upon notch to his overloaded shotgun. The limitless women he has known and the countless children he has fathered, form part and parcel of his recountable repertoire. As a hard seed, or village ram, he can be regarded as something of a hero and the subject of rum shop admiration." Many women began their discussions of their partners or husbands by commenting that theirs departed from the "usual Bajan man" or sometimes noted when they "behaved just like your usual Barbadian man."

The West Indian tradition of separate gendered spheres of sociality and leisure, noted in many classic ethnographies and a vivid part of the memories described by many of the entrepreneurs, was met by other women with profound frustration and sometimes outrage. As new conceptions of leisure time and participation in new realms of leisure activity in emerging leisure-oriented spaces are facilitated by the availability of disposable income, these provide key sites in which "coupling" is both enacted and inhabited as a way of being and feeling. These middle-class spaces, activities, and ways of being are often sought as a release from the rigors and stresses of business, and, as I will explore in chapter 4, a reprieve from the ever-growing demands for affective labor performed in both commercial and private life. It has always been the case that women have enjoyed the company of extended families and small groups of friends. However, most of the women entrepreneurs also articulated a desire for "quality time" (often using this exact formulation) with children, the nuclear family, or specifically denoting shared intimate time with a romantic partner or spouse. In addition to enjoying an expanding range of entertainment and leisure activities, their expectations for the kind of time, the emotional feeling produced in these shared pursuits, as integral to the life they wish to lead was marked. Expectations for how evenings and weekends should be experienced in relation to "non-work" time are in flux, and the nature of these distinctions are undergoing scrutiny and change. As Heather's remarks made plain, the ingredients for what constitutes a good husband and a good marriage have expanded well beyond those of earlier generations.

Debates and efforts to explain or refute "the marginal male" phenomenon in Barbados continue to be heated in both scholarly and popular arenas (Miller 1991; Barrow 1998; Barriteau 1998; Hodge 2002). In both the early kinship studies and women's own reports of their parents' and grandparents' generations, a "good father" or "good husband" was believed to be one who (in spite of the outside affairs and outside children) "looked after" or financially supported the family (Alexander 1977; Barrow 1996; Senior 1991; Smith 1996). Many entrepreneurial women across the age spectrum complained that their own and their friends' husbands still believe themselves beyond reproach if they "provide" well for their children (paying school fees, camps, extra lessons, travel, etc.) but show none of the other signs of emotional connection or fidelity. Indeed, this characterization of masculinity predominates in the literature and popular sphere. The notion that sentiment and the realm of emotions belong

primarily to women's spheres of kinship and domesticity is summarized
well by Wilson (1973): "Sentiment and affect are achieved through the kinship of women to each other and to certain male kin. Kinship is a principle
of social recognition in contexts essentially sentimental and affective and
in the main, involving only women. Such is the 'model' or the 'norm.'"
For men by contrast, "There is only one relationship which is ideally sen-
timentalized—a man's relation to his mother. Throughout his life he will
maintain, if not actually observe, that he loves his mother above all else,
and that he must show her the greatest respect . . . Yet the very idealism of
this relationship betrays something of its formal rather than spontaneous,
dutiful rather than passionate nature. A man rather more genuinely feels
a strong attachment to his children, particularly . . . when they are small.
Otherwise, a man's existential reference group, his sentimental community, lies outside his kinsmen" (135).

Ashanti commented upon the recent gender debates and what she perceived as a backlash against women with the new "men's movement" in
Barbados.

> There's an organization called MESA, the Men's Educational Support
> Association, I think it's called. It's wonderful that men get together
> and share among themselves whatever problems they may be having
> and so on, but what I resent is this . . . this sense that they're almost
> saying that if women weren't doing these things, if women weren't out
> there running businesses and buying cars, and buying land and being
> managers that we wouldn't be getting any problems with our children
> in schools! When men were running all over the place and leaving it
> completely up to women to deal with . . . bringing the family up . . .
> nobody was screaming. My point is that [raising a family] should be a
> shared responsibility . . . not considered women's work nor men's work.

Her own marriage and family life are structured around the goal of
partnership.

> I really don't see how I would commit my life's work without my hus-
> band's support, and I do believe he would say the same thing to you.
> Because it definitely is a shared responsibility at home, not just for
> caring for the kids' needs and making sure they have their doctors' visits
> and all those other things, but just being centered, being there for the
> boys and knowing that, okay, if something happens, the boys can come
> and say to either mummy or dad . . . it doesn't matter which one . . .
> something has happened, *this* has happened. It's not that we haven't

had our trials and tribulations in the ten years we've been married, but we've always been able to find our way through it. . . . I don't think either one of us is afraid to say sorry and if you can say sorry, you're okay. . . . It's been hard at times with the kids coming along and the businesses still growing but as I said, we do it together, and I never have to convince him that, "oh gosh it's been a tough day," he knows, he sees it and the same thing on his side.

The emerging resentment among women toward their husbands who are admittedly good "providers" but who continue to prioritize segregated gendered spheres of social life is not surprising. Historically it has been precisely the lack of basic provisioning and demonstration of economic support that has been waged against men as "marginal" partners and fathers throughout West Indian history (Miller 1991). However, among these middle-class couples, and for women entrepreneurs in particular, the grounds of conflict have shifted. They are no longer steeped in basic economic provisioning or even in more equitable divisions of labor (although this is often a point of contention) but increasingly revolve around other more emotional aspects of relatedness and intimacy. The idea that a "good husband" is now not only one who helps toward the financial support of the household but also is an intimate partner and emotional confidant, a soul mate who shares leisure time, consults in the rearing of children, and can be depended upon for mutual support, represents a significant redefinition and a radical generational departure in the minds of most of these entrepreneurs.[16]

The interpretation of patterns of kinship and marriage through an economic lens of support has led many analysts, myself included, to miss opportunities to delve more deeply into the nature and complexity of these affective bonds.[17] Indeed, in mining thousands of pages of interview transcripts, I found that allusions to love, and expressions of positive, relational affect more generally, among these entrepreneurs take on utilitarian terms. The degree to which a spouse is helpful and makes sacrifices economically or through volunteering time and skills to the business is conveyed as evidence of his or her love and caring. But a closer reading of their narratives reveals not merely the conventional understandings about marriage ensuring greater financial comfort and security, but a resounding articulation of other emotional aspects of desire, empathy and tenderness. While the lexicon of love I had searched for was elusive, between the lines I found the sentiments of intimacy and emotional connection that are under construction, and with them new understandings of what love is coming to mean in a climate of neoliberal projects of self making. And as I came to see the importance of these themes, their significance as both emotional desires and modes of labor became increasingly plain. Affective work is central to entrepreneurial life, whether in the intimate and personal relationships of private life or squarely at the heart of service exchanges and business deals.

Giddens (1992, 2) notes "the ethos of romantic love has had a double impact upon women's situation. On the one hand it has helped to put women 'in their place'—consigning them to the home while also sanctifying this space. On the other hand, however, romantic love can be seen as an active and radical engagement with the 'maleness of modern society.'" One could read Giddens's formulation directly through the Caribbean respectability-reputation paradigm and see just how radically women's growing desire for an intimate partnership in marriage and their entrepreneurial upward mobility fosters precisely such a "double impact"—they are at one and the same time drawn to the exciting (masculine) world of public trade while also subscribing to one of the prime markers of middle-class respectability. The ongoing expectation that married middle-class entrepreneurial women preside over the domestic sphere (even if as a manager rather than a labourer in this sphere) is coupled and sometimes in tension with their extensive and visible movement into the public masculine domain, a domain in which their freedom and flexibility (economic, social, sexual, emotional) can be unleashed.

THE ECONOMY OF SEX AND ROMANTIC LOVE

The idea that marriage is important to Caribbean women not for love but for security has been a persistent theme not just in the realm of social science but also in the region's literature and popular culture.[18] In a sense the contrastive emphases of Wilson's reputation-respectability paradigm may have contributed to this persistent dualistic understanding in which men and masculinity are associated with reputation, sexuality, flexibility, and "outside" relationships and children, while women and femininity are rooted in respectability, marriage, security and status, and "inside" or monogamous domestic life. Women's interest in security is commonly presented at odds with men's interest in sex and passion—women are condemned for mercenary approaches to relations with men, trading sex and affection for material rewards, while men are presented as having no choice in the matter but to "offer up the goods." In this matrix sex is portrayed as men's primary interest, whereas economic security or the acquisition of material "goodies" are women's primary goals. As Elisa Sobo

(1993, 187) writes about Jamaica, "to look [for] love is to search for sex," and as R. T. Smith (1988, 142) elaborates, "sexual relations are conceived as 'giving' one to the other rather than as the joint activity of a couple. Intense affect is not necessary." In Trinidad the tradition of men "begging" for sex in exchange for material rewards is described as part of the "smart rules" of village life in the mid-twentieth century. However, Birth and Freilich (1995) observe these patterns changing in the 1990s with the expansion of economic opportunities for women. With greater economic autonomy, as well as the threat of AIDS, the increased difficulty of sexual secrecy, and the influences of American television and popular culture, they argue that a new set of "smart rules" of romantic love has begun to supplant the "sex and begging system" with one of "sex and romance" (Birth and Freilich 1995, 269–70). Again, the interpretive anchoring of relationships (especially sex, since little mention is actually made of love) in terms of economic interest and the definitively nonemotional, manipulative associations of this economic interest has been a strong theme in Caribbean ethnography, especially of lower-class life (Rodman 1971; Wilson 1964). In literary works as well, Caribbean culture and identity is often presented as "so profoundly damaged by the impact of colonialism and the trauma of that initial loss of culture that any kind of love becomes an impossibility. . . . Sex 'stands in the place of love' as the first step to self-validation in a hostile and conformist Caribbean" (Hodge 2002). Jamaica Kincaid pronounces perhaps most boldly on the matter when she says that the violent ruptures perpetrated in the name of "discovery" in 1492 produced a "wrong" never to be "made right," a Caribbean "in which no love is possible," where "everything about us is held in doubt and we the defeated define all that is unreal, all that is not human, all that is without love, all that is without mercy" (De Caires Narain 2012, 204).

The picture is not much rosier in the ethnographic record of the middle classes, where love and affectionate courtship are described as ceding to obligation and social propriety of marriage (Alexander 1977).[19] The primary grounding of marriage in economic stability and support is also one reason that working-class couples have frequently delayed formal marriage until after the arrival of children. A couple often approaching middle-age will host a big wedding once they can demonstrate to the community that they have the economic means to support their family under the respectable rubric of formal marriage. Such an elaborate ceremony will often include their children, beautifully adorned, and forever memorialized in elaborate photo albums. Again, these practices are most often described as social demonstrations of economic wherewithal. They might also be read as gestures of what Berlant describes as "cruel optimism," the cautious commitment to institutions and promises (marriage, love) in the face of its frequent rupture and disappointment (2011).

Several forces converge in today's media-rich global arena that encourage exploration of these dimensions of experience as integral to our understanding of neoliberalism and the growing sway of entrepreneurship. As chapter 5 explores in greater detail, these middle-class entrepreneurs are increasingly drawn to an expanding array of services and activities that offer individual salve and comfort, pleasure and leisure. Yoga and massage, a range of therapies, including couples counselling, psychotherapy, iridology, reflexology, homeopathy, personal exercise training, and spiritual uplift, together with countless new cafés, boutiques, and entertainment venues are just a sampling of the services catering to local middle classes. These emerge in concert with widely popular self-help manuals for personal health, emotional fulfilment, spiritual uplift, and personal success. The simultaneously entrepreneurial and therapeutic dimensions of such endeavours and discourses are unmistakable. On one hand, these new services represent a growing domain of businesses catering specifically to the middle classes. But the nature of these businesses also signals new fields of experience, new realms of desire in which the self and the couple and family are envisioned as entities to be fashioned, soothed, entertained, and nourished. And for many, an integral part of such newly charted paths of personal fulfilment is a loving and mutually supportive partnership—emotionally, sexually, and economically.

OBEAH AND ROMANCE: LOVE AND MARRIAGE IN THE POPULAR SPHERE

The Afro-Caribbean marriage has historically been imbued with ambivalence, uneasily associated with the air of the colonial, the respectable, all the while seemingly out of reach. Over time the feeling has been that "marriage may be more respectable, but visiting relationships are easier to handle. They allow more personal autonomy and ensure an escape from conjugal violence" (Barrow 1996, 460). Views of marriage, like those toward work, parenting, religion, or the self, are always in formation, rooted deeply in cultural tradition, shaped by political economy, but alive and subject to dynamic change. Hodge's (2002, 481; emphasis added) evocative observations, with which the chapter begins, conclude by noting that "today, women's attitudes towards marriage are affected by the worldwide women's movement which has challenged the unequal relationship that existed within the traditional marriage. Moreover, with increasing access to higher education, women are gaining the economic independence that *allows them to change the rules of marriage. They can rewrite the marriage contract, making the relationship a more egalitarian one. Marriage becomes a more attractive option for women when men and women can be equal partners."* However, the influence of the global women's movement, the global film, television, and music industries, and women's economic independence are not, in and of themselves, adequate explanations for the kinds of transformations these Barbadian women today are seeking. The emotional mobility and entrepreneurial affectivity, which is part and parcel of women's adventurous market-based undertakings overall, imbues economic independence with other qualities that are sought in the marketplace and elsewhere. Through their market activities they also seek new bargaining power to imagine and ask for new modes of "partnership" or to adapt "matrifocality," single motherhood, or singlehood within a new middle-class context.

The testimonies by women entrepreneurs echo popular film narratives, fiction, and self-help manuals, in which marriage is characterized by romantic partnership rather than patriarchal systems of obligation. Such scripts are made all the more powerful when women are themselves able to provide economic stability. When women achieve economic independence, and especially an independence won in the wily domain of entrepreneurship, their marital desires turn toward romantic connection grounded in emotional synchrony and in the cultivation of new selves in large part supported by a new middle-class marketplace. Not dependent upon men for economic support, these women are empowered to dream of pleasure, leisure, and emotional satisfaction in new terms. Their new discourse of love is grounded in the language and structures of "support" but also intertwined with those of neoliberal flexibility, in the sense that they prioritize dynamic change, supple and mutual adaptability, and responsiveness. The new ideal highlights a mutual, intimate bond and shared experience that goes beyond economic provision, melding work and leisure and cutting across boundaries of private and public space.

Caribbean calypso has long provided a unique window into the cultural milieu, often with a distinctive combination of melodic sound and hard-edged lyrics. On the question of marriage and kinship, calypso classics provide telling social commentaries most often from the point of view of men. Where the "extended family" and the matrifocal household have been synonymous with Caribbean kinship, marriage has historically been portrayed as a foreign imposition and source of tension, sometimes at odds and in competition with kin relations. Here again, it is structure that is most emphasized in these relations. As R. T. Smith (1973, 141; emphasis added) boldly noted, in the Caribbean, "marriage is an act in the *status system* and not in the *kinship system*." And if marriage occupies an ambivalent relationship to the broad terrain of kinship in the Caribbean, its uneasy fit highlights all the more remarkably an absence of romantic love and feeling more generally in the ways in which all of these relationships have been characterized. I have emphasized the manner in which social scientists' own analytical preoccupations and theoretical orientations may have shaped this picture of a region relatively devoid of love, as well as the way in which the Caribbean's particular history of colonial conquest and plantation slavery has contributed to its own cultural emphasis on economy, structure, and support. Popular representations in calypso and the press frequently portray marriage as a plot set by women, ascribing to them a wide range of mercenary or bewitching tactics (obeah) to ensnare their male partners.[20] Here, the "ambivalence" Hodge referred to cedes to the downright demonization of marriage as entrapment. The popular portrayal of marriage is a snare, a hex, devised by women to capture unwitting men in the interest of their own desire for security and status. This theme is boldly drawn in the Mighty Sparrow's now classic calypso "Obeah Wedding," in which Melda's wedding bell dreams are simultaneously derided and unmasked as threatening witchcraft: "Girl you only waiting time; Obeah wedding bells don't chime . . . you can't trap me with necromancy!" In short, his deceptively sweet melodic chorus threatens, no matter how hard she tries, no matter how powerful the Obeah man she enlists, "All you do, can't get through, Ah still ain't gon marry you." Indeed not only is marriage portrayed as the work of the devil, it stands in direct opposition to peaceful and enjoyable love and sex. "Look how many nights, we hug up tight, tight, tight, all we ever know was love and peace, now every minute is only fight, fight, fight, till you using Obeah man for priest. Well you don't seem to understand, Obeah can't upset my plan." If Melda seeks out the Obeah man to help her win over her mate, she is not only destined to fail but also she is demeaned for her foul breath, makeup, and perspiration that suggest more than a whiff of witchcraft.

Where these pejorative portrayals of marriage are most often painted by men concerned to preserve their flexibility and reputation outside the confines of formal marriage, women too are known to express their own reservations toward marriage. The ambivalence about marriage is captured evocatively by Marie-Elena John-Smith (2007, 77–78).

She was the only one who did not understand that in the days before the wedding, these girls were finally forced to come to terms with the end of a life in which they had control over what they did, when they did it, and who they did it with. They would relinquish their ownership over their own selves, and they would swear in front of God to obey their new lord and master until death. These society girls cried because they knew that they were about to become a servant: worse, in fact, because servants were paid and could leave when they wanted. They were crying because they were about to become somebody's slave.

The women who had come in off the street . . . were too familiar with slavery to contemplate doing such a thing to themselves. For the next century or more, these Caribbean women, with their lack of interest in marrying their children's fathers, would generate a steady traffic in befuddled missionaries, curious sociologists, and excited anthropologists. . . . Theories would be put forward as to why they did this, studies would be undertaken. . . . All the big-brained people developing their theories and writing their arguments and counter arguments should have just talked to any of the women to understand that the reason they did not marry was simple. It was that the descendants of slaves had a natural aversion to slavery.

The popular "Dear Christine" column in the local *Daily Nation* newspaper is a veritable treasure trove in reference to the conflicting ideals and the many realities of love, sex, and marriage. Tensions between romance, sex, parenthood, and marriage, and the characterization of women as overly concerned with marriage, economic security, and commitment (respectability), while men prioritize reputation (virility, sexuality), constitute perennial themes. One recent column is suggestive:

Dear Christine,
I'll try to be as brief as possible because I know there is a great demand for space in your column. I have been going out with a man for the past six months and a lot of his conversation is about how much he wants a baby, but the word *marriage* never crossed his lips. I told him I did not want another child (I have a daughter from a former marriage). He promised if I give him a baby, he'll always support the child and provide for a good education. *He insists he loves me and that I can take his word to the bank. But I long to be married*, Christine. Should I take a chance that as time goes by and I give him a child, he'll marry me?

—WTK

Dear WTK,

Right now, this man wants what he wants, free and clear of any emotional commitment. If it is marriage you want (and that's not being unreasonable) don't go about getting a baby unless and until he marries you.

—Christine. (Dear Christine 2007)

Here, WTK wishes to marry the man she loves. He, by contrast, wants a baby from their union but not to wed. His assertion that his love and commitment can be "taken to the bank" signals the powerful equation of responsible and respectable fatherhood with financial support and the provision of a "good education." However, what she desires is *to be married*. She wants from her partner a public, formal demonstration of his love and commitment *to her*, not merely through his financial demonstration of responsible fatherhood.

West Indian literature and popular culture have engaged the affective and emotional dimensions of relationships and marriage more extensively than the social science literature. It is therefore notable that within these excerpts from calypso, literature, and the popular discursive sphere tensions and ambivalence surrounding marriage and its differential meanings and expectations abound. Certainly in recent decades the influence of Hollywood, popular world music, romance novels, soap operas,[21] and a global commercial sector have weighed heavily in favor of romance and models of companionate marriage. Wardlow's (1996, 2006) portrayal of Mills and Boon romances in Papua New Guinea and Larkin's (1997) discussion of Hausa audiences watching Indian films in Nigeria each reveal changing emphases on love and romance in the forging of marriage bonds in vastly different cultural contexts and diverse social and economic systems.

Intriguingly, in the realm of Barbadian popular culture the emergent model of partnership marriage amid an expanding terrain of entrepreneurship figures prominently in a recent series of romance novels, Caribbean Caresses. In this romance series, written specifically for a West Indian market by Caribbean authors, Jane Bryce (1998, 320–38) notes that deliberate efforts have been made to portray gender and romance in ways that counter persistent stereotypes and acknowledge romance, family, and class as dynamic relations. Since, as Bryce asserts, "representation is not only a matter of 'reflecting reality' but also an act of reclamation for these West Indian audiences," the heroes and heroines of these romances promise each other, for instance, "gender equality rather than swooning submission" (325). These authors attempt to subvert the traditional idealization of domesticated, submissive, pure, nurturing, virginal, or maternal femininity presented in European-derived notions of respectability, as well as the sometimes simplistic profile of the autonomous and tough Afro-West Indian woman who shoulders the responsibility of family and economy out of an ostensibly primordial grit and determination. The most successful of these novels echo the formulaic backdrop of an often glitzy and alluring setting and idealized characters (slim, attractive lovers) and reference points that feel familiarly Caribbean without being "too real." Indeed, too familiar a picture of the gritty social realities of poverty, unemployment, alcoholism, promiscuity, and domestic violence, and a protagonist with a plain "round, dark-brown face . . . nails short and unpolished . . . over-weight" as in one of the series' novels, *Merchant of Dreams*, made this the least successful of the series (Morgan 2003, 811).

The entrepreneurial couples in my study and many of the lovers of the Caribbean Caresses romances are intriguing in their deliberate counterimage to both the subservient and passive mythological feminine "ideal" from the colonial past, as well as to the portrait of Caribbean woman as mercenary, manipulative, dominating, and emasculating. The male heroic figures are also cleverly redrawn, departing from the male profile described in the well-known Women in the Caribbean Project studies (1986), and in much of the social science research generally, as almost irretrievably unreliable, unfaithful, and prone to drunkenness and violence (Senior 1991, 166). Instead, these romances are almost devoid of the common referents of an "outside woman," teenage pregnancy, male violence, presenting instead an "ideal man" who is sensitive, caring, trustworthy, and domesticated (Bryce 1998, 329).

The manner in which Barbadian couples today, in the new fiction and in real life, are imagining and attempting to redesign marriage, as an emotionally rich and more egalitarian relationship, resembles the "companionate" model described in other cultural contexts (India, Mexico, etc.). However, these new partnership marriages represent not only a change in form of marital expectations but also in prevalence—in other words, if partnership is attempting to rewrite patriarchy as the form for enacting marriage, it is also being forged in a cultural context in which marriage itself has been less dominant in practice. The specific meanings and historical underpinnings of the partnership marriage in Barbados as a dimension of contemporary globalization reminds us of the need to highlight "the particulars hidden by sameness" as Trouillot (1989) often advised. Companionate marriage, in each ethnographic and historical case, marks a particular kind of transformation, whether as Coontz (2005) describes "from obedience to intimacy," or as Collier (1997) observes in Andalusian Spain "from duty to desire." In most cases, where marriage remains normative, its forms and meanings are being redefined.[22]

In the recent romance novels, the protagonists are lovers who attain a highly sought fidelity and affection they mutually desire. They spend time together and value each others' company. Like many of the entrepreneurs I have studied, these couples engage in a wide range of social interactions in which their coupled status is visible—dinners in local restaurants, outings to movies, parties, and cultural events, holiday travel, attending social and family functions together as a pair—in contrast with the sex-segregated social spheres more common in lower-class as well as traditional and patriarchal middle-class life (Abrahams 1983; Wilson 1973). When entrepreneurial women and men place greater emphasis on partnership marriages, and on social life revolving increasingly around their nuclear families and small circles of friends, they hint at what may be a more dramatic shift in what have been traditionally kin-based social networks. Rayna Rapp observes in the American middle class that by prioritizing friendships over an extended network of kin, the middle-class couple or family concentrates its resources, reduces kinship exchanges, and in effect protects itself from or contravenes the social leveling fostered within lower-class *communitas*.

The heroines in the new romance novels, like the subjects of my study, are typically independent working women who are financially self-sufficient. Entrepreneurs figure prominently among them (Bryce 1998, 334). The protagonists are typically men and women of "ordinary families" who have propelled themselves upward socially and affectively as well as economically. Their emotional mobility articulated in their romantic relationships is one part, an affective dimension, of their economic mobility. Indeed, nearly half of the women in my research describe their business success as due in part to the involvement of husbands who offer emotional as well as practical support, such as handling the accounts, a role frequently performed by wives in old Barbadian firms of days gone by. The partnerships they strive for are simultaneously economic and romantic, and their desires for marriage, like their drive toward entrepreneurship, are permeated by a language of responsibility and self-realization that is enunciated in terms both "rational" and sentimental, about both duty and love.

The narratives of contemporary entrepreneurs in Barbados similarly elucidate some of the ways in which emerging models of marriage simultaneously draw upon and self-consciously rework long-standing kinship arrangements in West Indian culture. Love and support are conveyed not simply in the form of material security but also through expressions of emotional intimacy, desire, and comfort. The concept of "modern love" and the historical shift from marriage as primarily an economic arrangement to one steeped in emotional connection and romance has been described in many recent works as a relatively new dimension of modern social life (e.g., Coontz 2005; Illouz 1997; Giddens 1992; Birth and Freilich 1995; Hirsch and Wardlow 2006). These cases make clear that the trajectory from marriage as a vehicle for political alliance and economic interest to one initiated through love is not a necessary or evolutionary path to modernity. In Illouz's (1997) analysis of marriage in the United States, a shift from economic security to emotional satisfaction occurred in the early decades of the twentieth century with the expanding labor market and possibilities for decreasing women's economic dependence upon men. Like Collier's (1997) evocative ethnographic rendering of the shift "from duty to desire," from agrarian to wage labor, as the context in which companionate ideals for marriage grew in Spain, these reflected a shift toward individual achievement and changing modes of consumption as integral status markers. And it bears reminding that the shift in emphasis from economy to romance does not negate the economic dimensions of a loving and intimate partnership and the interdependence of economic and affective "support." What is at issue is a swing in the ideological weight given to one over the other.

THE COUPLE AS A SOCIAL FORM

Companionate marriage has generally been conceived to mark not only an emphasis on emotion and love as the basis for the conjugal relationship but also a kinship form in which *the couple* supersedes other family ties in importance (Hirsch and Wardlow 2006, 4). However, cultural differences emerge in the form and meaning of what appears to be the globalization of "companionate" or "love" marriage, and the rapid spread of such an idealized romantic norm is often experienced more as an absence, a longing, than as a realized institutional change.[23] In Barbados the growing emphasis on the couple as a social entity is a striking development, without a doubt. Indeed, so familiar and so powerful is this romantic ideal around the globe that again it is hard to emphasize adequately just how recent and dramatic a transformation this represents in the local social landscape.

Although Barbados proudly offers a luxurious setting for the romantic getaways for pop stars like its homegrown Rihanna, played host to Tiger Woods's wedding, and represents a desirable honeymoon destination for

European and North American couples alike, the divide between touristic romance and local public venues for couples' leisure has been stark. This has begun to change with the emergence of a range of new cafés, wine bars, galleries, and newly constructed public boardwalks, which have become popular venues for middle-class social life and recreation, including for couples. That said, the degree to which the couple has usurped traditions of sex-segregated social life and the extended family as the anchor of women's lives is less clear, as the stresses and strains of middle-class entrepreneurial parenting, and life more generally, frequently continue to call upon the support structure of the traditional kin network. In Barbados, and the West Indies more generally, marriage has been weighty ideologically but not the practical norm as elsewhere in the world, and to understand its newly idealized form we must also take this historical and cultural frame into account. It might be tempting to view these transformations as mere examples of the reach of global culture via American popular media, music, and travel, but to grasp their significance a deeper contextual understanding is essential.

In Barbadian history upward mobility has been subtly gendered. For men, movement into the middle class was most often achieved through education and occupation, whereas for women, especially from national independence onward, it was most accessible through marriage or within the narrowly prescribed feminine occupational domains of teaching and nursing. These positions, intriguingly, were predicated on women's single status, both officially and under the symbolic rubric of respectability (Greenfield 1966; Senior 1991). The government sector required that upon marriage women give up their employment, and social conventions of respectability mandated that a proper husband supported his household and family in such a manner in which his wife was not obliged to work. Such women were encouraged to devote their energies both to their children and households, as well as to social voluntarism. For women whose husbands owned businesses, their behind-the-scenes work managing books and accounts was (and is still today) a common and respectable means by which to extend this domesticity into the public sphere. In other words middle-class marriage and the values of respectability prescribed a feminine domesticity rooted in the patriarchal household. Independent entrepreneurship, as such, was not advanced as a sphere for women.

Entrepreneurial women today, who are attempting to forge new partnership marriages, present radical contradictions to these traditional expectations of middle-class femininity both in redefining the expectations for an egalitarian and emotionally enriching marriage relationship and in dramatically broadening the realms through which their middle-class livelihood and status are derived. As such, any inclination to read their marital status as a sign of their adopting conservative middle-class convention must be resisted. My own reading is quite the contrary—that these entrepreneurs' efforts to remake the project of marriage as a partnership is itself an example of the kinds of risk taking and innovative trajectories of upward mobility and self-definition they strive for overall. These independent businesswomen, whether as wives, partners, or individuals, are drawn to visions of relationships and new profiles of the self. Through their entrepreneurial projects in the personal realm and in the marketplace they are simultaneously challenging the boundaries of acceptable middle-class feminine work, middle-class respectable marriage relationships, and middle-class respectable femininity itself. The liberating qualities of these redefinitions are not evenly shared or appreciated, however. For some women whose entrepreneurial profits are insecure, the capacity to push for the new partnership may be curtailed by ongoing economic dependence upon a husband less eager for the change. For others, whose entrepreneurial success is met with a sense of threat and resentment by their husbands or partners, the integral relationship between neoliberal entrepreneurship and neoliberal marriage is tenuous at best.

For men, in general, the impetus toward the new partnership marriage tends to be less urgent, and even, for some, represents a source of irritation if it means changing what have been comfortable patterns of homosociality and patriarchal households. The degree to which class and gender together frame men's and women's conceptualization and valuation of what Derne (2008) calls "cosmopolitan gender arrangements" is critical to understanding these new partnership marriages as part of the globalization of love and romance ideals.[24] Also key are the local particularities of the cultural economy of kinship and marriage. As Barbadian women have become freer to brave domains of entrepreneurship, some have begun to achieve a remarkable degree of economic independence. At the same time, amid a global marketplace saturated by ideals of individualism as well as romance and intimacy, they become freer to define new contours of marriage, relationships, and selfhood in ways that feel meaningful to them.

Because of the complex historical meanings of marriage and its counterpart, matrifocality, in the Caribbean, this new partnership ideal cannot simply be interpreted as evidence of a generic, globalizing expression of "modern love" (Hirsch and Wardlow 2006). Rather, navigating the particular social and economic tightrope of entrepreneurship as a path to middle-classness, while managing the slippery slope of respectability, imbues their quests for emotional, romantic, and material partnership with distinct meanings. If marriage is neither socially nor economically imperative in the postcolonial Barbadian context, what then does the new partnership marriage represent among today's new entrepreneurs? The answers lie in an amorphous but powerful domain of emotional support, understanding, and sharing of the challenges and pleasures of their busy and challenging lives. What I am arguing is that marriage be understood as not only a structural resource (financial security, supportive labor, contacts, advice, etc.) but also as an affective goal, integral to the neoliberal project of self making so critical to these contemporary entrepreneurs. This goal, as I will explore in chapter 4, can only be met through investments in a variety of forms of emotional *work*, work that becomes intimately connected to the entrepreneurial work they are performing in their businesses.

While it was not *only* women who articulated ideals of new intimate partnerships in marriage in ways that reflect a wider entrepreneurial esprit, women do appear to be the primary drivers behind this affective movement. As I listened to many of these young and middle-aged women expressing unself-consciously their dreams and efforts to enact these new intimate partnerships, there was an unmistakably utopian, romantic ring to their narration and also something very "un-Barbadian" sounding to my ears. Their visions painted marital partnerships in which their businesses and their private lives were conceived creatively and mutually supported in a dynamic, flexible, and emotionally rich web of relations. This web included not only the romantic couple who listened to each other and shared aspirations, frustrations, practical challenges, leisure time, and so on but also a combination of children, extended family members, friends, church communities, and time alone for personal creative self-cultivation. The ubiquity of these themes raises several questions from the perspective of the neoliberal thrust toward middle-class entrepreneurialism. How does the search for intimacy and self-realization get melded to the entrepreneurial marketplace and what are the social effects of such a merger? Is the search for love and mutual recognition in the sphere of private intimacy a demand for a kind of "capital" of another form? There are intriguing resemblances here to the wages for housework proposals of early second-wave feminism. Kathi Weeks's (2011) return to this work is especially instructive. She suggests there is something about not just the demand itself (wages for housework) but the opportunity the demand offered to shed light on the importance of women's labor "as a force of demystification, an instrument of denaturalization and a tool of cognitive remapping" (Weeks 2011, 129). I explore similarly in chapter 4 how the search for intimacy suggests a similar lever on the tightly hinged relationship of productive and reproductive labor at a time in which intimate labor is an especially elusive but charged form of exchange. At a moment in which emotional work is increasingly critical to the largest growth sector of the global marketplace, *services*, how might we develop a critical reading that links these demands, desires, and enactments in the "non-work" realm of life to those of the marketplace?[25]

We might characterize the ideals of an intimate partnership marriage as part of a seemingly global thrust toward romantic love and companionate marriage, and on a broader plane, what I see as a neoliberal current of affect—a heightened "emotion-scape" to borrow Appadurai's (1991) rendering of globalization that now rings increasingly familiar across the world stage. The desire to imagine and enact such feelings is taking distinctive forms among middle-class women in Barbados and perhaps especially among entrepreneurial women. These transformations must be framed, as I have said, in relation to the plantation history of West Indian kinship and creole culture, for Caribbean marriage, new or old, egalitarian and partnered or traditionally patriarchal, is inextricable from matrifocality, its relational referent.

Since marriage has always been an ambivalent terrain for Barbadian women, their efforts at redefinition away from the constraints of traditional patriarchy are facilitated in part by the West Indian legacy of matrifocality. And the significance of matrifocality as a counterweight to marriage has both economic and emotional dimensions. Not only are women able to claim decision-making power and autonomy by virtue of their hard won economic achievements as entrepreneurs but also they are able to claim self-respect and feminine strength as they leverage the enduring cultural legacy of matrifocality within a new middle-class milieu.

CHAPTER 3

The Upward Mobility of Matrifocality

My mother who fathered me.
—GEORGE LAMMING, *IN THE CASTLE OF MY SKIN*, 11

The new intimate partnership marriage offers an evocative symbol of the desires and pressures associated with contemporary neoliberalism and the rise of entrepreneurialism in Barbados. Equally striking, and inextricably connected, is what I see as an "upward mobility" of matrifocality into this new entrepreneurial middle class. These social processes might be thought of as two sides of the same coin, together drawing upon potent cultural values in Barbadian tradition that are now immersed within, and giving new expression to, a neoliberal, affective esprit. Together they draw our attention to the growing saturation of economic enterprise with emotional desires and cultural sensibilities, the pursuit of flexibility, and the permeability of entrepreneurial work, family, and selfhood as signatures of life in the twenty-first century.

Throughout the history of anthropology, kinship has been a staple in the study of culture and social organization. Nowhere in the world is the preoccupation with kinship greater than in the Afro-Caribbean. Caribbean anthropology from its inception was anchored in a mission to explain the structure and function of the region's highly charged *matrifocal* or female-centered family. *Matrifocality* in the Caribbean and around the world has been defined in a variety of ways to signal the central importance played by women, and mothers in particular, in the spheres of kinship and domestic organization. The history of kinship studies in the Caribbean reflects a history of two primary analytical preoccupations: the matrifocal family and what has been called the "dual marriage system" of legally and religiously sanctioned "inside" conjugal relations and unsanctioned or "outside" relations.

Several decades of research have been devoted to the origins of the matrifocal family, the degree to which its form persists out of a legacy of African social organization (Herskovits 1947) or out of the ruptures and familial dissolution wrought by the brutal systems of plantation slavery (Frazier 1966). There has been little disagreement as to the distinguishing characteristics of these family forms: the "looseness of conjugal bonds, the nucleus of mother and child, the importance of family support to the individual, the peripheral status of the father and the rituals of courting, birth, and child socialization" (Barrow 1996, 459). Many scholars have noted and critiqued the preoccupation with matrifocality, a preoccupation that began among colonial administrators and social scientists intent upon identifying and rooting out what was believed to be the *pathology* of casual mating and family formations that threatened the European nuclear patriarchal norm (Barrow 1988, 1996; Morrissey 1998; Smith 1996; Gonzalez 1970, 1984; Smith 1996). Most observers in recent years have shifted away from the pathologizing stance and highlight the economic rationality and benefits of matrifocality in the face of persistent regional economic insecurity and circumstances in which men are unable to "fulfill the traditional economic role associated with patriarchy" (Morrissey 1998, 81). Its resilience, evocatively personified in Lamming's famous expression "my mother who really fathered me," continues to hail the profound importance of women and mothers as the anchor of kinship relations both within the confines of the domestic space and in Caribbean societies more broadly.[1]

My own intervention in the matrifocality discussion draws upon this robust literature with the hopes of opening up new lines of inquiry and connection. The shift in perspectives toward matrifocality from that of aberration to creative, flexible norm is expressed well by Christine Barrow (1996, 459–60), who has provided some of the most astute analysis and critique of the kinship literature in the past forty years: "In Caribbean circumstances of poverty and economic marginality, rigid nuclear family structures with specified roles and relationships were unrealistic and unworkable. If people were constrained by nuclear family expectations they would not be able to leave their marriages, delegate responsibilities to others and shift their children in order to take advantage of economic opportunities at home and abroad." In essence, visiting unions and non-marital, nonnuclear family forms in the Caribbean were not pathological but highly logical adaptations, "no longer a problem but a solution" (Barrow 1996, 463). Barrow says, "conjugal co-residence, especially marriage, is culturally defined as a segregated relationship, . . . a difficult relationship to manage and therefore best postponed until the partners are more mature and they have undergone a period of testing" (463). These struggles and adaptations have been especially pronounced for the Afro-Caribbean lower classes.

The emergence of new ideals of marriage which depart from those of patriarchal tradition, and of matrifocality, which extend beyond the survival strategies of lower-class Afro-Caribbean women to include both black and white middle-class women, invite a new examination of kinship and marriage today.[2] In this sense marriage and matrifocality together reveal and give expression to new facets of neoliberal entrepreneurialism. And as Caribbean matrifocality is increasingly understood as positively adaptive, it is also important to examine its reach not merely within the black lower classes but across class and racial boundaries. What kinds of possibilities as well as challenges are entailed for new middle-class entrepreneurs who find themselves at the center of such households and kinship relations, defining themselves through matrifocal terms? What roles are being played by the extended kin network, community, and the state in maintaining and supporting these flexible arrangements?

MARRIAGE, AMBIVALENCE, AND CARIBBEAN KINSHIP

If patriarchal marriage has been the ideological symbol of middle- and upper-class kinship in the West Indies, matrifocality has been the equivalent shorthand for kinship in the lower classes. Each has been analytically inscribed in systems of gender, race, and class in ways that might be elucidated in the heuristic model presented in table 3.1.

Historically, the emphasis on matrifocality has signaled the "salience of women," especially in their role as mothers in households in which men have been seen as marginal or "missing" (Smith 1988, 8; Rowley 2002, 24). Steeped in early structural functionalist analyses, the early kinship literature characterized the West Indian matrifocal family as an adaptive means by which to meet the basic needs of economic support, sex, child rearing, domestic services, and the overall management of the family group.[3] In its *ideological* hegemony, formal, respectable marriage has been implicitly juxtaposed with its more casual, flexible counterparts—visiting unions, cohabitation, and matrifocality.[4] This contrastive polarity is ironic

TABLE 3.1 **Patriarchal vs. matriarchal tradition**

TRADITIONAL MARRIAGE	TRADITIONAL MATRIFOCALITY
European roots/colonial	African roots/creole Caribbean
White and brown	Black
Middle class and elite	Lower class and poor
Patriarchal	Woman-/ mother-centered
Respectability	Reputation
Dependent femininity	Female autonomy and strength
Rigid/static	Resilient/flexible
Secure, aspirational/future-oriented	Insecure, survival-oriented
Ideological norm	Practical norm

in that virtually all analysts of kinship in the region have emphasized the flexible continuum of conjugal relations, of which marriage represents one possible stage.[5] Indeed, like the respectability-reputation complex itself, and its middle- and lower-class mappings, the contrasting institutions of marriage and matrifocality have been amenable to parallel oversimplifications that have masked their creative dialectical relationship.

While matrifocality has carried with it the aura of feminine strength, flexibility, and resilience, it is also the case that female-headed households have generally been poorer and more vulnerable economically than those headed by men. Women-centered kinship and household forms not only continue to represent nearly half of all households in Barbados but also they offer powerful symbols for the whole society of the age-old values and practices of flexibility in multiple realms (Smith 1996; Barrow 1998; Rowley 2002).[6] Over the past twenty-five years, *matrifocality* has come to refer not simply to household configuration (i.e., the female-headed household) but also more generally to the prominence of women and mothers as the anchor or engine of social and economic life, even when men are also present.[7]

The potency with which the analytical preoccupation with the female-headed household has dominated both popular culture and Caribbean social science goes beyond the mere structural form or numerical proportion of these domestic units. In Barbados, which ranks second after Botswana with the highest proportion of female-headed households in the world (46 percent), and where only 23 percent of the population is married, the scholarly focus on the survival strategies and resilience of such nonnuclear and/or matrifocal households has been well documented (Seager 1997). The matrifocal household has represented a kind of synecdoche for Afro-West Indian culture, a trope or cultural symbol of resiliency and flexibility.[8] Matrifocality in the Caribbean is interpreted not only as reflective of women's strength and tenacity but also more generally as integral to the region's resilient and adaptable creole culture as it emerged under plantation slavery, colonialism, and postcolonial dependency. Even with a gradual shift from pejorative to more positive value associated with matrifocality as integral to Caribbean society, there remains an enduring analytical association of matrifocality with the lower classes and marriage with middle-class respectability.

As increasing numbers of women in many countries assume a growing presence not only in the workplace but also as "breadwinners" of their households, the Caribbean legacy of matrifocality may offer an intriguing counterpoint and a wellspring of tradition.[9] As Shirley put it to me, women are used to taking one step at a time and working hard for what they need. They are used to having patience and sticking to their goal. Men, she and many others told me, are quick to want to make their mark in visible and public ways, buy a fancy car, show off the signs of their success. A woman, by contrast, will be more modest in growing her business. She will first reinvest, and continue to build slowly, often setting up another enterprise to offset her possible loss, manage the risks. She described these differences in bold and memorable terms,

> If any child came out of a mother's uterus and started running around, everybody around the child would freak out and run! The child has to creep, then it crawls, and then it stands up, and then it walks, then it runs and that's my whole attitude towards business. I think any women trying to start a business has got to research the business, go through the stages that you expect any business to go through . . . start at the very, very beginning. You don't have to hire somebody to do your market research, do your market research on your own if it's something you're interested in. . . . I mean look at the lady with the food vans . . . [she] started with a small Suzuki van then she got a bigger van . . . then, she put another van on the road then she got this humongous broad thing that could seat three or four people in the front. I mean it's unbelievable but she started small . . . she started cooking in her kitchen, she still cooks in her kitchen, she built a little room, at the side and she's cooking more stuff out there now.

Such stories about women's economic persistence, patience, and determination are common, not only in my interview transcripts but also in popular culture at large. They form a strong armory from which other women draw inspiration and a cultural model for self-realization. They typically highlight a small-scale enterprise involving traditional feminine activity—in this case the preparation and sale of food—and illustrate that by putting one foot in front of the other, a woman can support herself and her children. The poignancy of matrifocality as a critical resource for women, as both a structural kinship and household form and also a cultural model of femininity, became sharpest for me in witnessing and hearing testimonials about the tensions within, and dissolution of, the idealized partnership marriages. Matrifocality has certainly never been confined to the lower classes, just as marriage has never been exclusive to those of the middle and upper class, but a persistently bifurcated ideological association has long existed between them.

In alluding to the "upward mobility" of matrifocality, therefore, I am signalling not that middle-class women are for the first time enacting matrifocal households but that, as part of the neoliberal thrust toward entrepreneurialism, the reconfiguration of domestic life, relationships, and identities has given matrifocality a different footing, broadening its purview for women in this group. It is in this more capacious sense that I see an upward mobility of matrifocality as the expansion of a particular kind of strong, caring femininity that stands at the economic and emotional center of social life.

Almost every entrepreneurial woman I interviewed, regardless of her current conjugal or household arrangement, described previous frustrations and struggles in intimate relationships. Sheila's experience, as recounted in chapter 1, is one such telling illustration of the flexible model of matrifocality available to successful women today. Her husband's failure to conform to her desires for a true partnership lead Sheila to end her respectable marriage in favor of a looser relationship with an attentive "friend." She adopts the age-old "visiting relationship" not as an economic strategy but as an affective means for combining intimacy, leisure, and flexible autonomy in her entrepreneurial and private lives. She endures a female bank manager's disapproval and hires legal assistance to have her legitimacy recognized as the sole titleholder of the house she worked so hard to build. Such contemporary practices of middle-class entrepreneurialism reveal a familiar tenacity and resiliency women in the lower classes have long been hailed for, while at the same time moving them into new spheres and lifestyles of the middle classes. Their entrepreneurial independence was inextricably connected to these experiences and conjured up familiar references to female autonomy, resourcefulness, grit, and determination associated with strong Caribbean womanhood and the institution of matrifocality.

Many of those living without a spouse or partner described having "made their peace" alone.[10] Indeed, several cases of marital dissolution articulated especially dramatically and poignantly the qualities most at stake and hard to achieve in the forging of new affective selves and partnership relationships. They also illustrate the centrality of class within the very ideal of partnership itself. For underlying these entrepreneurial women's expressed desire for romance, compassion, and an equal partnership is the knowledge that if need be, they could support themselves and more than survive. While the new appeal of marriage and romantic partnerships privileged intimacy and emotional connection rather than financial stability, the often-elusive nature of emotional satisfaction meant that such quests also led to the downfall of these relationships.

The stories of Sheila, Colleen, and Suzanne in chapter 1 powerfully demonstrate that women's entrepreneurial independence (economic and otherwise) can inspire intimate partnerships and also provoke discord. It can foster new desires, new tensions, and also provide a great buffer in the face of marital rupture. Matrifocality, as a resilient gendered cultural model, emphasizes a woman-centered kinship and social network. It offers a template for a robust, flexible, independent femininity not only for the poor (who are often assumed to have no choice but to adopt these qualities and capacities) but for all women, even those imagined to be the staunchest gatekeepers of respectability. *Matrifocality*, in the broad sense in which I use it, does not imply, as some have imagined, a matriarchy, a society run by women.[11] Barbados, like the rest of the region, is still structured by many of the conventions and subtle ideological frameworks of patriarchy. However, women's critical importance in the formal economy, the informal market, as mothers, and their growing visibility on the political stage, together with the legacy of the matrifocal household, gives a particularly strong face to one model of Barbadian and Caribbean femininity. Where some women entrepreneurs like Sheila reconcile tensions exacerbated by their greater economic success by ending disappointing marriages and adopting a matrifocal model of household structure and selfhood, these struggles unfold in a variety of ways with no predictable outcome. Over the decade I conducted interviews and fieldwork, different dimensions of an entrepreneurial life, the external structural economic demands for flexibility, the internal desires for intimacy, flexibility, self-knowledge, and self-reflection, permeated women's relationships with their husbands, children, extended family, friends, community activism, and entrepreneurial life broadly understood. Lilliana's aspirations for intimacy and self-sufficiency, creative independence and family security stand as a poignant illustration of the complexities of economy and affect, desires for more mutual recognition and connectivity as well as independence and self-realization. Early in our conversations she reflected upon her husband's resentment at being the primary breadwinner, her own anxieties about financial security, and the implications of these tensions for both their marriage and her own independence and sense of self,

> I think every once in a while . . . he gets nervous that he's getting older and he hasn't done the thing that he wants to do. . . . He is pressured because he has the financial burden and he just thinks that I need to . . . contribute more . . . and he's right. I just feel like I'm in a career that doesn't lend itself so easily to that and so I have to figure out how I'm going to do that, you know because . . . he's getting to the point where he resents it. . . . I would like to think that we could share it more equitably. The truth is, I just think I have an enormous fear about it all. I am absolutely petrified about being poor and about having to be the wage earner, it is just a fear that I have . . . how am I going to do it?

Over subsequent years, their relationship and their financial situation have gone up and down, ultimately ending in a painful but amicable divorce. When his work was regular, her ex-husband continued to support her and the children. Meanwhile, Lilliana worked harder at diversifying her entrepreneurial energies in both her product lines, teaching, and community outreach. Since losing his job, money has gotten tighter. Lilliana now bears the burden of supporting her children and fully occupying the matrifocal role, financially and affectively. Her quest for creative self-definition and autonomy as well as intimate connection are not easily achieved, and economic precarity adds a layer of unease that puts some aspects of entrepreneurial viability into question; as she noted, "once you have the financial security . . . it buys you another kind of freedom."

Economic security and middle-class status, no doubt, offer critical ingredients in entrepreneurial women's capacities to make all sorts of choices about their work lives, households, relationships, the help they enlist, and their social and leisure time with less fear of economic marginality. On the other hand, the social costs of divorce and the stigma associated with being a woman alone would, according to many of my informants (like Heather and Ashanti in the preceding chapter), have kept their mothers and grandmothers from ending bad and even brutal relationships. At the same time, the legacy of matrifocality offers all Barbadian women, including middle-class white women like Lilliana, a potent model of feminine strength, independence and authenticity they can draw upon. Among the most striking aspects of more than ten years of fieldwork among these middle-class entrepreneurs were the confluences in both practice and ideology that *connected* middle-class women with these age-old matrifocal sensibilities and strategies.

Interestingly, while contemporary feminist kinship studies have adopted a stance in which Caribbean gender relations and kinship are understood within the rubric of dynamic, creole, or New World cultural innovation, Barrow (1996, 181) also contends that the legacy of the "plural society" model of Caribbean social organization has continued to "reinforce the ideas of cultural difference between black lower class and brown middle class. . . . Without any evidence to confirm or refute this . . . the brown middle class are assumed to conform to Eurocentric norms."[12] Still a half century later, we see the enduring notion that in Caribbean society at large, black, lower-class, African-derived, creole culture is counterpoised to white or brown, middle-class, European-derived (and therefore *inauthentic*) culture.

A notable shift in perspective has been underway, however.[13] Matrifocality remains squarely in the center of discussion but with a decidedly different value. Like the wider domain of reputation, as described in chapter 1, the matrifocal household is, in these new works, more commonly hailed for its flexibility and clever survival strategies than condemned as aberrant or dysfunctional. After decades of study and debate over both the origins and "solutions" to the "problem" of the Afro-Caribbean family, most contemporary analysts concur that kinship patterns in the Caribbean have demonstrated both continuity and stability over many generations. As Barrow (1996, 165) argues, lower-class family forms could neither be explained simply as a function of slave status nor of post-emancipation economic conditions:[14] "When the abolition of slavery removed legal distinctions on the basis of race and colour, there was no rush to marry among the ex-slaves despite pressure from missionaries and priests. Neither, it would appear, was there any reduction in 'outside' unions and 'outside' children. From a contemporary perspective, even though the standard of living and consumption patterns of the lower class in Caribbean societies have improved enormously since the 1940s and 1950s, marriage rates have hardly changed and illegitimacy remains high."[15]

Lisa Douglass (1992) offers a rare intersectional lens on race, class, and gender in her work on the Jamaican family elite and summarizes four ways in which gender, race, and class articulate. Echoing Wilson's key observations, Douglass (1992, 255) captures the essence of kinship in the Barbadian context and thus I quote her at length here:

> 1. Women of all classes are expected to wield a similar, centralizing authority inside their respective families. 2. Men of higher classes have greater authority inside the family than do lower class men. Upper class women turn over more of family authority to men. 3. Women of lower classes exercise greater individual autonomy outside the family than their upper class peers. Their movement and activity is not restricted by their relationships with men or their family responsibilities. 4. Men of all classes share a similar personal autonomy outside the family that is unaffected by their inside lives or by their relationships with women.

I witnessed the most dramatic challenges being posed by entrepreneurial women in the third of these generalizations, where the contest over respectability and the capacity to navigate public spheres was notable among these (aspiring) middle-class women. My fieldwork suggests a loosening of the boundaries circumscribing middle- and upper-class women's personal autonomy outside the family sphere in ways that resemble the freedom and autonomy long exercised by lower-class Caribbean women. Through their entrepreneurial enterprises, they occupy an ever-widening public domain within Barbados, across the region, and in the international arena at large. They give public presentations, sit on boards, write and communicate across a broad field of interlocutors, electronically as well as in person, and travel independently abroad.[16] In so doing, these women are changing the very terms in which public and private spaces are gendered. Gradually, they are loosening the confines of what has long been deemed a masculine public sphere, as they assume the podiums of public gatherings, the offices of trade and commerce, the airport and the street. Simultaneously, these women appear to be less inclined to turn over family authority to men than may once have been the case in higher-class households. And these changes are unfolding in two striking domains—within the context of partnership marriages and also in the context of middle-class matrifocal households.

In a climate of neoliberalism in which individuals must increasingly take responsibility for their own viability in the marketplace as well as in the personal and intimate realms of life, women who are able to achieve this dynamic economic self-sufficiency are increasingly articulating their desires for equal flexibility and responsiveness in their intimate and private lives. In doing so, these entrepreneurial women draw not simply upon global media representations of "modern" liberated women steeped in American-style individualism, as some might be inclined to suggest, but also from the matrifocal model of autonomous femininity rooted in more than three hundred years of West Indian history. I found that white and black Barbadian women articulate similar affective desires and partnership ideals today, and equally notable, they take similar paths when their desires and efforts to achieve this intimate partnership are dashed. The new marital partnerships ideally challenge conventional gendered norms of middle-class male authority in the household in favor of more egalitarian ones, and when these desires are not realized, as in Sheila's and Lilliana's case, women turn to other widespread and practical alternatives, including visiting unions, matrifocal households, and the age-old extended kin network.

It is in this sense that partnership marriage and matrifocality may be seen as two sides of a middle-class woman's coin, and taken together, they are reworking the local parameters of respectability and reputation. The metaphor denotes not only the relational interconnections between these desired forms of flexible intimacy and self-realization but also their significance as forms of value in the neoliberal economy. What we are witnessing is a decisive moment of economic and cultural transformation in which the logics of reputation and matrifocality that were long understood to be oppositional cultural expressions to the hegemonic colonial and capitalist order (respectability) are being profitably drawn upon and refashioned in the upward ascent to neoliberal middle-classness. All over the world understandings of *family* and *household* are in flux today. Along with new reproductive technologies, child fostering and adoption options, the gay marriage movement, "blended," "transnational," and "queer" families, the landscape of conjugality and kinship is changing both institutionally and affectively: household formations and ways of living and loving are more fluid and more various, transcending the confines of heterosexual marriage and nuclearization. If romantic love and marriage were constituted through the matrices of *modernity* in the last century (Giddens 1992, 255), the twenty-first century appears to also signal expanding neoliberal fragmentation and flexibility: rapidly changing global flows of labor and migration, longings for new commodities and lifestyles, and changing ways of relating to the marketplace, flexible blended families, transnational families, a growing number of people choosing to "go solo," and new ways of defining the self.

For entrepreneurial middle-class women and for some men as well, the much desired ideal of partnership marriage has offered a space of new affective experience as well as a structural redefinition of labor, material support, and kinship. For others, this intimate partnership has been elusive in practice but remains a potent imaginary, an aspirational ideal that melds in many ways with other dimensions of the entrepreneurial life—the flexible and constant reworking of themselves and their businesses simultaneously. Some have, by choice or circumstance, become divorced or separated from husbands and partners, maintained a "visiting" relationship, or remained single. Among these women I found there to be strong similarities in the ways in which they juggled their busy work and their domestic lives and embodied the kind of resourcefulness, flexibility, and strength long associated with poor and lower-class female household heads. For those entrepreneurs with children, even grown children leading relatively independent lives, women's homes remain significant loci of support and tangible provision (meals, laundry, financial support, child care, etc.). Just as matrifocality has offered flexibility to women in the lower classes to bargain for economic support, child fostering, sexual and emotional fluidity, and a certain degree of autonomy, these are also part of every middle-class woman's point of reference, and the manner in which flexible entrepreneurialism plays a critical role in the marketplace and in the private and domestic sphere is richly demonstrated across all of these conjugal and household configurations. These women and men boldly demonstrate concomitant changes underway in the constitution of the partnership marriage ideal discussed in the previous chapter and in the middle-class entrepreneurial enactments of matrifocality.

What is especially significant about these convergent transformations is that while many have assumed at least implicitly Rodman's (1971) notion of the "lower class value stretch," by which lower-class peoples are understood to subscribe to the values of middle-class respectability (even if the ideal is never realized), I am proposing that another set of identifications are simultaneously at work in the opposite direction. Just as lower-class women have long been known to imagine and idealize marriage and the "intact nuclear family" as stable, faithful, and secure (Senior 1991; Barrow 1996), women's autonomy within the matrifocal family has stood as a weighty countermodel of femininity. Having put to rest the legacy of early social scientists' concerns to solve the "pathology" or problem of matrifocality, what remains is an enduring profile of powerful, autonomous, and flexible femininity that offers an attractive alternative to that of demure dependence as imagined to be the heart of respectability. In short the reputational model of matrifocality is upwardly mobile.

These two models—the respectable lady or wife and the powerful woman head of household—have long represented competing sides of Caribbean femininity.[17] Gina Ulysse (2007) describes this contrast evocatively between the "uptown ladies" and the "downtown women" in her study of Jamaican suitcase traders, and Lisa Douglass (1992, 248) elaborates upon this contrast to elucidate how such competing articulations of femininity, class, and race reproduce a generalized pattern of gender hierarchy: "A lady cultivates a femininity that contrasts with the practices of men, whereas the lower-class black woman's aggressive and unrefined practices resemble those of a man. The same practices that bestow the cloak of authority upon a man, however, deny power to a woman. The higgler is devalued, not praised for lacking femininity." Indeed, Douglass notes that the higgler is a figure of great ambivalence for Jamaicans, and her observation could be made about Barbadians as well.

> She embodies many cultural traits that Jamaicans are proud of. She is black, clever, assertive and street smart. She is an exemplar of female autonomy. Jamaicans proudly point to such 'strong' women who work for a living, raise families alone, and stand up and speak for themselves. But Jamaicans are also critical of her . . . The higgler contradicts the feminine values that prevail among the powerful while embodying other cultural values of the society . . . In regard to femininity, Jamaicans ridicule the higgler and praise the lady. When they do this they are not simply expressing preferences about female style. The discourse surrounding these two contrasting images also encourages practices that help to reproduce a social order in which men dominate women, where whites rule over people of color, and where everyone is ranked by class. (248)

How then might we interpret the ways in which middle-class Barbadian entrepreneurialism offers a medium through which women may meld dimensions of respectable femininity with those of higgler-identified womanly strength, and what are the limits and possibilities of such blendings? On one hand, those who are married offset some of the "reputation-oriented" entrepreneurial costs to respectability via the symbolic value of their marriages. For others, the tightrope is negotiated in other ways, including active participation in religious or other spiritual communities, as I explore in chapter 5. For unmarried women, especially those with children, the manner in which entrepreneurship and motherhood are negotiated within the domain of middle-class life is especially illuminating. Other women I got to know ended relationships (visiting, common-law, and marriage) during their entrepreneurial careers, and they continue searching for a satisfying mix of romantic and emotional fulfillment in their lives. They express the appeal of nonresidential visiting relationships that afford them flexibility to weigh and recalibrate their priorities and desires without the structural constraints implied by cohabitation and marriage.[18] Together, these women are enacting new modes of matrifocality in ways that draw upon old forms of kinship and support, paving the way toward new articulations of relatedness and selfhood. In so doing, they are redefining the parameters of both respectable middle-classness and matrifocality itself. They face challenges in both the public and private domains of their lives, as signaled by Sheila's encounters with bank managers who simply refused to acknowledge her independent home ownership outside of her (dissolving) marriage and in her choice of an intimate but nonresidential relationship. Their efforts to manage the stresses and enhance the pleasures of their entrepreneurial lives, as we will see in the next two chapters, highlight resources and cultural traditions that give particular meaning to today's neoliberal ethos.

In the narratives below, I highlight entrepreneurial women who by circumstance and/or "choice" have come to head their own households. They embody matrifocality not only in structural household headship but also in broader cultural and ideological terms that bear emphasis. In some cases their paths echo the kinship and household patterns of these women's upbringing. I include women whose own family histories are rooted in matrifocality and who draw from the experience and model of their own grandmothers, aunties, and mothers in the ways in which they balance their work, extended kin networks, motherhood, and circuits of care. I also present cases of women whose matrifocality represents a dramatic departure from the households and families in which they were raised. For both white and black women reared in patriarchal households, the attempt to configure a balance in their own relationships, work, and motherhood in more egalitarian terms, and ultimately their embrace (by "choice" or default) of matrifocality, represents an intriguing new development in the parameters of Caribbean middle-class kinship. In these departures men too combine elements of respectability and reputation in the realm of conjugality and kinship. For some of the entrepreneurs, the enduring benefits of matrifocality are expressed in their relationships with both their mothers and their conjugal partners. The variety of cases I sketch briefly below demonstrates that, across class and racial boundaries, women and men today draw upon the creole continuum of kinship forms and give to these forms new meanings and inflections within the context of entrepreneurial middle-class life.

FROM MIDDLE-CLASS PATRIARCHAL RESPECTABILITY TO MIDDLE-CLASS MATRIFOCALITY: REDEFINING WHITE FEMININITY

Arguably, no group has been more closely associated with the normative model of respectability and middle-classness than white Barbadians, and at the same time no group has remained as ethnographically invisible in the kinship literature.[19] While small in number (the Barbadian population identified as "white" is listed as 3 percent in the Population Census of 2000, 93 percent "black," 2.6 percent "mixed," and 1 percent East Indian), this ethnic minority has held significant power both economically and in its symbolic associations with respectability. Unlike Trinidad and Jamaica, where mixture is celebrated within the national cultural rhetoric of "creolization" (Thomas 2004; Khan 2005; Munasinghe 2001), the self-selected identifiers of "black" and "white" are more pronounced in Barbados. And if white Barbadians have been elusive as an ethnographic subject, white women have been especially so. As I have already discussed, in relation to feminist scholarship and the weight of the reputation-respectability paradigm, and the association of *respectability* with *middle class* and *European*, there has been a long-standing avoidance of this group with the assumption that both the "place" and ideology of white femininity is already understood. Of the white women entrepreneurs I interviewed (twelve of seventy-two women entrepreneurs or 17 percent),[20] half (six) fit the domestic and conjugal profile one might have expected according to cultural stereotype—married, middle-upper or middle class, actively involved in civic and church life, and overseeing children and domestic responsibilities with the help of a paid domestic worker—all key elements in Wilson's understanding of respectability. Perhaps no group more alarmed me for their striking departures from conventional models and popular beliefs and for their explicit articulations of many of the neoliberal ideals of entrepreneurialism, desires for intimate partnership and introspective projects of self making.

When I first met Suzanne in 1999 she was married with one child and starting up a new business partnership in public relations. I was intrigued to note at the time that she was the self-described "head of her household." She said then, "well, I pretty much run things, do what needs to be done . . . now, if a census taker came to the door and said 'may I speak to the head of the household,' they'd probably go after the man . . . men boss women around, but I think the women basically cook, clean, maintain the house, maintain the children. . . . I consider my husband and me equal." By 2005 Suzanne had had a second child and had separated from her husband. Her story had run the gamut of the local rumor mill. Married for ten years, the mother of two school-age children, and the co-owner of a busy company, an affair with a foreigner had led her at thirty-three to end her marriage: "When I sit back and look at why I got married in the first place, I think I got married for the wrong reasons . . . I'm not saying I didn't love my husband, but . . . I think I was looking for something . . . security . . . I had lost my dad, and I was very close to him . . . I was looking also to fill that void. I was unhappy for a long time . . . I find that's what happens here a lot. People just stay in the marriage even if they're not happy. It's small . . . a small community, so to take that risk, to go out there again . . . ? And then there's the financial aspect about staying together for the children." For Suzanne, the appeal of her non-Barbadian boyfriend and the impetus to divorce revolved around precisely the kinds of marital frustration and romantic desire signalled above: "My husband used to always come home and complain about so and so's wife . . . nagging him to come home . . . but . . . I always was like . . . I don't want to be like that. So, I let him, I gave him a free rein and it backfired . . . because I realized well . . . this is not what I want . . . (being alone at home with the children while he was out with his friends). But at the same time, I was like . . . well, *I can't make you be something you don't want to be,* I can't make you *want* to come home or I didn't want it to be like that. I wanted him to come home . . . *because he wanted to.*"

Justine is the daughter of a prominent Barbadian businessman. She attended the island's top public school for girls (as did a striking number of the women entrepreneurs in this study),[21] went away briefly to university abroad, but did not complete her studies. Instead, she came home, worked in the tourism sector for a short time, got married, and had a child. Living in a cramped suburban subdivision and caring for her infant son, she started a small business "on the side," just to keep busy and have "something to do other than change nappies." For all intents and purposes, her trajectory looks like a predictably respectable path for a daughter of the island's white corporate elite. Ten years later, she now employs a staff of forty in her vibrant tourism supply and service business, is separated from her husband, and runs a second enterprise in her spare time. Her work involves waking at 4 A.M., driving a pick-up truck, working outside in the hot sun, as well as brokering several million-dollar contracts not only in Barbados but regionally as well. She straddles conventions of middle-class respectability with elements of the strong West Indian woman in striking terms. Her booming voice and forceful managerial hand with her primarily male staff are reminiscent of tough plantation overseers. In fact Justine's

roots are not in the plantation but in more modest stock of former indentured labor that worked their way into the island's middle and upper class
through commercial trade.[22] While her commanding voice and capacity
for the quick turn of phrase bear the confident wit of the calypsonian, her
homemade sushi platter and perfectly laid table signal an artful, polished
domesticity. Reputation and respectability converge. One particularly busy
Christmas season, she spent late nights sewing by hand outfits for all of
her nieces and cousins after winning the tender on a highly competitive
and lucrative job outside the island. Justine's enactment of matrifocality,
heading her household, employing her husband briefly, then divorcing
him in favor of a freer, flexible life, departs from the image of white respectable femininity. She sought a mutual emotional connection and the
desire to be together, while her husband found his social life among his
male friends. However, the picture is complex—sewing, gardening, and
especially riding horses are common features of middle-class white culture. But Justine's remarkable financial and emotional autonomy bespeak
an independence and strength more commonly rooted in lower-class black
Barbadian women's survival strategies.

Lilliana, from a large white planter family, expressed powerfully some
of the key ingredients of middle-class respectability and her efforts to find
security and "freedom" otherwise.

> Well, in my family the most important thing you could do is get mar-
> ried and get pregnant. So . . . you know, getting a first degree or a mas-
> ters or traveling to Washington or to India or producing the [kind of
> work I do] are, you know, congratulated . . . but the kind of *emotional*
> response that they would garner is *nothing* compared to the fact that
> you're gonna have a child. So . . . the most important thing you could
> tell somebody in my family—my mother and my grandparents or my
> aunts—is that you're *pregnant* and that's just, you know, the *best* thing
> that you could do, really. So, my expectations for myself were not . . .
> that I want to be able to make a mark, to produce meaningful work . . .
> You know if I'm invited to a workshop in India or I'm given a grant
> or I have an opportunity to go to university, those things give me an
> enormous sense of fulfillment because I feel as though, you know, in
> those very few moments that somebody is *interested* . . . it doesn't come
> very often . . . to me those were the most fulfilling and satisfying mo-
> ments. I love . . . to be able to work towards those things and I . . . I
> guess I feel differently about that [than my family]. I never saw myself
> being married and having children. It wasn't something that I really

longed to do . . . when I was at college, I wanted to be on the cover of a magazine and I wanted to be famous. . But, [she laughs, then sighs deeply] I keep falling out of it, you know? Going away to school . . . the States [vs. England or Canada]. . . . Then separating the marriage and then . . . you know it just seems like a whole series of backward things that didn't work out! So, hopefully there'll be a . . . little bit more security. I think . . . once you have the *financial security*, it buys you another kind of *freedom*.

Lilliana's sense of social shame associated with marital separation lead her to keep this reality a secret from her family for many months. The power of certain key ingredients of respectability such as marriage remain strong. One might say that Lilliana's socialization within the secure web of respectable white Barbadian culture and large close-knit family presented her with a patriarchal tradition and expectations for conformity she found confining and impossible to uphold. Yet Lilliana balances an unconventional career and conjugal path. Her middle-class matrifocality combines elements of classic respectability: maintaining a tasteful home with a traditional verandah on which she hosts friends and family as well as potential customers and clients for tea and homemade cakes, employing domestic help, nurturing her children's emotional lives and educational opportunities, and being a dutiful and attentive daughter, sister, and teacher. However, her strength to remain part of, but also define herself against, prescribed social traditions is reflected in her extraordinary entrepreneurial resilience and determination. She navigates between the world of her upbringing and new professional and social worlds with a markedly diverse mix of people who cut across cultural, national, racial, gender, class, religious, and sexual identifications. In many ways, Lilliana has configured a middle-class life that is the very embodiment of reputational flexibility: combining income-generating activities from multiple sources, and spreading risk and reward opportunities across a number of market-oriented production projects, government and international agency grants, community service activities, travel and international contacts. This is done in conjunction with single motherhood, reliance upon her extended kin network for help, emotional support, and a close circle of female friends with whom she spends leisure time, shares her frustrations, emotional desires, and dreams. She also pursues autonomous and introspective self-care through various therapeutic means. For Lilliana, just as education, travel, and her professional world give her enactment of reputational flexibility a new shape, so too is she redefining respectable middle-classness with new referents and meaning. Matrifocality, in short, offers white middle-class Barbadian women, like black Barbadian women, a critical set of resources and ways of being in the world that fit squarely into the entrepreneurial fold.

The creolization of both marriage and matrifocality that I see among this new entrepreneurial middle class reminds us that just as respectable femininity is not reducible to a single static formula, neither can matrifocality be simplified to just one profile (black and lower class) or one set of meanings (whether oppressed or heroic). Just as feminist critics amply demonstrated the flaws in characterizing the family in Euro-American contexts as unilaterally oppressive for women, failing to capture the most important kin ties and affective experience for African American women (Collins 1992), so too have Caribbean feminists critiqued the "heroic matriarch" characterization of the black female-headed household. Indeed many have pointed out that resilient as woman-headed households are, they also tend to be among the poorest of the poor (Massiah 1983). In this sense the seemingly natural strength and limitless flexibility ascribed to female household heads has also relieved the state and society from addressing well-entrenched patterns of gendered occupational stratification, the absence of state-subsidized child care, and the provision of further social supports. By turning to the lives of black and white women together inhabiting the new middle-class sphere of entrepreneurialism, we see how dynamic and mutually transformative the contours of reputation and respectability are.

ENTREPRENEURIAL MOBILITY: THE LEGACY OF MATRIFOCALITY AMONG BLACK BARBADIAN WOMEN

For Afro-Barbadian women, especially those who have risen to the middle class from modest and often matrifocal households, the model of matrifocality is one of both struggle and strength. The memory and reflection upon their mothers' difficult lives permeates their own musings and choices and also represents a source of confident self-directed decision making. Nadia is the successful owner of two women's boutiques in prime locations on the island. Forty-six when we met, she was divorced with one nineteen-year-old daughter. Nadia owns a comfortable suburban home that she now rents out since her daughter left for university abroad. She lives in a modern rental apartment on her own and reflected in generous detail and with calm emotion about her life, marriage, and work. Nadia's story bears the scars of many West Indian families whose transnational labor migrations of the 1950s separated and rejoined parents and children in ways that forever shaped, and sometimes scarred, them. I include Nadia's testimony at some length as she evokes the pain and determination that many others, men as well as women, bring to their entrepreneurial journey and the manner in which entrepreneurship becomes not only a means of earning a living (financially) but also of *making a life* more generally. Her story is not only one of upward mobility through self-employment and business acumen but also of the complex dynamics of West Indian kinship, female-support networks, and parental rejection that have shaped the trajectories of many others. The consonant desire to prove her worth and ability to an absent and/or harsh, unloving parent is one that appeared painfully often in the entrepreneurial narratives I collected of both men and women: "My mother left me to go to England when I was about five. She went with her cousins to my family there, and at that point in time she and my dad had separated and she just take off and run away from all the heartaches and everything else. She left four of us with my grandmother, so my grandmother kind of raised us. I next saw my mother when I was sixteen." After eleven years apart, Nadia's mother sent for two of her four children, Nadia and a brother, leaving her sisters behind with their grandmother. "I spent three years with her and then *I left* . . . I don't know . . . she had already started a new family that we didn't really know about, you see. . . . Three years that I was there . . . I feel that you should show me more love and embrace me. . . . *That* I did not get from her . . . it was so miserable. Those were the worst three years I've had in my life, those three years when I went to England, you know, separated you from the person that was your mother [her grandmother]. You are in a strange country and *there is no love.*"

Not only was Nadia rejected by her mother when she moved away to England, but she is rejected again in their reunion, as her mother's life had moved on. In joining her mother in England, she loses the only mother she has really known, her grandmother. In the absence of that bond, and determined to survive, Nadia envisions her own upward mobility through education, and against her mother's wishes, she is determined to go to school. Emotion rises in her voice when she recounts the story, "I couldn't go to school! She tell me I have to go and *work*, support my own keep, but I *make sure* that I go to school. I went to school in the evenings . . . I was always determined . . . I asked questions and I went and signed up to do evening courses. But, my mother? What I always say about her is that she didn't know any better. She was just doing what she thought was okay, you see? So . . . I don't hate her, I kinda forgive her, *cause I love her*, but I don't think that we have a mother and daughter *relationship* because I *can't call her and talk to her, we don't have a rapport,* I can more go sit down and talk to my grandmother still about things that might be bothering me, but *not her.*" Nadia's emphasis on emotional rapport and love, the feelings of betrayal and her mother's cold, harsh rejection highlight a ruptured parental (as opposed to conjugal) bond. The longing and desire for closeness and emotional support are equally palpable, however, and are intertwined with Nadia's story of self-invention, self-determination, and her own maternal sacrifice and care for her daughter.

Nadia's story echoed that of at least a dozen other entrepreneurs whose parents (usually their fathers, but sometimes mothers like Nadia's) had left them for work abroad and/or for another relationship. What is notable in her retelling is the acknowledgment of emotional damage wrought by this lack of recognition, and its tie to her own determination to *become someone*—not an object due material support and "sending for" but a subject to recognize, *a feeling* subject and a *worthy* subject (Benjamin 1988).[23] At the same time, her story highlights a key feature of West Indian kinship and a central theme in the life of most others I interviewed: the extended kin network. Nadia's rescue from her painful alienation in England was enabled by a half sister who sent for her and offered her a new life.

> It's amazing . . . how I got into Canada, well, my sister . . . a half sister by my father, I met her when I was like thirteen years old and we would write each other and correspond and she was doing pretty good in Canada. I invite her to come over to England for a holiday . . . I would write and I would always tell her about how miserable I was, and she came over for three weeks and . . . at the end of those three weeks she said I can't let you stay like this. She went back to Canada, filed papers for me. Nobody knew that she was doing that, she sent my ticket for me, to get me out of that misery . . . you know I don't even think that she realized how much she did for me even though I would write and I would tell her "thanks for changing my life," because *she changed my life.* I went to work [as a bank teller] and I went to school part time. . . . But, that was like my savior. I think all *this* [she waves her hands to indicate her thriving business] is to *prove to my mother that I can succeed without her.* Sometimes I think that all my success is to prove to her that I can do it without her. It's amazing. Every time I think about it, it's that, because not having her support in anything that I do or if you call on her to help in any way she never would help. So, it's like I'm gonna do it to show you that I can do it . . . if I didn't have that [conviction and determination] I don't know if I would be here.

For Nadia the pride she feels in her own tremendous achievement is tempered by a sad past and her mother's continued refusal to show her love and affirmation:

> She came back here for a holiday but, you know it's funny, . . . I have 2 sisters here, and she would come and praise one other sister so much, then when she look at me she don't say anything, you know? She would see my house, she don't say it's nice, nothing. But yet, everybody would say "Nadia you're doing very well! da da da da . . ." No, she don't say nothing, she would come look and she would criticize, but that's her way, you see, I'm glad that I've grown to the level that I accept her for the way she is and don't, like, hate her because if I hate her I'd be carrying that with me and I don't think that I would succeed. God won't allow me to succeed.

While Nadia's mother deprived her of love she craved, other women in her life—her grandmother and her half sister—stepped forward with affection, support, and nurturing. She credits them for keeping her going and locates her business success and the recognition others give her to the determination borne out of struggle. Her network of female kin has been integral to her achievements. A half sister in Canada, and another sister in Barbados loaned her money to get her business started and consistently helped her to raise her daughter and juggle the multiple demands of family, work, and personal life.

In many ways early childhood rejection and a sense of abandonment led her to approach motherhood with a particular form of independence and determination. Her own marriage to a "Trickidadian," as she called him (a gloss for his Trinidadian origins), ended in divorce and without child support. As with her mother's rejection, Nadia expressed, retrospectively, a sense of resolve this abandonment presented, giving her the liberty to raise her child in her own way. As a single mother, she did not have the perpetual disappointments of a disengaged husband and an uninvolved father for her child.

> I'm a professional and I'm working and I'm out there trying to *make a business work*. If I had a husband in the house that did not put in his part in raising [my child] that would have been a disaster. Sometimes it's best just to let them go their way and you deal with your child and your business because the husband is *just there* . . . not putting in what he is supposed to put in, like discipline the child, be part of his life, take him to swimming, do all these other things with him. What is the point,

then? The child will grow up now thinking, "Wait, he is my father? He is *just here?* He is not showing any interest?" It affects children, but I don't think a lot of parents understand that, you know? And I'm glad, in a way, that I had her withdraw from her dad and I just raised her by myself with the help of God and . . . that is why she is the way she is.

At another point, however, Nadia described with unveiled wonder and admiration the relationship of one of her friends, a fellow entrepreneur who is married with several children. This man she praised as "loving being with his kids, spending quality time with his kids," remarking about the easy balance struck by the couple to cover the demands of the business. Nadia has struggled to find a meaningful relationship and in a sense seems to have given up on the kind of intimate partnership she has wanted. Now that her daughter is grown and off in university, she is especially aware of being alone.

> No this is not my choice . . . but I find that the quality of men that we have in Barbados I don't think that they ready for independent women. They might *say* that, but they not. They feel threatened somehow. You know, a gentleman walked in here Saturday, right? A nice gentleman, talking to me, right? And he was talking very smooth, everything, and I'm listening to him and talking to him . . . and talking to him, when he asked me my name and I . . . told him! And then? He saw the name outside before he walked in cause he looked in and he . . . he couldn't talk to me anymore . . . the same way he was talking to me, right? Even though he was saying to me that he was a business man and all this. But he thought that I was *just working* at the store, not its *owner!* I should not have told him my name and then see what would happen!

Sadly, she describes feeling ready for a meaningful relationship but unable to find that:

> I think at the stage that I am at in my life right, if I should have a part-ner, I think that it would be easier because I don't have my child to worry about. . . . It's just me and my business . . . I . . . have more time . . . to share my evenings . . . to have companionship, that's the only thing that's missing from my life that I miss, but I don't make it a priority because sometimes it can be very frustrating so I just let that go, I know that God will work that out when the time is right.

Nadia's predicament is echoed by numerous other successful entre-preneurs. The effort to prioritize the demands of her business and the needs of her daughter as she was growing up left little room for the cultivation of an intimate relationship, especially when the men she knew were unwilling to offer her the kind of shared partnership she wanted. While matrifocality offers to entrepreneurial women a path in which to retain flexibility and independence both economically and emotionally, there are also women entrepreneurs who made clear that being single and their own household head was not their preference but rather their predicament. Myra, a fashionable and vivacious woman in her late forties, has never married and has had relationships but not fully satisfying or lasting ones. She says plainly that "she has always loved her work too much for men to take her on," and she seemed a bit wistful now about being alone. She sees being single less as a conscious choice, than the outcome of her drive and ambition in the world of work.[24] Myra was dynamic, open, and very clear about the tradeoffs she has made. Her now grown daughter was "really raised by her grandmother and aunt," since she was traveling so much of her life for work. Recently, her grown daughter was made financial controller of the major company at which her own mother had worked as a maid—another of the many instances of dramatic upward mobility I encountered among these dynamic entrepreneurs. Her evident pride and satisfaction about her own business success and even more about her daughter's tremendous achievement were also dampened by her own longings for companionship and intimate connection.

A common story among these middle-class entrepreneurs, many of these experiences and desires are also shared by salaried professional women. Among a much smaller sample of ten middle-class professional women, I heard similar struggles among almost half. Madeline, for example, is a highly ranked civil servant and the first woman to occupy her particular government position. She is forty-two, single, and the mother of one young child. Like Justine, she suggests a multifaceted portrait of Barbadian femininity. She is both entrepreneurial and an embodiment of traditional respectability in her own right, sewing her own clothes and enjoying cooking and baking, "very domestic" and at the same time a highly trained professional with advanced education and a job overseeing a staff of more than a hundred. She noted with pride, "people were shocked that a woman got this job!" While her friends think she should move into the private sector where she would earn significantly more money, Madeline likes the security and prestige of her position. Ironically, she came into the public sector "because I said I wanted to have kids but I also wanted a job . . . at the time I was in a serious relationship for about five years and I thought we would have gotten married and have kids and I wanted to be in a position where I could still have a good salary but have time to devote to having a family, raising a family and keeping a household, so I came into government thinking government work finishes at 4:15 and starts at 8:15, you don't have to take home work or anything. . . . Little did I know!" As a single mother, the challenges are great, juggling workdays that often run from 8 A.M. to 7 P.M. or later. Her mother looks after her child but the question of a relationship seems to Madeline almost incomprehensible.

> Oh, Lordy. Sometimes I work such long hours I don't meet anybody . . . and by the time I get home I'm so tired I just want to be home, I don't want to socialize. I hope it won't be forever but I know that right now with all the problems and stress and the issues which come with a relationship and the demands . . . I don't know if there's enough of me to do my job, be a mother, and Madeline, *and* have a significant other . . . I don't know if there's enough of me, and since the first three can't go away, what will happen to the last? *I'm a mother and I don't have the choice, because if you have no father you better have a mother, you know?*

Like the vast majority of all of my interviewees (entrepreneurs and others alike), she relies heavily upon her extended kin network for help along several lines.

> I'm fairly fortunate cause my sister has no kids and with two of our brothers here, my son gets his father figures and gets a lot of attention . . . they play cricket and football and . . . we take him to the beach so he does all those masculine things but *he* is not there . . . *his dad* is not there . . . I still try to say good things about his dad, shouldn't but we say them anyway as he's only little, and you never know what could happen . . . there's always hope . . . Well that's typical Bajan society where the guy works very hard and he feels it's okay to go out . . . don't spend time with your kids . . . you find the higher the profile job . . . the higher up they go, the less time they seem to spend with those children.

Dawn, a former Barbados beauty queen and successful owner of a manufacturing firm, is outspoken about her own challenges to maintain the kind of relationship she desires and quick to assert her refusal to tolerate the "beatings, infidelity, and traditional expectations of marriage" that Heather referred to in the last chapter. At forty, Dawn is unmarried, a self-declared single woman who reflects upon some bad relationships as well as her continued commitment to forming a fulfilling relationship and "settling down."

At the end of the day, I realize, it's me, I've made some wrong choices . . .
I realize too that I know what I want and I'm not going to settle for
anything different. I'm not saying that you going to find the perfect
person, but there's certain basic criteria. . . . You must have something
in common with the person, you must be able to communicate with
that person . . . and be comfortable with that person . . . and share a
common goal. Sex is very important and that will come out of mutual
love for each other. . . . And that person must be your friend. You want
to grow together . . . and you must be strong enough to recognize that if
this person is not moving how I want them to move, what am I gonna
do!? (Leave!)

Like Heather, whose explication of generational shifts lead her to seek out
and reflect upon her own remarkable partnership marriage, Dawn speaks
boldly about women of her mother's and grandmothers' day who "frankly
were willing to endure the outside affairs and outside children because
they already had so many children of their own . . . this was a way of satisfying their husbands without more and more pregnancies—so long as
the outside relationship didn't get too serious, that was almost convenient
from a woman's perspective." The argument that a man's sexual appetite
is insatiable, requiring more than one women to quench, was as common
a reference to the sexual double standard among the women I interviewed
as it is in popular parlance. Indeed, as important as marriage has been
in the pursuit of respectability, neither marriage nor middle-class status
has protected women from their husbands' proclivity toward outside relationships (reputation).[25] The manner in which formal marriage and other
conjugal relationships are enacted involves both structural and affective
dimensions, and the two become closely intertwined.

The capacity to move between visiting relationships and marriage, or in
the other direction, from marriage to more flexible modes of conjugality,
is afforded by a culture steeped in matrifocality. When Sheila's desires
for a partnership marriage failed to be realized by her husband, and despite efforts by her female bank manager to ensure her wifely dependence
(symbolically if not materially by denying her the independent title to her
home), Sheila was able to break away from her marriage and "hold her
head high." Her self-worth and self-regard, and her ability to walk away,
were fostered precisely by her hard-won economic independence and entrepreneurial acclaim. As Lilliana remarked earlier, "once you have that
financial security, it buys you another kind of freedom." With these combined economic and status autonomies, Sheila is free to pursue a "friend-

ship" with an older man with whom she enjoys outings, dinners, and intimacy but feels no particular desire to marry. She adopts the long-standing "visiting union" as a way to flexibly combine her motherhood and extended kin relationships, her business, friendships, and her desires for intimacy and support. Where the visiting union is often portrayed as a kind of "stepping stone" toward marriage in which couples share all of the elements of an ongoing relationship (sex, companionship, etc.) without living together, for Sheila, there are no particular advantages posed by formal marriage and co-residence. The matrifocal household is increasingly recognized not only as viable but also as potentially advantageous to women, and as the expectations for marital partnership grow, marriage and matrifocality, and in turn the values long ascribed to respectability and reputation, are in the process of being redefined.

THE GENDERED SEGREGATION OF SOCIAL LIFE

Even more contentious than the long-standing threat of "outside" relationships in middle-class marriages and all manner of relationships today is the question of shared social time. A striking majority of the married entrepreneurial women expressed at least mild frustration with, and in some cases a wholesale denunciation of, the traditionally gender-segregated social sphere (Greenfield 1977; Wilson 1973; Smith 1996; Senior 1991). Even when socializing as couples or families in each other's homes, traditional modes of gender segregation continue to be expressed in the divisions of labor (e.g., men pour drinks and women cook, clean up, and attend to the children) as well as in the arrangement of social space and conversation itself. I witnessed this pattern time and again, and personally shared these women's frustrations. In the course of social evenings, especially dinners in people's homes, it did often seem that the interesting discussions about island politics and the rest of the world, full of loud and jocular debate, emanated from the masculine spaces of breezy verandahs, while the women and I cleaned up in the warmer confines of kitchens or sitting rooms. Patricia, a white Barbadian entrepreneur in her thirties, described with visible aggravation the continued experience of being "stuck in the kitchen talking about children . . . while the men are off talking politics on the patio." On one hand, she was intent to assert that in structural terms there were significant changes from her parents' generation to her own, in the determination of household headship:

> My father is, without a doubt, the head of his household, so to speak. You know, my mother looks up to him; he's the *ultimate* decision maker.

He pays all the bills. Now in *our* house, it's *completely different. I* pay all the bills, *I* know about the finances. My husband looks after the investments because that's his thing, he likes to do that, but other than that? I handle the doctor's appointments . . . all the bills, all the house renovations, *I do it myself.* Things like that, my mother doesn't *touch.* My father doesn't believe that she's capable of doing it . . . he's that type of mentality and his father is like that, too.

While Patricia and her husband are both university-educated, busy, and successful entrepreneurs in their own right, her weekends are spent at the beach and home with sisters, sisters-in-law, and their respective children, while their husbands join their male friends on the cricket pitch, polo fields, and in sports bars. She remarked, "they do like their own company . . . when I think about it my husband goes every Friday to [a local sports bar] and it's just a group of men who sit down there and drink together. . . . And he's, right now, away on a golf trip—just a group of men, again, and no wives. I think that the Bajan man likes to hang out in the Bajan-man company, so to speak. They don't necessarily look to female company for friendship, you know." In fact, so familiar is the spatial and social segregation of men's and women's lives that in some senses the trajectory to matrifocality for many women suggests little in the way of transformation in the social sphere.

Ashanti, a black Barbadian woman of about the same age, whose marriage I described in the last chapter, echoed both Patricia's observation and mentioned that her husband too enjoys going out with his male friends to the same sports bar at the end of the week. For Ashanti, however, there is little frustration or resentment associated with her husband's desire for separate social time with his male friends. She appreciates his involvement in the family and enjoys the opportunity these outings give her for some quiet time to read and relax alone once the children are asleep. By enjoying her own autonomy as well as the sharing of family time, she happily combines elements of partnership marriage and matrifocality.

Historically, the expectation that men of all social classes participate in homosocial activity in the public sphere—whether it be the rum shop, the draughts table, or the polo field—while women, by and large, attend to children and the domestic domain and find their social networks among other female kin, neighbors, and church or work associates has been well documented ethnographically, and was an element of living in Barbados I was often struck by. I recall my own surprise during fieldwork in the early 1990s in Barbados that women in the informatics industry, who had eagerly pushed their employers to host elaborate Christmas dinner dances and evening dinner cruises, planned and invested in spectacular outfits and attended these events not, most often, with husbands or boyfriends but with female friends and relations with whom they said they could better relax and enjoy themselves. On the other hand, growing desires among women for mixed social experiences, especially those in which the intimate couple is together, stood in direct challenge to the traditional order of homosociality. Veronica, another young, white, and married Barbadian entrepreneur, described what she sees as the age-old sexual division of activities and interests:

> Men and women in Barbados are exceedingly different. . . . They do different sports and different hobbies and talk about different things and when you go to a party there's always men on one side of the room and women on the other. They are very happy to be separate because we have such a large group of family and friends, then it's very easy to be separate from your husband. People do things separately, meaning they go to a hobby or social gathering separately . . . most of the time they never do the same sport or hobby. They are very together, they are happy, there is nothing *wrong* in their marriage, but. . . . Birthday parties are a good example. I take my son to birthday parties and my husband hardly ever goes. . . . Because we have *other* people . . . I've realized after knowing a lot more people that are American and English. We don't need the companionships so you tend to do a lot of things separately. Even going to the gym. Even if they both go to the gym, they'll go at different times.

But later on in her interview, she contradicts the ease and comfort of this rhythm and the gendered separation of leisure and social life, noting,

> I think men still very much believe that the women do the home things and they "work," and even if their income is the same as their wife, they are still on that kind of a *level.* They are allowed to have a hobby, and they don't feel the responsibility as much and then they say their wives are nagging at them because the women now aren't taking it. So I've got that all in my age group. "All the girls, *they all nag,* my wife nags, my wife quarrels with me because I went to football, quarrels with me because I went to hockey," but they aren't seeing that it's not the hockey or the football that they have a problem with or the cricket, it's the "*you aren't spending enough time with the family.*" You know what I mean?

They're not seeing that part. They are just seeing that their wife doesn't like them to be out.

Women's complaints centered less around the threat of other women and "outside" affairs (though that is always an implicit reality) than on the dashed desires to share experiences, conversation, and intimate connection. A resounding theme in my interviews with women centered on the desire to both challenge the tradition of sex-segregated social spheres in order to emphasize the importance of a new social construct, "the intimate couple" and its temporal companion: intimate "quality time." As I explore in closer detail in chapter 4, the taxonomy of time and its particular "qualities" becomes a locus of conflict as well as transformation. Together, this new couple, defined simultaneously as a private and also a public unit, and the formulation of time in which to attend to intimate relationships and the cultivation of the self, are growing in importance especially for entrepreneurial women.

Taken together, these chapters highlight two intersecting phenomena that emerge in the entrepreneurial lives of Barbadians today—a new articulation of partnership (versus patriarchal) marriage that highlights intimacy and emotional relatedness, and what I am describing as the "upward mobility" of matrifocality. As both a household formation and structure of kinship, matrifocality has long signaled the adaptive, flexible strategies with which Caribbean women, and especially lower class Afro-Caribbean women, combine sources of support through both formal and informal economic activities and a network of kin and others to ensure the livelihood of themselves, their children, and often other relations (Barrow 1986; Senior 1991; Bolles 1986). Alongside the female centeredness of matrifocality has been an enduring popular as well as academic discourse of "male marginality"—sometimes castigating men for not being responsible providers, sometimes blaming women for usurping too much control over the household and thereby placing men "at risk" (Miller 1991). I found that both within the new constellation of the intimate partnership marriages as well as in the upwardly mobile matrifocal ones that men too are engaging in a more expressive, participatory affective culture.

MASCULINITY AND MATRIFOCALITY

In the narratives of male entrepreneurs, the tensions and unevenness of these changes are also apparent. Patrick, for example, is the son of a well-known and highly respectable family, as he said, "chock-a-block with professionals." By living at home with his mother, he saved and worked hard to build his business, fighting off his family's worries at his leaving a "secure" job with a private firm in favor of self-employment. His mother, he reports, encouraged his siblings to choose their path without pressuring them in one or another direction: "She always allowed us to date who we wanted and do what we want . . . the one thing she's asked us to do is to stay out of drugs, alcohol, and umm . . . becoming criminals." At thirty-eight, the owner of a highly successful consultancy firm with forty employees, Patrick got himself "in a lot of hot water" on the personal front. Muttering with some embarrassment, he revealed that he is the father of three children, two of exactly the same age by different mothers. Patrick's reliance on his mother for financial support, hot meals, and a home well into his thirties is not what he had planned on, but it's not uncommon in Barbadian patterns of kinship. His affairs and different mothers of his children are familiar elements of West Indian masculinity, highlighted among the lower classes, though not unusual across all classes. The fact that he fathers two children out of wedlock while maintaining two different relationships concurrently could threaten his respectable status. However, as Smith (1988, 118) has argued, for established middle-class men, having "outside" children "seems to be no disgrace, and might have quite the opposite effect as such 'irresponsibility' enhances their masculinity." These are among the vaunted gestures of reputational flexibility.[26] Jack Alexander (1984, 62–63) notes that what distinguishes middle-class Jamaican males from working class men is "that the middle class male operates on two tracks at the same time . . . a 'responsible' legal family and an 'irresponsible' illegitimate, 'outside' relationship." And it is precisely his economic success that culturally demands this romantic multiplicity. Ultimately, Patrick's "hot water" held little consequence. His business success increased alongside some lucrative real estate investments, and so long as he maintains these dual households responsibly, his respectable masculinity remains intact. Whereas middle-class women have historically faced a measure of "shame and silence" by out-of-wedlock births, men of all classes accrue accolades of masculine reputation (Alexander 1984, 158–59; Barrow 1996, 177).

One of the fascinating dimensions of the upward mobility of matrifocality relates specifically to this sexual double standard and what appear to be gradual changes underway. Single, married, separated, and divorced entrepreneurial mothers reveal intriguing ways in which they are unwilling, as Heather put it, to endure what their grandmothers and mothers suffered—*neither* the "lash" *nor* the "outside women." However, as Suzanne discovered, there are still social limits to a *woman's* capacity to enjoy flexibility and self-fulfillment in sexual spheres as men have long been able and encouraged to do. Patrick's case, on the other hand, is illustrative of changing gender roles, gender relations, and gender ideologies expressed in his intimate management and involvement with his children, their different households, and his common-law relationship. Such cases are remarkable not only structurally in the sense that they represent changing *roles* for fathers, and thus a new set of definitions of masculinity that includes more active parenting. Perhaps even more remarkable than the scheduling adaptations and physical involvement of these fathers in their children's daily lives (e.g., bathing, picking up from school, etc.) are the marked ways in which they are attentive to the developmental needs, their emotional growth, and are engaged in sharing and working collaboratively on these with their intimate partners.

Patrick alludes to his current girlfriend's preference for marriage in contrast to his own emotional commitment but nonmarital preference. He says, "she's not the overly demanding type for time." The children "keep her so busy that . . . it keeps her mind away from sitting and worrying about me [i.e., the threat of infidelity and/or his reluctance to marry, and perhaps other aspects of their relationship]. I mean, I still try to make a dinner a week and a night out. Saturday nights we go out together and probably once during the week we go out for dinner. . . . Sunday's we just lounge around and go to the beach." Meanwhile he is intent to provide not just economic support to his "outside" girlfriend but also nurturing care for his "outside" child whom he bathes and readies for bed each night en route to his residential family. Regardless of his unmarried status, this melding of a coupled way of life, including "family time" at the beach and intimate restaurant dinners on Saturday nights, are integral parts of the relationship he works to foster and maintain. Patrick enacts several of the most familiar markers of reputation (sexual freedom for men, outside relations, and outside children), along with daily involvement in the nurturing care of his children, regular dinner dates with his partner, and the ownership of a thriving firm. He provides a window into new configurations of reputation and respectability, support and intimacy, matrifocality and marriage in which new forms of middle-class masculinity emerge. Indeed, when one examines the middle classes, especially the entrepreneurial middle classes, it is clear that these conjugal forms are not only relationally defined but also that they are mutually constitutive; they shape one another in a dynamic that is at once steeped in a particular plantation history and in neoliberal flux before our very eyes. Together, these processes suggest not merely a reformulation of economic and social structures—household forms, conjugal relationships, and kinship arrangements—but of gendered sensibilities, feelings, and practices more broadly.

Even though scholars have hinted at changes in some of the signature forms of Caribbean kinship, the participation of fathers in more aspects of child rearing, the adaptive qualities of female-headed households, and the emerging "couple" as a social form, assumptions about marriage as a static patriarchal union form, and matrifocality as somehow provoking male marginality remain powerful tropes.[27] In fact, the resiliency and tangible weight of the "patriarchal man" model of marriage is reflected in the power Suzanne's husband exerted in attempting to deport her foreign boyfriend from the island and in the previous chapter the capacity for a female bank manager to insist upon Sheila's ex-husband's signature on the legal title of *her* house.[28] However, just as the long-marginalized single woman-headed household and the extended family are being reimagined and refigured as emblems of a proud creole heritage of adaptability and creativity, the contemporary articulation of marriage as a partnership is emerging in what I see as a new dialectical engagement. As the value orientation of one changes, so too is the other redefined; both become imbricated in the dynamic culture of neoliberal flexibility. By engaging the new partnership marriage ideal together with contemporary matrifocality as part of not just a continuum of household forms and kin arrangements, but as fields of intimacy, affect, care, and self making, we stand to unhinge the respectability/marriage, reputation/matrifocality binaries and to highlight their more dynamic, creole forms. In so doing, this case also offers a rich illustration of theoretical specificities of neoliberalism. Equally, our capacity to craft "work-family" or "work-life" models that might make the stresses of modern life more viable, more manageable, might profitably draw upon parts of the world that have a long history of nonpatriarchal kinship and household forms.

CHAPTER 4

Neoliberal Work and Life

Woman is a donkey. She work at work . . . she go home and work again.
—WEST INDIAN ADAGE (SENIOR 1991, 116)

THE LOGISTICS OF WORK/LIFE

Caribbean women, like men, have *always* worked. What interests me about the contemporary moment, and the rise of neoliberal entrepreneurialism as a way of middle-class life and subjectivity, are the ways in which the *nature of work* and its meanings in peoples' lives are in flux. Owning and running a business, whether a small hair salon, manufacturing plant, or a trendy new wine bar, requires vision, constant attention to detail, both long- and short-term economic savvy, and a willingness to be "on call" most of the time, day or night. As one woman described it, the business "seeps into all of the crevices" of an entrepreneur's life. This "seepage" is, in large part, a matter of *time* and the porous logistical boundaries around *work* for the self-employed and the tendency for its sheer demands to spill over into *nonwork* time and space. Delays in delivery of a product or service, problems clearing goods and supplies at the port, broken equipment, a sick employee, a last-minute client request were all among the kinds of unexpected interruptions encroaching upon nonwork time, time spent with family or friends, leisure time, time for prayer or exercise, time alone. As many individuals described to me, being an entrepreneur meant being one's "own boss" and brought with it autonomy and self-satisfaction at "running one's own show" and not being "accountable to anyone." The boredom, rigid hierarchy, and domineering bosses that made them chafe in their prior jobs in local banks, insurance companies, and public sector offices had also been associated with jobs they had happily left behind at 4:00 when the workday ended. As a business owner, their work was seldom far from their thoughts, or they from its practical goings on. I heard some say they "lived and breathed" their business, carrying it with them "24/7." Some described the preoccupation with their business as akin to having an affair, always on their minds and full of the excitement and risks of the unknown; others were "married to the business." I now realize that the intimate analogies of these entrepreneurs unlock a key dimension of the notion of neoliberal entrepreneurialism—the central role of *affective* or *emotional labor* that permeates the lives of these new middle classes.

When I began this research I was interested in how entrepreneurs managed the various facets of their lives—their businesses, as well as activities, responsibilities and relationships outside of them. I deliberately sought out entrepreneurs engaged in both "traditional" as well as nontraditional enterprises, and I was eager to survey as wide ranging a demographic group and entrepreneurial field as possible. As I reviewed the broad spectrum of household configurations and marital and conjugal arrangements of more than a hundred entrepreneurs (male and female, black and white, young, middle-aged, and older), the presence of young and school-aged children posed the greatest challenges and highlighted what seemed to be particularly fraught about the growing entrepreneurialism, especially for women. I engaged both women and men in lengthy discussions about these challenges and derived insights about the kinds of struggles and desires that appear to be especially heightened in today's economic and cultural environment. As in the previous chapters' analysis of the new intimate partnership marriage, it was women entrepreneurs who most explicitly confronted and articulated these struggles and from whom I derived a palpable sense of social transformation. As we will see in this chapter, mothers are clearly grappling most directly with the challenges and implications of entrepreneurial life, though their accounts and reflections reflect the dialogic involvement of fathers, husbands, and partners. Social scientists and policy makers in the United States and elsewhere, meanwhile, were paying increased analytical attention to questions of "work-life balance," and based on these assumptions, I took detailed surveys of entrepreneurial "divisions of labor."[1] Who did which household chores? How did entrepreneurs carve up the planning, financing, accounting, marketing, and running of their businesses? Were there patterns of conflict and change, and did these relate to the particular life stages and household or conjugal forms? Was the age-old extended family network in decline, as the local media warned? Were fathers playing a more active role in child rearing, as some feminist accounts and the local Barbadian "men's movement" claimed?[2] I was interested in the gendering of these divisions of labor and curious about how women and men might manage these complex undertakings differently in conjunction with their businesses. What did the *work* of entrepreneurship entail and how did it relate to other dimensions of their lives: relationships, families, children, community involvements, leisure activities?

The discussion must begin, however, with a fundamental difference of Barbadian history and culture that flies in the face of the premise of the work-life rhetoric: that work and family, work and motherhood, and work and life are fundamentally at odds. In essence, as the old saying at the start of the chapter notes, in the Caribbean, "woman is a donkey," her life is defined by work "at work" and work "at home." The "double day" (productive and reproductive work) and even the "triple shift" (waged work, informal sector work, and reproductive work) are not new concepts for Barbadian women. My earlier fieldwork and a voluminous scholarly literature in the Caribbean had taught me that the very notion of separating work from life was spurious, not only for today's international "creative classes," for whom work constitutes a pleasurable and meaningful outlet of self-definition (Florida 2002), but also for ordinary folks, for whom formal employment, informal sector activities, and "leisure" are typically closely intertwined.[3] In short, the pursuit of a "livelihood" in the Barbadian and wider Caribbean context has described the ways in which *work is life* and *life is work.* Labor performed within the spheres of kinship relations and social reproduction, wage earning, informal trade, leisure, social life, and community service, is all interconnected and has arguably been for hundreds of years. The country higgler trades in provision crops, fruits, and vegetables as well as gossip and camaraderie, a group of fishermen out for a day's catch share rum and stories along with the labor of their trade, the ubiquitous kitchen garden and fruit tree yard provided systems of exchange and social glue among middle and lower classes, whose lives intersect via residential proximity, through employment, or otherwise. The Masons or YMCA organize gatherings that raise money for vulnerable orphans or marginal youth, while at the same time cementing social ties and business contacts for each other; the babysitting provided by a sister or aunt allows one woman to earn wages that contribute to the livelihood of all of their kin; the labors in one domain contribute to the support and maintenance of another, whether formally remunerated or exchanged more casually "in kind." Few people—male or female, lower or middle class—operate solely within either the realm of "formal" or "informal," "productive" or "reproductive" economies alone, and most engage in multiple ways of getting by within and across these apparent divides.

In essence, the concept of reputational flexibility that I discussed in chapter 1 expresses precisely this convergence of work and life, in that being adaptable and responsive to new conditions economically, socially, environmentally, and so on has been prized as a quality of resourceful opposition to systems of oppression, an opposition that has run counter, according to Wilson, to the dominant forces of colonialism and capitalism. But what is striking in these entrepreneurial narratives and in this neoliberal era is not just that work and life both span public and private, productive and reproductive spheres. Increasingly the divisions as they have been traditionally formulated are becoming not just more permeable but also more evidently saturated by an economy of emotion that has become part of the labor process in and across these spheres, offering enrichment and solace, as well as worry and stress, for those most involved in these pursuits. Not only are many of today's entrepreneurial enterprises highlighting a new range of emotional engagements and new expressive forms in the lives being worked upon. These transformations are all the more powerful in a society not known for expressive emotionality.

Contemporary forms of middle-class entrepreneurialism highlight new ways in which work is performed, as well as new meanings and categories of time itself. Put simply, in Barbados today it is not the fact of women working outside the home that, as in some places, is held in awkward balance against the rest of life today. Rather, it is the nature of the labor they perform and the "quality" of the time they seek and spend in these different pursuits that are undergoing dramatic change.[4] These changes are manifest both in the kinds of businesses these new entrepreneurs are creating and in the new ways in which they are crafting their roles as mothers and fathers, intimate partners, and persons or *selves*.

Among the women I studied, the single most powerful motivation for becoming an entrepreneur was this self-described promise of *flexibility*. This quest is echoed in other studies of women entrepreneurs around the world, along with the disheartening but not surprising discovery of the promise denied (Coughlin and Thomas 2002; Bruni 2005; Hughes 2005). It bears reminding, however, that concepts such as flexibility carry particular meanings when they travel the world. As I discuss in chapter 1, flexibility is also one of the Caribbean region's signature cultural elements that is steeped in lower-class culture of creative ingenuity, autonomy, and *opposition to the colonial-capitalist order* (Freeman 2007; Mantz 2007). However ubiquitous the search for work-family or work-life flexibility appears, and however widely this quest is portrayed as primarily and universally *women's* concern, I want to highlight some of the subtle distinctions in how this flexibility is being imagined and attempted and ways in which its particular dimensions and meanings have culturally specific importance. I focus this chapter, therefore, on not simply the challenge of combining business enterprise with raising children (as in much of the work-life discourse) but also on the ways in which, when read together, these entrepreneurial projects are suggestive of a new, neoliberal way of living, working, and feeling. I want to highlight several aspects of the affective *work* involved in these new entrepreneurial middle-class lives and the subtle ways in which this kind of work is being desired, coerced, and enacted in spheres that are permeable and expanding.

AFFECTIVE LABORS OF WORK/LIFE

The melding of work *as* life and life *as* work is conveyed by the entrepreneurs not as a matter of spatial or temporal intrusions, as the usual work-life rhetoric would have it, but more a matter of growing intensification of all aspects of life, an intensification characterized by its emotional core. The spillover or intermingling of emotional energy, care, and contemplation associated with running a business—worry, anticipation, fear, doubt, excitement, pride, pleasure, and deep absorption spurred by bidding on a new contract, a troublesome employee, a late order, a slow sales period, mounting bills, and so on—with those thoughts and affects that permeate the rest of life—pride in a child's school report or a hard-won business contract; worry over a sick parent or mounting bills; love for a spouse, partner, or another; anxiety about one's health or the hint of infidelity; happy exhilaration melded with a spiritual revelation; consumer or sexual longings—become intensified, intertwined, and indistinguishable in both emotional form and weight.[5] The desires for more open expression of emotions and, as we will see in the following chapter, the search for therapeutic interventions, along with the appeal of new embodied experiences and salve formed an integral part of these entrepreneurial processes. My conversations with men and women entrepreneurs were layered by explicit references to feelings and embodied states, and their importance was also conveyed in the *ways* in which they spoke, the timbre and lilt of their voices, the intensity of their expression, and the look in their eyes.

Sometimes their emotions overflowed in tears or laughter, dramatic hand gestures and evocative sayings.

Arlie Hochschild's groundbreaking *The Managed Heart* (1983) expanded C. Wright Mills's (1951) investigation of the "personality market" of white-collar occupations by examining not just the growing significance of emotion, demeanor, and personality in the white-collar marketplace but also *the labor* entailed in the production of these required affects, as Hochschild said, labor that demands "one to induce or suppress feeling in order to sustain the outward countenance that produces the proper state of mind in others" (1983, 7). Today, affective labor—the production of "a feeling of ease, well-being, satisfaction, excitement, passion" (Hardt 1999, 96)—is gaining prominence across systems of exchange and occupies an ever-expanding dimension of labor and life more generally under neoliberalism.[6] Greater attention to the significance of "immaterial" labor as an increasingly dominant labor form under advanced capitalism has led a number of scholars back to the concept of emotional labor to interrogate these current formulations (Hardt and Negri 2004).

When considering the production of affect as an active form of *labor* (versus a temperament or natural quality associated with femininity, for example), it is helpful to be reminded of the skills and techniques this kind of work requires. Hochschild (1983) noted that these skills entail "surface acting" (the mask actors and others put on in order to feign an expected emotional demeanor) and "deep acting" (in which the individual so relates to the real or imagined state of another that she conjures up deep emotional empathy or feeling with which to respond). These became critical tools with which flight attendants *managed* their emotions and their employer's demands that they retain an ever pleasant, helpful, and friendly demeanor in their work. What is the difference between the requirement of affective labor demanded by one's corporate employer, as in Hochschild's flight attendants, the demands as set by the clients of one's service occupation, as in the case of many of the Barbadian entrepreneurs, and the demands they set for themselves? How does the history of the plantation and the dominance of a tourism economy lend a particular set of meanings to such emotional labors in the current service economy? As Lazzarato (1996, 135) noted of such affective labor, "the prescription and definition of tasks transforms into a prescription of subjectivities." How are these labors and subjectivities related to those forged in the intimate and personal spheres of children, extended kin, friends, domestic workers, neighbors, and so on? In essence, how are affective labors articulated within and across public and private arenas? Affects today are suggestive of the very fabric of neoliberal culture, its aspirations, desires, and sense of entrepreneurial possibility. Affect, as Stewart (2010) describes it, "is the commonplace, labor-intensive process of sensing modes of living as they come into being." The current entrepreneurialism, I want to suggest, centers much of its energies in these modes of work and illustrates precisely the difficulty of thinking about life outside work and vice versa.

The emphasis on certain kinds of emotions, and labor required to foster these emotions, is increasing across all dimensions of middle-class life. This intensity is reflected in the articulation of new intimate partnerships (chapter 2) and more broadly in the demands for a growing array of entrepreneurial services offering a variety of personalized care and emotional labor for these middle classes. Today, especially for those in health-related fields, education, management, and other services whose work depends heavily upon electronic communications and new media, work has few discernible boundaries of time or space. A middle-class professional with a smart phone can, for example, participate in an important conference call in real time, confirm a doctor's appointment, check traffic patterns for her afternoon commute, and instant message a child about homework and the after-school pickup, virtually all at once. Indeed, it is precisely such a picture of multitasking middle-class working families, two parents with active school-aged children, who are conceived as the primary subjects of work-life balance agendas, whether in the United States, the European Union, or in Barbados. Worry about this "spillover" of work into private life lies at the heart of most such programs. As such, much of the discussion about work-life and work-family "balance" is predicated upon not just the separation of these spheres of activity and feeling and the need to protect one from the other but also, importantly for my purposes, the notion that the growing importance of *emotional labor* in the workplace and economy is fundamentally subsidized by (and thus a drain upon) the emotional reservoir of private life.

"Work-life balance" campaigns hail a fairer equation between two ostensibly separate things, something called *work* and something called *life*. They promote several goals, from higher productivity at "work" to better health and well-being of workers and their families. The more we examine the relationship between these so-imagined spheres, the more we see their increasing entanglement in structural, spatial, and temporal terms.[7] Over thirty years of socialist feminist scholarship has illuminated the critical economic and social significance of *reproductive* labor within the domestic sphere that not only subsidizes the realm of production but also perpetuates in gendered terms the differential value associated with these two spheres of activity (Hartmann 1979; Weeks 2007). Indeed, the very concept of reproductive labor, or the work required to both biologically and socially reproduce the labor force, entails not only the birthing of babies, rearing of children, and the relentless tasks of cooking, cleaning, laundry, and the like, but as the recent Italian autonomists emphasize, the affective labor of socialization: cultivating and emotionally soothing and nourishing as well as disciplining the household and family (Hardt and Negri 2000; Clough and Halley 2007). The turn toward affective labor as it circulates across public and private life allows us to challenge a long persistent bifurcation between "emotion and interest, expressiveness and instrumentality . . . (and) critique the notion that households (and workplaces) can be analyzed exclusively as *either* economic or emotional units" (Lutz and White 1986, 422).

The forms of emotional labor performed in the nonremunerated sphere of life include both the management and the experience of positive and negative, enhancing and depleting feelings. Again, Hochschild (1997) has contributed importantly to this perspective in her discussion of working mothers, whose greatest calm came not in the form of a daily homecoming after work to their familial "haven in a heartless world" but rather when they reached their offices in the mornings and found a quiet and orderly reprieve from the numerous demands of their "second shift." On the other hand, even Hochschild is susceptible to the persistent bifurcation in the work and life discussion that inevitably characterizes the engine of the marketplace as tampering with, de-skilling, homogenizing, and commodifying sacred elements of the family. In short, if for liberal second-wave feminism the entrance into the waged economy offered the tools of women's liberation, today the burdens of restrictive workplaces and long hours flip the prescription in favor of prioritizing a rather idealized family-centered life (Weeks 2007, 158–60).

Just as every constellation of home and family life—patriarchal, matrifocal, hetero- or homosexual, single, nuclear, or multigenerational—faces constraints of time and contains stresses as well as salve, pleasure along with pressure, so too do we find competing currents across the continuum of remunerated and nonremunerated *emotional* labor. However, the simple assumption that the natural reservoir of emotional capital to fuel the market-based demands for this kind of labor is to be found in the private, feminine, domestic sphere is a premise that the Barbadian case helps to question, since the domestic sphere, again, has never been featured as the antithesis to work or envisioned as a particularly emotional sphere itself. Further at stake in the cultural specificity of this case is a shifting emphasis toward certain kinds of emotions that are ever critical to and desired within commercial and private life.

West Indian history hails its *strong*, rebel women (Mathurin 1975; Beckles 1989). Physical strength and mental fortitude have also been associated with an inclination to avoid emotional display, to hide feelings except anger and toughness (Schreiber, Stern, and Wilson 2000). Plantation slavery formed the scaffolding for culture and political economy in the Caribbean, and one of its vaunted legacies is purportedly a more egalitarian ethic due to the equality of male and female labor under the whip. One quality of this complex legacy has been a reverence and pride attached to certain affects and certain kinds of affective labor: emotional toughness, restraint, and stoicism for Afro-Caribbean women as well as men. Interestingly, according to early accounts of white indentured labor as well as those who rose to the status of plantation mistresses in Barbados, toughness and emotional discipline were qualities best adapted to plantation life. White women, hardly symbols of a "haven in a heartless world," are described in early accounts as "tetchy" and "unhappy," their "marriages cemented by property rather than affection" (Bush 1981, 256). In short, matrifocality as a primarily lower-class social form associated with black women signaled women's capacity to work and be mothers, to "cut and contrive," to be strong and resourceful materially as well as emotionally. The value complex of respectability also called for a kind of emotional strength and severity. Even the plantation mistress was known for her stiff upper lip. If these are, in a sense, two sides of the coin of Barbadian femininity, neither is particularly suggestive of the kinds of emotions increasingly being called for today. Just as the plantation model of culture and political economy indisputably shaped the island's social contours, it seems fair to suggest it shaped its "structure of feeling" as steeped in economic exchange. For white and black Barbadians alike, the emphasis on the cultivation of an inner life of feelings and expressive intimacy suggests a new terrain in both public and private life. Among many of the women entrepreneurs, especially those involved in the expanding sphere of services, we find a new depth and form of labor expectation that mirrors and, I will argue, becomes integrally tied up with the affective desires they are aspiring to and/or expressing in their personal lives.

Certainly those businesses involving the direct delivery of service—whether in design houses or dining establishments and even more so in the delivery of bodily treatment and care, such as salons, health and wellness services, spas, and the like—require the most explicit and obvious emotional attunement and expression of care and attentiveness to tastes, preferences, and feelings. However, even in traditionally masculine spheres of manufacturing, or other forms of production where the delivery of a product is concrete, less "immaterial" entrepreneurs take time over the cultivation of customers' desires, involving aspects of their lives outside of these transactions, in a holistic approach toward their customers and their staff that required many of the emotional elements of service enterprises. When Nicole (a forty-five-year-old "life coach") holds teamwork seminars for client groups, she is offering not only recommended guidelines for streamlining business processes but also a range of therapeutic interventions and exercises for enhancing owners' and managers' own introspection, self-reflection, and capacity to build empathy for their customers, thereby improving productivity, profits, and self-worth.[8]

For a culture in which *service* has been symbolically shackled to *servitude* and a three-hundred-year history of plantation slavery, the "friendly" Barbados rhetoric of the nation's tourism industry should be read less as a transparent reflection of cultural authenticity than a mandate, the state's attempt to coerce friendliness or at least the appearance of friendliness from an otherwise reluctant, reserved populace. When I first began doing fieldwork in Barbados in the late 1980s, an extensive ad campaign by the government's Barbados Tourism Authority more than hinted at the need for emotional labor and the challenges of extracting such labor in this Caribbean island. "Tourism is Our Business! Let's Do Our Part!" billboards and signs proclaimed, in the airport, near the cruise-ship terminal, and on busy commercial streets of Bridgetown, especially Broad Street, home to many duty-free shopping venues. The campaign was aimed at the local Barbadian, instructing her or him to *be nice*! Smile! Do your part! This campaign demanded what Hochschild refers to as surface acting, the façade of friendliness, a performance of pleasantries, a mask of a smile regardless of the true (and probably contradictory) feelings underneath.

West Indians are familiar with the adage "All skinned teeth ain't a smile," noting that an upturned mouth and the showing of teeth, apparent grins, are not always genuine smiles. The art of dissembling in a former slave society is well understood. Indeed, despite a more than fifty-year history of tourism as a dominant economic mainstay of the island's economy, the fact that the state tourism board needed to mount an explicit campaign to entreat such pleasantries foreshadowed comments I heard years later in almost every interview with entrepreneurs, regardless of the nature of their business—about "poor attitudes," "surliness," and the challenge of instilling an ethic of customer service not only in tourism-oriented niches but also in retail outlets and other services catering to the local population.

Indeed, a recent volume titled *Best Practice Guide for Customer Service Professionals* was published by the National Initiative for Service Excellence, a joint venture of the Government of Barbados, the trade unions, and the private sector, as part of the goal of the country attaining its "vision of becoming a developed country by 2025" (2006). The provision of friendly service continues to be a challenge for the highly competitive tourism sector, without a doubt, but attention to questions of service are growing in other economic sectors as well.

Indeed, the expansion today beyond the requisite "surface acting" of a smile to a deeper level of emotional engagement is a growing dimension of entrepreneurial life today. A new niche of novel businesses specialize in precisely such affect-laden services—from Colleen's "team building and wellness" center and other similar (and mostly woman-owned) firms geared toward helping local businesses maximize productivity, organizational teamwork, and enhance service skills. Each of these highlights neoliberal elements of corporate rationality and organizational structure as well as understanding and empathy toward one's coworkers and customers and the management of *selfhood*: enhancing "self-knowledge and life-mastery" as one such website asserts.

For Barbadian women entrepreneurs like Nicole, Colleen, and most others in the service sector, a central aspect of their businesses, along with many dimensions of their so-called nonwork lives, features the production of *nurturing feelings*; emotional exchanges are integral to the services they provide. These emotional expressions are, in the Barbadian context, like elsewhere, gendered. The delivery of caring labor is imbued with femininity. However, if along with other aspects of the domestic sphere, which are ascribed a feminine value, the nature of femininity and in particular its emotional core cannot be taken to be universal or static. Whereas caring labor in cases such as Hochschild's female flight attendants of the 1970s had gone largely unnoticed *as labor*,[9] precisely because of the assumption that care is a natural feminine quality, the expectations for what constitutes "emotionally attentive" service, and in this case, what expressive forms "care" takes, are not everywhere the same. Considering the wider scope of emotional culture and gender in Caribbean societies such as Barbados, we must ask then what is entailed in the production of these emotions and how do they in turn reshape the meanings of gender and gendered labor? The deep acting required by Hochschild's flight attendants led to their "going robot"—alienation from their own emotional selves. In the case of the entrepreneurs, the production of these caring emotional exchanges in both market-oriented and private spheres might be understood together as forging new kinds of feelings as well as new kinds of feeling exchanges. And as we will see in the next chapter, the desires for such affective experience, and the strains created by these desires, become closely intertwined with new therapeutic and spiritual interventions geared specifically toward their alleviation.

The melding of emotional labor and emotional desire between commercial and private life is not performed along one single or predictable path or in a singular direction. The interactions, the activities they perform, the skills involved and the ways in which they enact them, feelings and desires produced in both themselves and their relational others that together form the basis of *work* (i.e., the paid, formal activity recognized as entrepreneurial work) increasingly mirror entrepreneurial life itself and vice versa. One aspect of the current entrepreneurial impetus not only in the marketplace but also in the otherwise private projects of intimate relationships, parenting, and self making is the manner in which all elements of life become subject to similarly emotional labor regimes. As an owner of a budding business enterprise, the new entrepreneur invests herself in cultivating relationships, offering empathic and caring service, being friendly and attentive not because she is commanded to do so by a boss but because she is aware that her own reputation and the success of her enterprise are enhanced through such modes of rapport. In essence, the *self-regulation* of emotional labor gives it a different dimension for the entrepreneur than for one of her employees, as for one of Hochschild's flight attendants. While the work of producing these feelings in herself and in her client resembles in kind that of any of her staff, her stakes as the owner and proprietor are greater not only financially but also in terms of reputation and status, as a reflection of herself.

Grace illustrates this distinction well when she described a recent exchange with a client over the design of a new project. What she signals are the subtle skills with which she deploys her own emotional sensibilities to elicit and then interpret a client's mood, tastes, and desires, even when they are murky or unknown to the client himself:

> I don't listen with my ears, I listen with eyes, *I listen with my heart*, and that may sound a little corny but it's one of the things that has made us as a company successful . . . it is not an easy thing to listen and interpret. You can *train* someone to do it, because I actually trained my husband to do it. . . . A client . . . wants something with his mouth and the inference behind it in his body language or the tone he uses or the words he uses, he may say he wants more or may say he wants less, in

fact my husband had a client who said to him she wants all these pretty colors, she wants purples and greens and yellow she wants all these colors and he came back after meeting with the client and started trying this thing. . . . It's obviously impossible for him to do! And I said to him "but you're not?! Listen to what she saying, she wants the *right* colors, she wants something to grab the attention, she not actually *wants* purple, pinks and all these!" You've got to *listen*, you've got to move beneath those words and listen!

Others writing about the United States have begun to describe a new emotional discourse of capitalism and market exchange that foregrounds the kinds of feelings—sympathy, care, nurturance, love—that have historically been associated with private, intimate relationships (Reber 2012). Equally, in "nonwork" spheres, such as marriage and family life, parenting, intimate and sexual relationships that might be considered "outside" of market relations and immune to the nomenclature of the market, is a growing ethic and language of entrepreneurial, DIY-oriented, *labor* that depends upon emotional exchange. I encountered these converging discourses among Barbadian entrepreneurs in expectations to "work" on their marriages, cultivate children, mold and discipline their bodies, craft and individualize their houses and themselves in much the way they were compelled to work on their marketing, sales pitches, budgets, hiring plans, their management of staff, suppliers, government officers, and clients. In one sense "private" realms of life and thought are subtly yet increasingly amenable to Weberian rationalization, and the inducement to bring individuality, character, emotion, and care to the formal capitalist marketplace of service has become an ever-growing expectation of paid labor and market exchanges.[10]

Weber (1958) himself, and later Giddens (1991, 74–81), mapped the concept of self-identity and many of its key elements (the notion of the self as a reflexive project, a trajectory of development from the past to an imagined future, as coherent and amenable to narrativization, etc.) as signs of the late modern era. And while striking in their resonances with many of the transformations at work in today's Barbadian neoliberalism, I want to suggest that these modes of emotional work, and the feelings being produced and embodied, be foregrounded in ways that highlight their distinctive cultural and historical implications. Many historians, anthropologists, and sociologists write about the cultural and historical particularities of emotion to demonstrate not only the breadth of emotionally expressive forms different people give to the same stable of affective experience but also the difference in the very feelings themselves (Lutz 1986; Lutz and White 1986; McMahon 2005). As Hochschild (2003, 122) aptly describes:

> Love in a New England farming village of the 1790s, say, is not the same old love as in upper class Beverly Hills, California, in 1995, or among working class Catholic miners in Saarbrucken, Germany. Each culture has its unique emotional dictionary, which defines what is and isn't, and its emotional bible, which defines *should* and *shouldn't*. As aspects of "civilizing" culture, they determine our *stance toward* emotional experience. They shape the pre-dispositions with which we interact with ourselves over time. Some feelings in the ongoing stream of emotional life we gladly acknowledge, welcome, foster. Others we grudgingly acknowledge, and still others the culture invites us to completely deny. And the dictionary, the bible, the stance alter to some extent what we feel.

The lack of a vocabulary or lexicon for particular feelings influences our capacity and inclination to recognize, and indeed feel, those feelings. Equally, the availability and circulation of a new discourse of feeling, the kind of affective air that people breathe today, has a suggestive effect in awakening and heightening new affective sensibilities. The growing significance of emotional labor at the center of neoliberal entrepreneurialism in Barbados illuminates dramatic cultural change that cannot be captured by the usual structural analyses of Caribbean political economy. And these transformations are equally instructive in our broader understanding of the nature of work and life more generally in the contemporary era. Subtly, these kinds of entrepreneurial service work might also be understood to be producing and giving expression to (not only taxing) affects that are also desirable, pleasurable, and enhancing of "nonwork" lives and selfhood.

Lilliana's reflections about her life are evocative of many of the familiar struggles and expressed the kinds of tensions I was primed to expect. Her use of the very term *balance* intrigued me, for like so many others, it suggests the slippery discursive terrain of fieldwork today and the easy misrecognition of familiar tropes. At the time of that interview, I did not probe any further about the amendments she had made to her own life's goals, but as our conversations continued over several years, I came to better understand just how dramatic her new path was to become. Then married and with one child about to sit the Common Entrance exam and another in preschool, her description of her life and her daily rhythms are saturated by logistical juggling and a heavy dose of flexibility discourse.

Just doing all of this stuff that keeps the house running . . . drives me nuts. I hate the domestic stuff . . . the supermarket! I feel like I *live* in a frigging supermarket! The bank, the bills, you know, it's just all of that stuff. I find it just takes up space in my head and I probably need to detach emotionally from it and just go through the process of doing it, but, I find the combination of raising two children, you know, trying to give your partner time in the evening, running the household . . . [exhausting!] My *work*? [it's treated] almost like a hobby! I mean, during school time . . . I'm up pretty early. I practice yoga in the morning, then I get the children ready for school; I do the lunch boxes, give them breakfast and . . . you know, one of us will take them to school . . . I usually then have a couple of hours between 9 and 12, dropping her and picking her up where I . . . I try to work . . . and then once she's home I find it quite difficult to do anything . . . because it's lunch and, you know, there is chaos and up until very recently I was working in the house, in the kitchen and in that little office space and so it's a communal space and it was almost impossible to really have a thought. . . . And then, at 2:30 [my son] comes home and there's homework and then . . . dinner and bed and umm for a long time I've really been getting up between 4 and 5 and would then not be able to stay up very late so [my husband] would sort of say "well, you know, you need to work late at night!" and I just found it very difficult to do that.

Lilliana's description of her daily rhythm of managing both the logistics of her own entrepreneurial work and the work of caring for her children, household, husband, and her own well-being was echoed through the narratives of almost every other woman entrepreneur with school-aged children whom I interviewed. In her narrative, *work* refers to her efforts to earn a livelihood, her entrepreneurial enterprise launched from her kitchen table and eventually expanding into the studio she built off the back door of her modest house. However, the work of fixing meals and shuttling children, participating in a complex web of kinship, a child's chronic illness, and an increasingly difficult marriage, took an equal toll on her time and energies. Her day holds all the ingredients she and most other entrepreneurial middle-class women are trying to combine—care for their businesses, customers, employees, children, husbands, extended families, and themselves. Historically, despite Caribbean women's simultaneous prominence as mothers and in the realm of paid labor, it has also gone without question that the domestic realm and domestic *labor are primarily a woman's duty*—cooking, cleaning, laundry, grocery shopping, child care, and the like (Hodge 2002; Senior 1991). The growing contemporary importance of emotion work in the care of children, intimates, and customers, as I want to suggest in this chapter, represents yet another dimension.

Ashanti, whose intimate partnership marriage I related in chapter 2, is also illuminating here. In business with her husband when I met her in 2001, and the mother of two young girls, she described some of the ways in which her entrepreneurial endeavors and life more generally had changed by 2005. The first entailed a structural separation of the two business enterprises she and her husband had been running together. They continue to work out of the same building but have separated the businesses.

> I don't have to convince my husband how tough my days are, he *knows*. [Working in the same place] and having that sort of connection during the day is good because we know where the other one is in terms of how the day has been and where we may have to pick up and cut the other one some slack at home . . . because my days can be really, really long. I start later in the morning generally because I would take kids to school, get them ready, and so on . . . and in the evening I've got some meeting or the other, that can go on interminably . . . and so he is at home for them in the evenings. He is there to take them down at night and get them settled and so on. . . . We've been able to split the responsibilities at home.

However, as Ashanti described in more detail the logistical challenges of child care, her voice became more emotional and intense.

> Jasmine, my elder daughter, finishes school at 2:30 in the afternoon and that is, for all intents and purposes, *smack dab in the middle* of my work day, so I couldn't drop everything and go home and stay with her. Rose, my younger one, at two, she is in a nursery so umm she can be picked up (any time), *her time is a bit more flexible.* . . . [So,] Jasmine would come to the office with us and she would stay there until one of us would leave to pick Jane up, which is probably around 5. For Jasmine that was a *terrible* time because from 2:30 or 3:00 when we get her back to the office, until 5 o'clock she's got two hours of having to be disciplined in the office after having been disciplined all day in school, so no time to run around and play, you know, and that kind of thing. . . . It was tough on us too because we still have to work so we try to get her to be occupied with something. The attention span of a five-year-old is notoriously short, right? So we can't get her to sit still for two hours! It

was just absolute madness and so one day I said to my husband, "this has to stop, we can't keep going like this! It's not fair on Jasmine, it's not fair on us, everybody is *stressed* and *whacked* at the end of the day and everybody is screaming and that doesn't make any sense!" *So, we set about trying to find a nanny*!

What often began as detailed and dizzying schedules and enumeration of tasks quickly radiated unmistakable emotion—worry, stress, anxiety, hope, desire—that I came to see as an integral part of the work of life itself. Here, Ashanti and Lilliana are not merely "stressed" and exhausted by their long days. Their stress is produced out of an orbit of emotional labor within which they conduct their business and their family life. These stressful feelings, like the contented, soothed, and pleasurable feelings of intimacy described earlier, are evidence of the affective economy that increasingly permeates their contemporary, often anxious, middle-class life. This emotional field is nourished in large part through the hidden but indispensable labor of paid domestic workers—the nanny-housekeeper whom many women confessed that they depend upon for their very sanity. Indeed, the ways in which middle-class women entrepreneurs spoke about their domestic workers and nannies, and their expectations for a newly intensified and changing understanding of "care," equally revealed the entrepreneurial aspects of parenting and the project of rearing a middle-class child in Barbadian culture today. What we see here are the converging dimensions of new middle-class practices and subjectivities—expectations for ways of being and feeling that also entail new modes of labor.

NANNIES, HOUSEKEEPERS, AND THE NEW "QUALITY" TIME

Middle-class respectability in Barbados and the wider Caribbean has been marked historically by several key features: home ownership, the marital ideal, and a paid domestic worker. While hiring a domestic worker is a long-standing marker of middle-class Barbadian status, the manner in which this figure fits within the entrepreneurialism of today adds vital dimensions to our understanding of what is new under Barbadian neoliberalism. For in women's entrepreneurial accounts the "nanny-housekeeper" held far greater importance for the maintenance of their businesses and their sense of equilibrium than government marketing programs and NGO seminars on business plans or finances. While male entrepreneurs also noted employing domestic help when asked about their household divisions of labor and the management of their "nonwork" lives, not a single male entrepreneur brought up this hidden figure independently or emphasized their critical role in their capacity to run their business. In other words, so ingrained is the assumption that domestic work is women's work, and middle-class households hire domestic workers to perform this work, they required little comment by men. By contrast, women tied the hiring of a variety of types of domestic workers directly to their capacity to be entrepreneurs. Lilliana reflected upon this phenomenon early in our conversations,

> Frankly, I don't think that I'd be married if I didn't have a housekeeper . . . because *I hate* . . . no, *we both hate* to do domestic things. You know, like a lot of things that I complain about? If we had more money, I could pay people to do more things. I complain a lot that he [her husband] doesn't do enough around the house . . . and he keeps saying, "I work too blasted hard to come home and do anything else," if we could have two housekeepers, he wouldn't have to lift a finger. *I'd sooner give up my husband than my maid!*

As a white Barbadian woman, her pronouncement about hating housework and the essential role of a housekeeper might not come as a surprise. Maids were a common fixture in her plantation upbringing, and in the households of most she knew. "Both my parents worked at home, we were not latchkey children. . . . Although my parents didn't play with us, . . . there was an enormous sense of security . . . there was always somebody there. We had two housekeepers, somebody who cooked and cleaned downstairs and somebody who did laundry and cleaned upstairs, and we never lifted a finger . . . and then there was staff in the yard, so there was always somebody around."[11] However, as her testimony and that of many black Barbadian women will demonstrate, the importance of paid domestic help for entrepreneurial women today far transcends the parameters of housework alone. Grace is an Afro-Barbadian entrepreneur in her forties, and like Ashanti and over half of the married women entrepreneurs, her husband is also an entrepreneur. They are partners in business and work side by side most of the day. With one daughter in her early teens, and a business "now really taking off," Grace was candid about the indispensable role played in their lives by their paid domestic help. She began her remarks with a pronouncement as memorable as that of Lilliana, "I firmly believe that every female, executive, entrepreneur, whatever, should have a housekeeper!" In her case it was her husband who first insisted upon this help. His rationale was financial; however, his reasoning spoke powerfully of the affective economy in which they are enacting their business and their lives.

He said, "let us look at it financially, I can bill for one hour of your time $250.00. You can pay that person (the domestic helper) less than that for a *week* of half days! Cut to the chase; one hour of your time, alright?" I mean . . . I'm tired, and just this morning he said to me, "I'm exhausted, and you know if *I'm* exhausted *you've really* got to be more exhausted, so what for? The house is still gonna be there, and you're not, and you want me more than you want the house," so that's his [thinking]. I'm the idiot who took a long time to accept that, because a woman's supposed to keep the house clean, is supposed to feed her husband, is supposed to do this, is supposed to do that, and do the work and still work like a dog in the business too. . . . Something has *got* to give. I don't want it to be *me*, because I want to be around to enjoy life! I don't think it's a matter of . . . people in the past, older people have said, a matter of *laziness*, or a matter of being *organized*, or a matter of . . . *priorities.* . . . They [domestic workers] need work too; I'm helping the environment, I'm helping the whole situation here in employment. They need work too, they have to survive, and I have better things to do than to do laundry! I mean, much better! Last night I was with a client til 10; after I finish that, *really? Excuse me? I'm going home to do what? Sweep, vacuum, clean windows?* I think if men have a problem with that, they got to look at the correct way, you want your *wife*, you want your *woman*, that's more important than keeping the place clean! By far! Get someone, it's not . . . expensive, house help here is not an expensive thing.

While others have begun to suggest that gender roles and ideologies in today's Caribbean middle classes are shifting and that men are participating more in the lives of their children and families (Hodge 2002; Barrow 2001), it is still the case, as Grace herself articulated, that the management of the domestic sphere continues to be seen primarily as women's responsibility. Women entrepreneurs, in other words, continue to be held responsible for the domestic domain, even if they themselves are not performing all the labor within this sphere. Women entrepreneurs like Lilliana, Ashanti, Grace, and almost all of those with children whom I interviewed, seek flexibility to manage a harmonious balance of family duty and their desire for self-fulfillment and autonomy in work. This flexibility constitutes a powerful force behind their new enterprises. The new intimate partnerships and middle-class matrifocal lifestyles each include efforts to achieve this harmony. However, the kinds of flexibility they seek are attainable not solely through the self-defined hours, the home-based or proximate location of their businesses, or the willingness of husbands or partners and other kin to pitch-in, as they are quick to highlight, but through the critical presence and increasing skill base of a paid domestic worker or "nanny-housekeeper." Their management of domestic workers and nannies, enlistment of extended kin, and a growing array of market-based services for a wide range of domestically related needs (food provisioning and preparation, transportation of children to and from school, child care, etc.) are critical to their ability to keep all of the elements of their lives afloat. However, if we regard the logistical arrangements of domestic life and work alone, we miss what I see as the equally crucial aspects of neoliberal change afoot.

The fact that Lilliana, like Ashanti, spent much of her day managing school pickups and homework, grocery shopping, preparing breakfast and packing the lunches, and squeezing her work not only temporally but also physically into the domestic rhythm and space were not unexpected challenges. In the past decade or more, debates about work-life and work-family "balance" have occupied increasing public policy and popular media attention in the United States and beyond. The familiar discourses of balance, flexibility, and "having it all," like other elements of neoliberal policies and culture, have a way of echoing and bouncing back with new insights and formulations from elsewhere in the world, in places such as the Caribbean. They are assumed to be universal struggles or at least universally middle-class struggles. However, while many of the structural challenges of working mothers sounded familiar, and while even the lexicon is the same, something about these debates about work and life as framed in the popular press and the social science literature did not fully capture what I sensed were the most dramatic transformations and challenges within these Barbadian entrepreneurs' testimonies.

Something distinctive reverberated through women's remarks and musings about entrepreneurial life that at the time I found difficult to name or analyze beyond the sense that it had a markedly different timbre from working women's narratives with which I was familiar. And reading between the lines of Lilliana's, Ashanti's, and Grace's efforts to streamline their work schedules to fit around the priorities of their households and children, the commuting and school runs, are elements not reflected in the globalizing language of work-life balance. First, the importance of maids and housekeepers, as well as up-scale, cell phone–toting nannies with driver's licenses and CPR training, rings of both tradition and newness. Hiring domestic workers was explicitly described as a key to marital harmony, however, not only in the sense that her labor would free up women entrepreneurs from these exhausting duties but also in absolving husbands or partners entirely from sharing responsibility for domestic work. Lilliana's remarks ended with an explicit acknowledgment of this long-standing feminist conundrum: paid domestic work leaves intact the traditional feminine/inside, masculine/outside gendered binary divisions of labor and the feminization of housework—and upholds the system in which reproductive labor remains women's preserve. The rationales and expectations for hiring a nanny-housekeeper include not just the need to get help with the daily "dirty work" but also to free women up from these chores in order that they can participate more freely in *other* sorts of activities, including not just their income-generating businesses but also new bodily pursuits such as yoga, personal training sessions at the gym, walks with friends, and spending time and emotional energy on husbands, intimate partners, children, and the like. As Grace's final remark makes plain, "you want your *wife*, you want your *woman*, that's more important than keeping the place clean!" In essence, all of these divisions of labor, as I will attempt to show, hinge increasingly upon expectations for more and different kinds of affective exchange.

With some husbands like Ashanti's and even unmarried fathers like Patrick playing more and more visible roles picking children up from school and involving themselves in other aspects of their socialization, one might miss the hidden but indispensable figure of the "nanny-housekeeper." However, just as expectations for marriage and intimacy are becoming more layered beyond the traditional economy of material support, so too are the expectations for domestic workers expanding to include not just cleaning and cooking but "speaking proper English," modeling good decorum, and extending more nurturing forms of care. What is critical in this combination is not only that there are resemblances in the kinds of expectations for emotional engagement and attunement but also that the hiring of a nanny-housekeeper can diffuse tensions over domestic divisions of household labor and meanwhile foster men's inclinations and capacities to become more involved in other aspects of domestic and kin-based life.

In Barbados, and the Caribbean more generally, the gendered divisions of public and private space, whereby men occupy the "outside" and women inhabit the domestic "inside," have been so well articulated in the region's ethnography they almost go without saying. However, Ashanti and many of these other women entrepreneurs paint not only dramatic spatial transformations, in which husbands are now participating in more aspects of domestic life such as bathing children and readying them for school, but also equally dramatic affective changes in fathers' participation in the crafting of children's life experiences as a whole—the quality of their interactions and the content of their day. Her description of the rationalization of their two businesses, streamlining and separating out their different interests, is echoed, in a sense, on the domestic front. Each takes charge of a portion of the day, Ashanti the morning and her husband the evenings, attending to some of the aspects of their family life and child care. Efforts to juggle the children and their two businesses led to tensions and struggle. By separating out their companies, each has a clearer idea of their responsibilities and manages things more independently. By hiring a highly skilled nanny-housekeeper, they have help shuttling their kids to after-school activities and the reassurance that their daughters are being cared for and nurtured, not only safe but also stimulated and engaged emotionally.

While the hiring of a domestic worker is not a new element of middle-class life, the nature of the exchange or calculation behind this paid labor holds new meanings. The contemporary nanny-housekeeper is a key factor in the entrepreneurial work-life picture, as Grace's husband asserts, in that she can be paid for nearly a week's work what Grace can bill in an hour. In financial terms, Grace's time, according to her husband, is too valuable to warrant exhausting herself with a second shift of laundry and cleaning. But this calculation alone does not capture the picture entirely. As I will try to illustrate through this and the following chapter, the desires and stresses of entrepreneurial lives are not just a matter of finding a "balance" of tasks or activities carried out in different spheres of offices, businesses, and homes. The affective qualities defining *work* and *time* are at the heart of these changes, and they define these arrangements beyond conventionally economic terms in this era of "emotional capitalism" (Illouz 2007). The neoliberal flexibility these entrepreneurs are attempting includes not only a more efficient or rational division of labor per se. For them, the very *nature* of labor and the *quality* of time are being radically redefined and self-consciously prioritized. Grace put this shift in succinct and compelling terms: "I think we made a decision . . . we looked at our priorities, with twenty-four hours in a day. Business is a priority, our daughter is a priority, we are a priority, and then *we as individuals, we* are a priority: *four* priorities." It is precisely the effort to achieve these combined priorities and the degree to which the energies and labor required by each become not just intertwined but also how they come to *resemble* each other, which is what I see as the crux of a dramatic set of changes in contemporary middle-class life. These efforts involve earning money and juggling time in order to find the space for each set of priorities, but they are also about valuing and giving expression to certain kinds of activities and certain ways of being that are particularly expressive of middle-class life in this neoliberal era.

Lilliana, Grace, and Ashanti, quoted above, illustrate that for both white and black middle-class women today, in addition to the practical challenges of domestic chores, cooking, shopping, and managing their businesses, the search for flexibility embodies a struggle to more ably manage their desires for stimulating, self-defining, and income-generating work while nurturing a fulfilling relationship, motherhood, close friendships, intimate connections to a spiritual community, and a desire to reflect on themselves. The flexibility they desire is not only defined structurally in the allocation of time for work and nonwork but also in affective terms that relate to the *quality* of that time, the quality of relationships, and the subjective experience they foster. Recasting time and relationships in these ways in turn reproduces a particular affective climate and orientation toward self making for the children growing up in this new milieu.

These new modes of flexibility include, as I have suggested, new formulations of marriage or romantic relationships forged in concert with a self-directed and creative realm in which to work and define oneself. As we will see, this also produces a particular kind of leisure time in which to nourish new formulations of motherhood, intimacy, and self. Especially among the women entrepreneurs, these efforts at flexibility expressed themselves not only through pragmatic, structural juggling of kids' school drop-offs and pickups, grocery shopping, employee schedules, client deliveries, phone calls to a sister or a mother, a session with a personal trainer or new-age pastor, but through subtler entrepreneurial gestures in which emotional energy, foresight, consideration and worry were all integral to and shaped by these practical activities of work and life. As the entrepreneurial narratives suggest, these changes reflect subtle but significant redefinitions and valuations of time. The recent and growing emphasis on "quality" family time, time with an intimate partner, or even time for oneself, reflects a new conceptualization of time and how it should be spent in the enactment of a fulfilling middle-class life (Gregson and Lowe 1994). The distinction is not only that of demarcating work from nonwork (play, leisure, etc.). This conscious effort of reserving free time for specific relationships, not only leisure but also the active work of fostering intimacy, pleasure, connectedness, is bound up with a broader social landscape of neoliberalism in which the individual, the couple, and the family are believed to require particular kinds of nurturing and engagement. The creation of such designated forms of "quality time" and the emotional capital, skills, and labor

FIGURE 4.1. Family time. Photo by Carla Freeman

these new categories of time require[12] reflects several convergent and interconnected processes, including a growing emphasis on certain kinds of emotionally laden service in the marketplace, a host of subjective markers of middle-class belonging and modes of subjectivity, and the (often hidden) presence of dependable domestic workers who free up both time but also emotional energy for entrepreneurs to invest as they wish.

For the women entrepreneurs who most effusively described their marital and/or conjugal "partnerships" as intimate and supportive (e.g., Heather in chapter 2 and Ashanti in this chapter), the presence of a reliable domestic worker and/or nanny-housekeeper was, whether they acknowledged it or not, a key ingredient to the domestic harmony they valued. Like these entrepreneurial households, more and more middle-class households around the world today are relying upon paid domestic workers to pick up the slack of household cleaning as well as many aspects of child care. In Latin America and the Caribbean at large, domestic work continues to constitute the single largest category of paid work for women (Osirim 1997, 53). However, these trends reflect not simply the increase in working women and mothers in the waged economy. They also provide clues to the nature of the kinds of work and ways of living being newly fashioned under neoliberalism. If the neoliberal enterprise requires supple flexibility in responding to client and market demands, and if the entrepreneurial household equally requires fashioning individualized activity, talents, and modes of involvement, these Barbadian parents, and mothers in particular, are faced with even greater demands on their time and emotional reservoirs. If, as in the case of Lilliana and Ashanti, a competent and skilled domestic worker can be entrusted with several key elements of the domestic sphere, such as cooking healthy meals, doing laundry, and cleaning, more time and energy are left for these energetic women to spend nourishing close relationships with their children, stimulating their talents and interests, and so on. Meanwhile, as Ashanti's narrative illustrates, the nature of the nanny-housekeeper or domestic worker job is also in flux and demanding increasing elements of tailored emotional labor.

Often in fieldwork one becomes most aware of new patterns when they are contradicted. Beyond their numerical significance, I became most conscious of the growing desires for intimate partnership marriages when I began to hear about separations and divorces. Equally, I have become even more attuned to the powerful relationship between intimate partnerships and the hidden but indispensable role of paid domestic workers in the few cases I encountered of women entrepreneurs who did not employ such help. Jacqueline runs a busy daycare center with the assistance of her eighteen-year-old daughter. She related with bitterness and resentment that her husband has been of "no help" or support in her business or in their life more generally. Jackie takes care of all domestic responsibilities. Their finances are kept entirely separate. She has no idea what he earns in his construction business, and he seems to contribute little financially or otherwise to the running of their household. Jacqueline would like to buy a house; she sees the ownership of one's own home as the single most important sign of independence and middle-class security, but her modest daycare business has not made that possible, and she resents her husband's lack of help. Indeed, she suggested fairly plainly that she would be better off without him. If she and her daughter were on their own, they would likely rely a bit more upon "her family" (i.e., her extended network of a sister, cousins, and the like).

I found that among many of the married women entrepreneurs, as among married women in the informatics sector I studied more than a decade ago, being married and living in a nuclear family household impinged upon women's capacity to depend upon the kinds of extended-kin support that other women in matrifocal households more readily relied upon. For married middle-class women, the employment of a domestic worker provided critical labor and household support that poorer women sought among their extended kin. Despite their seemingly respectable middle-class privilege, in the absence of a paid domestic worker, married entrepreneurial women faced notable stresses and exhaustion brought about by their double day. While their greater financial resources allow them to buy labor saving household technologies, prepared food, and other conveniences to ease some of these burdens, the simple fact of their second shift is not unlike that faced by working-class women (Chaney and Castro 1989; Mohammed 1988). With no domestic helper, Jacqueline was bitterly aware of the absence of support from her husband, and her discontent focused more upon the conventional economic measures of "support" than the more emotional elements of many other women.

For those women who were able to depend upon the paid labor of domestic workers, the capacity to outsource domestic work to a nanny-housekeeper was essential, freeing them as middle-class women to enjoy the mobility and empowerment of higher levels of remuneration and also allowing them to develop other aspects of life equally important to them and to contemporary expectations of middle-classness. This "freeing up" gives middle-class entrepreneurial women and men the capacity to engage in their demanding market-oriented work and new leisure pursuits and activities while also fostering the growing impetus to expend emotional energy and imagination toward each other, toward their customers and children, and to engage with themselves as subjects in their own right, as new loci of entrepreneurialism.

One might compare the relationship of the nanny-housekeeper and expanding expectations for emotional labor with an earlier era of domestic enhancements. Just as many had anticipated that women's work would be dramatically reduced with the arrival of washing machines, vacuum cleaners, and the like, we found instead that these technologies only increased the expectations for cleanliness and further inscribed these domestic activities as women's duty (Schwartz Cowan 1983). Similarly, while paid domestic workers indisputably absorb much of the onerous labor and strain on middle-class entrepreneurial women's double day, their importance coincides with mounting expectations for new and often hidden layers of nurturing, affective work that is equally feminized and specialized. Certain forms of work—the crux of what makes emotional labor special—simply cannot be "outsourced." Lilliana alluded to the subtle but palpable strains she felt even with the support of paid domestic help: "we *do* have maids and babysitters. . . . They do a lot . . . but there are some things the children don't want a maid to do . . . there are some things that you *can't* ask a maid to do in your home. . . . All the little details. And you know? They're always telling me, 'don't sweat the small stuff,' but *somebody* has to sweat the small stuff or everything is going to fall apart!"[13] Articulating precisely the distinction Iris Marion Young (2005) drew between "housework" and "homemaking," the "loving work" of homemaking works on two tracks: on one hand, this work fosters "quality" time among intimates—the intimate couple and an increasingly nuclearized family with close parental bonds—on the other hand, this work constitutes another layer of emotionally saturated labor that fuels the pleasures and stresses of this entrepreneurial life.

EMOTIONAL CAPITAL AND THE ENTREPRENEURIAL CULTIVATION OF CHILDREN

In very much the same ways I found myself surprised by the growing emphasis on romance, intimate communication, and "the couple" as a locus for investing work, attention, time, and cultivation today, I was equally struck by a shifting discourse surrounding children and their care. The kinds of emotional labor invested in Ashanti's search for the perfect nanny for her children, and her particular emphasis on care and nurturing attention as opposed to discipline, for example, denoted what I sensed were marked shifts in Caribbean tradition. They suggest both a changing emotional economy as well as the commodification and privatization of care that is integral to this entrepreneurial landscape. Ashanti related having received over two hundred calls when she advertised for a nanny, and she commented extensively on her determination to find someone with excellent references and evidence of both polished manners as well as all the nurturing qualities she wanted her children to experience in her absence: "We drew up this brief questionnaire that we could do on the phone and what their experience was especially dealing with children, and so on, and if that looked okay then we would invite them in for a first chat and then if that kind of went okay we would have them in for a second chat and make our decision from there. In like three days we were trying to wean out, you know, two hundred and something callers . . . almost three hundred callers we had!" Each evening, she plans out with the nanny what she should cook for the kids' supper the next day:

> She has her routine. . . . They're sitting down to eat by 6:30, which is great, compared to what it was before. We were really eating a lot later in the evening because we got home late, and there wasn't any time to play . . . it was mostly trying to get dinner ready and get them off to bed, so they missed out on a lot of afternoon activity and a chance to run around. . . . Everything is more settled now, because . . . after supper is bath time, time for them to calm down and listen to their tapes or have a story read to them. She does all that.

In essence, most accounts of child rearing in the region highlight strict discipline above and beyond all other elements of socialization. When social scientists compare the roles and importance of mothers and fathers, mothers are generally portrayed as more significant in children's lives; they are also understood as more caring, loving, and nurturing in contrast to fathers' contributions of financial support and discipline (Barrow 2010, 137). Although parenting and childhood have not been studied extensively in the region, UNICEF summarizes the Caribbean as a place in which "children are to be seen and not heard" (13). Indeed, the high value placed on having children is closely wedded to the expectation of children's obedience.

However, just as the desires for intimate partnerships suggest new models for enacting conjugal relationships and new ways of envisioning "the couple" as a social entity, I noticed equally dramatic transformations in relation to parenting and new ways of conceiving of, relating to, and cultivating children that draw upon a new emotional register. Children become important loci for class anxieties and desires that permeate entrepreneurial narratives, while at the same time they are subjects of growing affective expectations and affinity. A new language is emerging from the lips of these middle-class entrepreneurs that, while familiar to my American ear, carried a notably un-Barbadian accent. Ashanti and Grace employed expressions such as "date night" to describe their deliberate efforts to set aside specific time for intimacy with their husbands and to plan outings to particular kinds of venues that would allow them to focus on their marriage, separate from their busy and intertwining entrepreneurial and domestic lives and household activities. So too did more and more entrepreneurs mention the desire for "quality" family time as a focus of their leisure pursuits. Where a recent review of studies of working-class Jamaican parenting noted that "parents do not tolerate or see as necessary children's expressive and assertive behavior, [and] almost 80 percent of parents in [one study] admitted that they beat their three-year-olds with an implement such as a stick or belt" (Evans 1996, 422), the shifting emphasis toward children's individuality and emotional lives was striking. These observations call for a brief historical discussion. For on one hand, as I have noted, children have always been highly valued in Caribbean society. Parenthood has symbolized a central ingredient to adulthood for both women and men. Generally speaking, for women, biological motherhood or the common practice of child fostering, and for men, fathering children, surpasses marriage in importance to adult status. It is widely held that, despite the challenges of poverty, education, healthcare, precarious economic development, and the social problems of drugs and violence across this region, children are "universally loved and cared for if not by their own parents then by extended kin, friends and neighbors." On the other hand, many an expert and casual visitor alike have noted with alarm the commonplace corporal punishment, "sharing licks," "lashes," and "flogging" by parents, teachers, and any other adult figures on children of all ages. The biblical dictum "spare the rod, spoil the child" is familiar in all West Indian circles, rich and poor, black and white (Barrow 2001:145).[14] One official report from the Child Care Department of Barbados noted "a 'property mentality' among parents and guardians according to which they assume the right to deal with their own children as they see fit, combined with the belief that the physical punishment which they themselves received as children 'didn't do me nothing' [did me no harm]" (Epstein and Limage 2008, 425). Among other references, my informants used the expression "beatings and blows" to describe the means by which their elders induced proper manners and behavior.

So legendary is the harshness of Barbadian discipline in the realm of child rearing that a popular BBC reality TV series titled *The World's Strictest Parents* sent two unruly English teens to endure proper Bajan parenting in the home of a middle-class Seventh Day Adventist family. The mother, a primary school teacher, and the father, an IT specialist, live in a modest "wall house" in a suburban neighborhood, drive a comfortable SUV, and have two well-groomed and well-disciplined daughters who are depicted diligently practicing the violin, sweeping the yard, washing the car, enumerating their household chores, attending one of the island's top public schools, and, most importantly, defending their parents' mode of discipline and demand for respect. The father describes his family's values, "God first, then . . . family . . . we believe in strict but fair discipline . . . we believe in our children living to the fullest of their potential." The mother says, "number one discipline in the house is lashes . . . my voice raised, my body language is more in a fighting mode," but what they demonstrate over the course of a rocky week with these two sullen and disobedient teenagers is the value of tough love—rules that are enforced, respectable codes of behavior that involve modest dress, decorum, and speech—and the pride associated with education, including the education of the self, "knowing who you are."

Many aspects of this reality show, along with the interview narratives and my own eyewitness to child rearing over the past twenty years, reveal important shifts in the emotional tenor of these relationships and ways of relating to children. In the TV episode, the visiting teens grumpily attend school (trying to run off, their host father chases them down on foot and returns them), scoffing at their classmates' compliance and quaint pride. In an English class assignment they are asked to write a self-revelatory essay reflecting upon mistakes they have made in their lives and the lessons learned from those experiences. Reciting these essays aloud brings not only these jaded teens but many of their classmates to tears. What moves the English youth seems to be a recognition of the emotional pain they have caused their families, and a sense of loss they feel when confronted by their Barbadian peers' comparative self-respect and respect for parents, schooling, and authority. I offer this vignette not to paint a rosy picture of Barbadian youth or Barbadian schools today, for local discourse about rude kids with "no broughtupsy" and chaotic classrooms echo similar missives the world over. Instead, the story suggests a new emotional register has entered even those institutions most known for their discipline and order. I discussed this episode with several alumni of this same school, and what struck them most was the nature of the assignment itself. Self-revelatory essay writing and emotional discussions were not assigned in their day, when strict discipline, memorization, and recitation—as opposed to discussion, the sharing of feelings and personal thoughts—were the pedagogical norms.

The prioritizing of "quality family time" with a focus on children stood in sharp contrast with descriptions entrepreneurs offered of their own childhood experiences. For some, these new ways took the form of regular trips to the beach, picnics, and a deliberate effort to talk about school and hear about their day, beyond just the provisioning of dinner on the table, books, and supplies required. In addition to expensive family holiday trips to Florida's Disney World, Toronto, or New York to visit "gone-away" family, black and white middle-class entrepreneurs alike described a new concept of "stay-cations" in which they took advantage of new deals offered by local hotels during the slower summer tourist season to woo Barbadian customers. Equally, the treat of ordering a pizza and having a family movie night was mentioned often as an end of the week ritual. Almost without exception, entrepreneurs described these experiences with their children as something they had not grown up with, but that they were intent to share with their children. Their desires to craft enriching experiences for their children and time to bond emotionally reflected both class anxieties as well as desires for closeness and the capacity to relate to their intimate partners and children in newly expressive ways. Lilliana expressed the melding of affective desires and anxieties that I heard from dozens of other parents. Speaking about her eldest daughter, she said,

I want her to feel confident that her parents are able to offer her opportunities and experiences that are *valuable* and *exciting* and *fun* and so the family dynamic can change, because I think if the stress is taken off . . . the need to acquire money, just to sort of get through, to survive, and then to have some excess, I think that that would create a healthier kind of family dynamic, because then we can *do more fun things*. You know, when you're struggling to make money all the time it . . . there's not a lot of time for the fun things . . . I'm not interested in huge quantities of wealth, I just think it would be nice to take a really nice family trip every year, to a new place you know, to take them to South America, to go to Costa Rica . . . go to a place where there's snow, umm, and to let her feel that we can afford to send her to a good university, or maybe to let her do her "A" levels in England . . . I think it would inspire confidence in the children and expose them to diverse places and diverse people and to contribute to them being more confident and, you know, more socialized and . . . I think that it would be very healthy.

Lilliana's narrative was as much about her own worries and desires about her earning potential and the future of her business as it was about her hopes and dreams for her children and for them together as a family. Ashanti feels confident of the partnership she and her husband share as fellow entrepreneurs as well as on the domestic front, having some separate time in which to enjoy different interests is a priority, so long as the needs of the children are met first. For her, shared involvement in *the family* and special time together with her children is primary. Women as well as men, such as Patrick, mentioned the importance of "date nights" for couples and "quality time" for children and family as part of the entrepreneurial project of self making and the making of the intimate couple and family.

Just as the growing sphere of wine bars and galleries, boardwalks and restaurants offer new venues to cultivate intimate romantic relationships with a spouse or partner, the past decade has seen a sudden expansion of new venues in which to nourish and train creative and artistic, athletic and academic abilities in children. Not only are there new extracurricular activities, camps, lessons, and experiences being offered for the enrichment of a new generation of supple, flexible would-be entrepreneurs but there are equally dramatic emphases on ways of *relating to* and developing a deep and intimate understanding of children. There is a notable transformation in the ways in which children are seen, cultivated, and invited to participate within middle-class family life and society more

FIGURE 4.2. Leisure and activity on the new boardwalk. Photo by Carla Freeman

generally that suggest both neoliberal ethics and a changing reputation-respectability logic.

A recent emphasis on children as "projects," requiring not only strict discipline, good manners, and proper behavior but also the cultivation of new modes of expression and creativity, the fostering of open communication, warmth, and care, reflects a notable cultural reorientation toward many of the central qualities and values of neoliberalism—individualism, expressiveness, flexibility, and adaptability in an ever-changing marketplace. These radical revisions of the affective culture of child rearing were expressed often to me as entrepreneurs recalled their own childhood traumas and efforts to foster different kinds of relationships with their own children. As Reynaldo, a successful and well-established black entrepreneur in his sixties, recounted in tears during our interview, his father visibly favored his brothers and ignored him: "I always loved my father, you know, and my father never told me he loved me. . . . I make certain every day I tell my little son I love him."

Ashanti's story evokes many dimensions of the changing affective landscape of child rearing, coupling, and selfhood. Like dozens of my entrepreneurial subjects, her story is framed by the relationships and hurts of her early upbringing: her mother and siblings who raised her, her father's desertion and the continued scars of that experience, and her conscious or unconscious desires to move forward, establish a different kind of primary relationship with a partner and a different model of parenting. Ashanti was like many of the men and women that I interviewed, whose narratives echoed pain, loss, and determination to prove themselves worthy and successful to an absent parent (mostly fathers, but in some cases mothers who migrated abroad and left them with other kin). Ashanti's father left the family when she was seven years old:

> I never really understood what happened. And as I grew older I got bitter about it and I just didn't care to even know or understand. He just disappeared. . . . I used to get a book from him every year until I turned eighteen and then that stopped. . . . But as I said, you know your focus changes, I think, as you get older and a little bit more experienced, starting up a family of your own. . . . You know, it's not easy . . . because you know in Barbadian families you don't explain things like this to children. Maybe you do now with the more modern families but certainly you don't talk to children about splitting in the family and stuff like that.

Ashanti's narrative is permeated by pain and sadness, as well as the determination and drive to create and live out a different way of being when it comes to her own marriage, her relationship with her daughters, her capacity to realize her dreams as an entrepreneur, and as a social actor and introspective subject more generally. Part of this process of entrepreneurial self-exploration, coupling, and parenting entails a decisively different communicative set of tools and inclinations, the desire to talk through problems and express emotions in ways that her own parents, and Barbadian families more generally in the past, did not.

Ashanti signals that traditional Bajan sensibilities and practices are gradually making room for, or giving way to, new mores for relating to kin, partners, and children that reflect the shifting affective landscape. If children were once akin to "property" over which parents and the wider networks of kin have had control and responsibility, as suggested in the report of the Barbados Child Care Board, they are cast increasingly as active partners in a dynamic intersubjective relationship, one that requires the *labor* of planning, care, nurturance, and communication, and one that is privatized within the bounds of an increasingly nuclearized family. Children require not simply basic support in the form of financial inputs (school books and uniforms, food, shelter) but also other forms of emotional, cultural, and material investments and labor. And while extended-kin networks remain integral to family life, the primary responsibility for the cultivation and care is concentrated in the hands of parents. In this sense children are seen as projects, inextricably connected to the project of self making: they are a reflection of the labor and investments (emotional, financial, cultural, social) made for them.

Like many other entrepreneurial mothers, Ashanti describes new and radically different activities and experiences she is keen to offer their children. I became more and more aware that these activities reflected precisely the entrepreneurial landscape I was undertaking to study. The second time we met, I was struggling to find a summer camp or babysitter for my own six-year-old daughter in order to conduct my fieldwork and interviews each day. Ashanti recommended two camps that her own children were enjoying. Both were offered by women entrepreneurs I had previously interviewed, each tapping into a growing set of needs and new desires for enrichment experiences and physical activity. One offered weekly fieldtrips to each of the different parishes on the island, historical sites, a tour of the local milk-processing plant, horseback riding. Another was Colleen's adventure business, tailoring hikes and high ropes courses, team-building exercises and outdoorsy activities for kids. These new camps and activities give middle-class entrepreneurial parents the assurance that, while they are working longer hours, their children are not only being kept busy and "out of trouble" as many put it, but they are learning new skills and being exposed to sports and knowledge that are increasingly associated with global middle-class values. Any number of parents commented to me that their children were learning to sail, kayak, surf, and ride horses, while they themselves could barely swim.

One new brightly painted art camp, housed in a renovated and gracious old plantation-style home on the island's south coast, offers a growing array of activities and sensibilities that reflect this cultural shift. I continue to receive their email updates announcing new services, classes, and themed camp sessions from *Alice in Wonderland* and *Charlie and the Chocolate Factory* to Halloween and Easter. During the summer parents can send their children for full- or half-day sessions of mixed-media art projects and creative activities along with yoga, dance, drumming sessions, treasure hunts, and the like. Like other modes of leisure and consumption, the flourishing of American-style camps in so many metropolitan areas is unmistakable. The enterprise is owned and run by a young married couple from the United Kingdom, the wife a "qualified art teacher and therapist," with a "deep interest in art, healing, and people," and her husband the financial director who handles the business end, with a "keen interest in the arts." Here, children enjoy indoor art and outdoor recreational activities, with souvenir T-shirts and final art projects taken home at the end of each session. Week-long and shorter camps during school holidays facilitate

FIGURE 4.3. New children's summer camp. Photo by Carla Freeman

working parents' schedules, and the facility is now also home to a weekend "farmer's market" with fresh food, specialty coffees, fruit smoothies, and "fun for the whole family." Studio space for local artists and rental space with air-conditioning, polished wood floors, and views of the sea are envisioned as a venue for group meetings, yoga classes, or conferences. The outdoor play park with jungle-gym equipment and zip lines can be rented for birthday parties. An art gallery and café on the premises offer a gathering place and "hive of activity for the community to come and relax and meet up with friends." This is a new, multifaceted institutional structure designed to accommodate the busy work schedules of parents with school-aged children, the growing desire to foster creativity and expressive extracurricular outlets for both children and adults, and the need for leisure activity and space for all to gather outside of the home. Like the island's new wine bars, restaurants, cafes, ice-cream shops, malls, and popular coastal boardwalk, venues such as this offer a host of new physical spaces for new kinds of social engagement as well as individual expression and contemplation.

These new extracurricular activities, languages, clothes, electronic devices, and travel experiences are all suggestive of the kinds of flexible youth being conjured in this neoliberal middle-class milieu; however, the transformations are also embedded within the affective shifts toward more emotional connections and communicative engagement. As Ashanti explained it to me, things that were not traditionally spoken about with children, for example, her own father's desertion of the family and the trauma this entailed for herself, her siblings, and her mother, had left a wound she now hoped to correct in the raising of her own children. So conscious was she of the need to foster a different kind of nurturing and emotional self, in addition to a new model of parenting, that she vetted hundreds of applicants in her search for just the right nanny for her young daughters. Her requirements included not only a capable and experienced babysitter with a cell phone but also a nurturing caregiver who would "speak well" and engage her child in meaningful activities, nutritious meals, and conversation. The intensifying affective labor involved in the middle-class "concerted cultivation" of childhood (Lareau 2003) echoes many of the other modes of affective labor in entrepreneurial life. They reflect new sets of desires as well as anxieties. Parents such as Ashanti express an intent determination to create a different emotional milieu for her children than the harsh experience of her own childhood, and she is also keenly aware of the need to foster in them new skills (e.g., Spanish language, artistic creativity) and the flexibility that will ensure their future in a rapidly changing labor market and world.

The emotional attunement and labor invested in this new, more intimate middle-class relationship of parent and child entails resources of time, physical and emotional energy, and multiple forms of capital—social, cultural, and financial. As Cindi Katz (2012, 186) argues, the notion of childhood as a commodity and a strategy of accumulation has multiple effects on today's children, parents, and the society at large, most notably the increasing stress and discipline of intensive parenting that runs counter to an ethos of a collective good (the communitas of reputation). Some parents bemoaned this privatization process as signaling the loss of the "social" responsibility of parenting and socializing children in Barbados, however, their regrets were framed without exception in terms of discipline. In the old days, when they were "coming up," anybody's parent, any adult, could give a child "a lash" and put them in line. Today, by contrast, there is a greater sense of individual parenting styles and responsibility and a growing reluctance to "interfere" with other people's (nonkin) children. The significance of neoliberal parenting in the Barbadian context is equally expressed in the thrust toward newly expressive affective bonds that many of these same middle-aged entrepreneurs described having longed for in their own upbringing. Their desires to enact loving and attuned relationships with their children and to foster their individual growth and development by talking with them, sharing their thoughts and feelings, and cultivating their particular interests and talents in new activities, classes, and camps fit indisputably into the neoliberal entrepreneurial fold.

The cultivation of the child is certainly not entirely new in Barbados. Indeed, the Caribbean bildungsroman is the story of education as a means to upward mobility for the lower classes and the promise of a good life (Zobel 1980; Marshall 1970; Lamming 1983; Hodge 1981). Middle-class parents have, for decades, arranged extra coaching prior to the Eleven-plus exam with the dream of their children landing a coveted spot in one of the island's top state secondary schools. Middle-class privilege also afforded sporting opportunities and travel, and for some, boarding school education abroad. However, those privileges were investments akin to the kinds of "support" that marked traditionally respectable households. They fit, one might say hand in glove, in the hierarchical order of bureaucratic respectability.

Today's neoliberal parenting involves prioritizing not only cultural enrichment, sport, and the arts but also the cultivation of childhood through more intimate, expressive, and emotionally attuned relationships as opposed to harsh discipline. Equally, as we will see in the next chapter, forms of therapeutic intervention and spiritual life represent not just a growing sphere of middle-class investment and labor but also a changing, intensifying affective landscape. These organized activities, therapeutic and embodied practices also represent fertile ground for the kinds of new entrepreneurial enterprises many of these new business people are creating in Barbados, from shuttle services designed to get children from school to camps or after-school programs, to art studios, sports and aquatic programs, dance schools, and every variety of spa service imaginable. Just as entrepreneurial parents flexibly respond to economic fluctuations and the pressure to "niche market" their businesses' goods and services, they are becoming increasingly aware of the competitive landscape in which their children are coming of age and are seeing in these very spheres new business possibilities at the same time. The entrepreneurialism of the self, the child, and the business enterprise converge.

WORK/LIFE AFFECTS

I see the growth of a new affective milieu surrounding child rearing, intimate relationships, and desires for self-reflection and self-actualization as intimately connected to the general culture of neoliberal entrepreneurialism taking hold in Barbados today. Its resonances are especially powerful among these entrepreneurs whose lives straddle the work world of their businesses, their intimate relationships, and their sense of self. What interests me most about these affective "spillovers" in the private and work-related lives of Barbadian entrepreneurs is not simply the capacity of work to sap affective energy from the emotional reservoirs of vulnerable workers (Gregg 2011). For such a formulation assumes that care, intimacy, and emotion emerge from within the "private" sphere and are at risk of being siphoned and encroached upon by the marketplace that increasingly finds value in (and hence commodifies) these affects. The picture presented by the Barbadian entrepreneurs is a messier, more dynamic, and multidirectional one in which the very premise of a *prior* reservoir of emotion, love, and empathy from which the capitalist market now endeavors to extract such affective resources is less clear. Rather, desires for intimacy, care, affection, and the impetus to express such feelings today emerge within and across private and market exchanges. These processes and the affective esprit of which they are apart are experienced not by middle-class entrepreneurs alone; however, this group, perhaps more than others, boldly demonstrates their evocative interconnections. All who witness, long for, and participate in these emotionally rich encounters and spheres of activity are privy to their influence, whatever their class, occupational pursuits, race, age, religion, gender, or sexuality. The work of *work* and the work of *life* are not only becoming more and more intertwined but also, for most of these entrepreneurs, the forms this labor takes are increasingly the same. Care, attunement, and nurturing lie at the heart of much of life and work today. However, it is important to emphasize that this economy of emotion is taking hold across vastly different emotional fields, and for Barbados and likely elsewhere in the Caribbean, it is growing within a milieu not known for expressive feelings of care and intimacy.

Others have commented on the centrality of emotions and affective labor to modernity and late capitalism (Illouz 2007; Giddens 1991). However, these accounts tend to hold constant or assume universal the cultural footings upon which these transformations rest. In the Barbadian context, where an emphasis on interior life and on expressive intimacy has not been the dominant affective tradition, we see that these practices and ways of being, whether in the market exchange or in private with kin, intimates, and children, become mutually constitutive. These exchanges permeate life in its broadest sense, across all spheres of activity, relationships, subject positions, and the manner in which these, in turn, are managed and felt. They signify new burdens and pleasures. As we will see in the following chapter, the growing rationalization and commodification of feelings can heighten desire as well as alienation, requiring entrepreneurial interventions of new sorts and, at the same time, the capacity for defining and asserting the self in meaningful new ways.

CHAPTER 5

The Therapeutic Ethic and the Spirit of Neoliberalism

We were taught women should be in church every Sunday; we shouldn't party, nor should we drink . . . nor should we consider smoking. Those were not things that were considered ladylike. It didn't matter that you were hurting; *you were told to grin and bear. . . . You grin and you bear, and that's it.*
—COLLEEN

The previous three chapters have turned a spotlight on the new inti-mate partnership, matrifocality, and new modes of parenting as illus-trations of a growing neoliberal structure of feeling in the Caribbean that is bound up in its current entrepreneurial ethos. In each sphere we find a heightened set of emotional desires and demands for af-fective labor that spans public and private life and appears especially charged in the middle-classes. In this chapter I turn toward other di-mensions of entrepreneurialism and new middle-class subjectivities in contemporary Barbados that I see as intimately connected to the changing neoliberal landscape—a growing appeal of new forms of spiritual practice and belonging, including new middle-class "pros-perity" churches, a flourishing marketplace of self-help, counsel-ing, bodily treatments, and what might broadly be understood as an incipient "therapeutic culture" (Illouz 2008). In these expand-ing realms lie opportunities to experience new modes of sociability, embodied practices, and subjectivities that are all bound up closely with the neoliberal esprit. Today a burgeoning arena of therapies and treatments related to holistic well-being, personal individual growth, and healthy relationships and families has emerged almost from thin air. Together, new churches and spiritual communities as well as an expanding field of psychotherapy, yoga, meditation, and a multitude of bodily practices, spa facilities, and treatments aimed at soothing and connecting the mind and body are evidence of both the new entrepreneurial thrust and an affect-laden culture that are decidedly novel. I see these as part and parcel of the new middle-class entrepreneurialism that are unsettling a country both caricatured and praised as the most orderly, conservative, and quintessentially "respectable" of Caribbean nations (Lewis 1968).[1]

Such practices and their embeddedness in the neoliberal ethos denote what Nikolas Rose has called the psy–effect, the twin technologies of psychology and its affiliated experts, and modern, liberal structures of governmentality by which the "regulative ideal of the self has been invented" (1990, 2). Eva Illouz (2007, 5) describes the rise of therapeutic culture and its associated "language of the self" as "qualitatively new" with "virtually no antecedent in American or European culture." These new discourses, according to Illouz, reflect a radical remapping of social relations and self-understandings in the twentieth century. In brief, capitalist modernity together with the rise of middle-class culture fostered an ethos of emotionality both in the workplace and in the private sphere. She argues that "middle class men and women were made to focus intensely on their emotional life, both in the workplace and the family, by using similar techniques to foreground the self and its relation to others" (4). In this process there has been an intimate mingling and intertwining of the economic and the psychological, the market and the interpersonal. With the early influence of Sigmund Freud, and the midcentury rise of second-wave feminism, Illouz argues, a distinctive therapeutic emotional style transcended boundaries of popular and elite culture. This new emotional style would characterize American culture at large. Indeed, the intensity of psy-culture is illustrated boldly in the fact that almost half of the entire population of the United States had been under the care of a mental health practitioner (Illouz 2008, 6). For Illouz the modern shift toward a therapeutic culture in the United States is expressed today in various forms, from introspective psychoanalysis to "assertiveness training," "new age mind-body" therapies and "life coaches." Not only has therapeutic discourse become a trademark of American culture but also, according to Illouz, it has traveled the globe as a new "transnational language of selfhood." This is a point that requires closer scrutiny—the manner by which understandings of selfhood and mechanisms and techniques of therapeutic discourse travel. In its travels, therapeutic culture takes on new meanings and significance. If these are the signatures of modernity (Giddens 1991; Rose 1992), they take specific expressions that have seldom been captured in ways that expose the complexities of culture, geography, and historical specificity (Watters 2010). While rich traditions of psychological anthropology and cross-cultural psychology have treated these aspects of cultural life for more than half a century, the manner in which the neoliberal therapeutic preoccupation takes hold in culturally specific ways has received little analytical engagement.

Notably for the Barbadian point of comparison, this interpersonal framework and model for self-understanding was founded upon a specific point of origin: the nuclear family, an unconscious "epicenter . . . [of] sex, sexual pleasure, and sexuality" (8). If these triple forces—feminism, Freud, and the primacy of the nuclear family—have constituted the root of American emotional capitalism, their collective weight in Anglophone-Caribbean cultural history could hardly be less pronounced. Regional feminists have examined why American second-wave feminism, and its urging of women into the paid labor force as the primary avenue to gender equality had less relevance and appeal in the Caribbean (Barriteau 2003). To my knowledge, there has been no parallel attempt to examine why Freud fared similarly, though such a study might provide interesting clues for interpreting today's emotional currents. For my purposes here, suffice it to say that if for both Freud and second-wave feminism, the nuclear family constituted the "origin of the self and that which the self had to be liberated from" (Illouz 2007, 7), and this therapeutic premise helped to anchor modern, capitalist American emotional culture, its relevance has been much less pronounced in the cultural imagination of post-colonial capitalist Barbados. As we attempt to theorize contemporary neoliberalism, the significance of these differences bears close and careful study.

Summarizing the rise of "therapeutics" in the United States, the United Kingdom, and Europe, Rose (1992, 149) notes that "contemporary individuals are incited to live as if making a project of themselves: they are to work on their emotional world, their domestic and conjugal arrangements, their relations with employment and techniques of sexual pleasure, to develop a 'style' of living that will maximize the worth of their existence to themselves." This intertwining of therapeutic culture and entrepreneurialism highlights the individual as both the engine of economic growth and the site of potential alienation, processes that converge especially powerfully around concepts of middle class-ness and efforts to enact middle-class lifestyles. Here again, the Caribbean cultural model of reputation-respectability is of interest, for the current reworking of entrepreneurship as a middle-class pursuit (versus the oppositional, scrappy means of survival for the lower classes), marks a new aspirational trajectory of business enterprise and self making. In this sense, the figure of the Barbadian entrepreneur both builds from but also transforms earlier understandings. Put simply, the industrious and flexible economic agent of reputation utilized "occupational multiplicity" in piecing together a livelihood (e.g., informal marketing, fishing, a job here, a job there) and derived social support from networks of kin and congregation (women) or "crew" (men). When propelled onto a middle-class stage in the contemporary cultural economy of neoliberalism, entrepreneurial flexibility is bolstered by a new system of support—that of an individualized and embodied, affect-rich, therapeutic milieu.

Like the pursuit of self-employment and entrepreneurship itself, these spheres of leisure, spiritual practice, and "body work" in Barbados today represent a blending of both new and old. Novel experiences and ideas travel through global media circuits, and build upon long-standing cultural traditions themselves layered by global processes—colonialism, slavery, tourism, and other circuits of labor migration. In each case the pursuit of these practices by middle-class entrepreneurs (among others) is intricately connected to their entrepreneurial lifestyle and contemporary modes of enacting middle-classness. For example, a growing awareness of health and physical fitness among busy middle-class business owners who spend their days rushing between client meetings and suppliers, home and work, often well into the evening hours, has spurred interest in their own bodies and at the same time the growth of new businesses: spas, holistic salons, gyms, personal trainers and workout coaches, fitness, sport and adventure camps, and so on. For a society in which hard physical labor and the hot sun have long been associated with the sweat and toil of the slave-based sugar plantation, deliberate exercise in bright tropical daylight were anathema to most of the women I got to know in my early fieldwork more than twenty years ago. I recall with embarrassment my brief attempt to go running along the busy West Coast Highway where I lived. Passersby in carefully pressed work clothes stared in disapproval of my running shorts and the preposterousness of my recreation. Similarly, when I had proposed weekend outings to the beach with some of the working women I was studying at the time, their idea of a day at the beach involved a "sea bath" close to shore and a picnic under a tree, not the long, goggle-wearing, exercise-oriented swimming I enjoyed. Most avoided getting their heads wet; many could not swim.

Today, however, many of the entrepreneurs I studied, men and women

FIGURE 5.1. Personal training session. Photo by Dondré Trotman

alike, actively seek out exercise and the outdoors—walks and swimming in the sea—as means to "calm themselves," stay fit, and to nourish their well-being. In addition to greater knowledge about obesity and common diseases such as diabetes, many (especially women) alluded to other new anxieties and sources of unease: their own or their children's consumer desires, mounting credit-card debt, and the pressure to uphold new middle-class lifestyles. These everyday strains of hectic middle-class entrepreneurial life are, meanwhile, being salved in part by the services of new enterprises being started by equally savvy entrepreneurs opening appealing new spas, restaurants, health centers, or living-room based spiritual communities. In fact, over the decade in which I conducted my interviews, the webs of interconnection between my research subjects became increasingly complex, as they referred to each other's businesses and services as indispensable parts of their respective lifestyles.

As women and men follow the new path of middle-class entrepreneurship, it is clear that these pursuits entail new forms of labor and new subjectivities that in turn offer new pleasures, possibilities, and sources of alienation. These desires and stresses faced by busy, aspirational middle-class Barbadians are reflected in the range of new businesses cropping up across this small island nation, especially along its densely populated south and west coasts—carpool services to help manage school pickups, catering and specialty prepared food services for entertaining as well as impromptu take-out food for dinners, cafés and ice-cream shops for quick after-work meals and treats, event planners for work events as well as children's birthdays, and an elaborate array of salons and clinics offering acupuncture, massage, and nutritional supplements and bodily and psychological treatments of a wide variety of forms. As familiar as these kinds of businesses and consumer and leisure activities are to the tourists who arrive by cruise boat or plane, I cannot overstate how remarkable they are to Bajans and repeat visitors, ethnographers such as myself, and others. While Kentucky Fried Chicken and Chefette, a local fast food chain, as well as a couple of tiny strip malls and beach bars marked the South Coast "highway" development when I first arrived in Barbados in 1989, the landscape of the island is being redrawn in every sense, physical, commercial, and cultural, with today's entrepreneurial explosion.

In several striking cases entrepreneurs reshaped the nature of their businesses in line with the kinds of everyday struggles they themselves were experiencing. Colleen and Lilliana were cases in point. These two women, a black Barbadian from modest, working-class roots and a white Barbadian from the planter elite, follow similar entrepreneurial trajectories in leaving jobs solidly anchored in the orbit of traditional respectability (a bank, a prominent secondary school) in favor of their own independent businesses (team building and outdoor adventure, and a gallery and home furnishings business). In both cases, as we will see, their own personal struggles also led them to develop awareness of others' shared plights and to extend their entrepreneurial endeavors beyond their original businesses in the direction of therapeutic intervention and holistic self-care. Their work led them on journeys of introspection and enterprise, toward greater self-awareness and concern for those around them. Foucault saw the "care of the self" anchored in early Greek tradition, as meditative, reflective, enacted through thought and through the act of speaking as well as through bodily care. Care of the self "implies labor" and "takes time"—a few moments for "introspection . . . for reflecting on the day that has gone by . . . turning one's thoughts to oneself," enabling "one to commune with oneself, to recollect one's bygone days, to place the whole of one's past life before one's eyes, to get to know oneself. . . . Add to this the correspondence in which one reveals the state of one's soul, solicits advice, gives advice . . . *the work of oneself on oneself* and communication with others" (Foucault 1986, 50–51; emphasis added). How such modes of self-care become a means for financial enterprise and for generating new middle-class subjectivities became unexpected but especially rich fields to explore entrepreneurship. The growing emphasis on

FIGURE 5.2. New sites of leisure and middle-class consumption, a popular ice cream café. Photo by Carla Freeman

self-improvement and self-knowledge is part of the continuum I have been charting in the preceding chapters, including the cultivation of an emotionally attuned child-parent relationship, intimate relationships with partners and spouses, and attention paid to the care of the body and cultivation of the self. Grace, in the previous chapter, articulated these interconnected affective projects simply and efficiently. She and her husband have mapped out their priorities much as she would a new design project in her business. Her entrepreneurial formulation reflects the sense that time is a precious and limited resource and that apportioning how it is spent, the *quality* of that time, is integrally related to the fostering of life's most important elements: the business, their daughter, their marriage, and them*selves*.

> In terms of going out and socializing . . . we socialize with [the extended] family but [given] where the business is at, where our daughter is at, in her stage of development . . . it is not an easy thing to do, and because we are focused . . . we made a decision . . . we looked at our priorities with twenty-four hours in a day: business is a priority, our daughter is a priority, *we* are a priority. . . . We skimp on the *we*! . . . and then we as *individuals*—four priorities. This year has been great because [our daughter has] been sleeping over at my parents every

Friday night. . . . Friday night is our night, which has been good! I can get to go out with my husband, have a date. . . . We skimp on *we as individuals* a lot . . . which is a big issue . . . and we try to pull back . . . we'll do it . . . for a month or two and then we slip back [into the busy routine].

The impetus toward care of the self constitutes a largely hidden but central key to the entrepreneurial quest. Virtually all of entrepreneurs I interviewed, like Colleen and Lilliana, vigorously embrace the neoliberal mantra of *flexibility* and *autonomy*, using these terms often as well as highlighting their various meanings. They articulate a passionate desire to break out of and move beyond the limits set for them by bosses and by bureaucratic institutional frameworks, seeking self-realization, greater economic rewards, and, in the case of women, the pressing goal of managing competing demands of work and "personal" life, by which they meant family, children, time with friends, and the opportunity to pursue a range of their own interests and desires for *themselves*. As we have seen in previous chapters, for Colleen, the decision to marry and the kind of intimate "partnership" she is working to build with her husband depart dramatically from the female-headed household of her upbringing and from the patriarchal norms of "traditional" Barbadian middle-class respectability. Her rejection of the respectability of her bank job, with its requirement of politely measured affect and carefully pressed uniform, in favor of the sweaty athletic gear and the riskier and more emotive enterprise of her wellness retreat and adventure camp speaks to the marked shifts of neoliberalism in Barbados.

Clearing brush and climbing high ropes courses in the hot sun are far from her former air-conditioned bank job with its set hours, hierarchy, uniform, and middle-class aura of feminine respectability. Indeed, as we heard in chapter 1, by relinquishing some of these traditional elements of conventionally respectable femininity, and developing the island's first such business of its kind, she has veered into the realm of reputation in her entrepreneurial climb. Her youthful determination and success are not embraced and supported by everyone around her. She struggles to keep up with her financial commitments and with multiple demands for her attention—to be responsive to clients and groups when they are on site, to market her business to prospective groups and anticipate new niche markets, to manage her staff and train them to deliver the kinds of service she has in mind, and to maintain her sideline business growing and packaging herbs and vegetables for supermarkets from her roof-top garden in addition to tending to her partnership marriage and friendships, as well as her own emotional, spiritual, and physical needs.

The stresses and strains of her entrepreneurial life and the intensity with which affective labor permeates all of its dimensions led to an array of health problems and exhaustion that prompted Colleen to seek medical intervention, as well as individual guidance, from the pastor of the new church she had recently joined. The search for intimacy and partnership in her relationship, for self-understanding and self-actualization, and the commitment to foster personalized service for her clients, as the previous chapter explored, entail the constant management and production of feelings—comfort, affirmation, support, care—a heightened demand for affective labor. As meaningful and pleasurable as many aspects of these pursuits are, they are also elements of daily *work* that take a toll on top of the more easily recognizable efforts to manage her accounts, keep up with her bills, supervise staff, and deal with a number of unexpected problems with soil erosion and the physical structure of her business location. Several years into her new adventure tourism business, she spent a year feeling very unwell, with lower back pain from lifting heavy objects and being "overstressed" and "psychologically spent." Her musings about her own personal path toward wellness and the new trajectory of her business are revealing of an intricate and emotional intermingling of neoliberal restructuring and self-management. She vocalizes the strains produced: "I was in a lot of pain; I was exhausted. My doctor kept saying, 'take some pain killers . . .,' but I pulled back, probably about nine months ago and really [started] looking at what was happening with me."

Ultimately, Colleen's own health problems became closely intertwined with her approach to her business. She enrolled in the island's first sports management program, a three-year course offered through the community college and committed herself to juggling her studies with her growing business. As part of her course, she started to

> study the problem and found that a lot of professional people, young women, middle-aged women were having a lot of challenges with their health, but . . . were not willing to confront them. Women who'd had cancer, women who'd had things like ulcers and endometriosis, all sorts of things . . . were popping up. I also found that people were suffering with hypertension, diabetes, and we were relatively . . . young people . . . I mean we were saying "Oh God!" "Oh AIDS and HIV!' But hypertension and obesity and all these other strains . . . they are more prevalent among black people and this is the majority of our population . . . so

you have to do something about it! . . . More people are stressed, so even though we have this growing middle class, a lot of them don't eat well 'cause they can't afford to . . . it's too expensive! Have you seen the prices in the stores? So I started working toward cleaning up my health, which has improved a hundred fold, and as a result of that study I've been able to get down more support to help me structure a wellness-based program based in the outdoors targeting these groups. Out of doing the study, and going to meet different people and getting their feedback . . . oh my goodness, it's sort of taken on a life of its own!

These personal experiences and Colleen's growing awareness of others' suffering—especially middle-class women much like herself—led her to expand her adventure tourism business and to offer a range of new programs, from children's wilderness camps and corporate team-building retreats to wellness programs of integrated health and fitness. Following in the time-honored Caribbean tradition of "occupational multiplicity," well known within the lower classes, Colleen maintains another "side" business inspired by the wellness approach she pursues and her concern about food, diet, and nutrition. From her kitchen and rooftop garden, she grows vegetables and herbs for local hotels and grocery stores, starting her seedlings in a line of bathtubs and other containers that adorn the back of her home, and packages and labels them from the crowded space of her kitchen counters.

The convergence of illness narratives amid entrepreneurial journeys was not anomalous. Justine, whose story I introduced in chapter 3, told me that she had begun getting "panic attacks": "I'd just all of a sudden get totally panicked. My heart would start racing, I thought I was having a heart attack or something. I felt dizzy and awful, and out of control." More than a dozen other women, most in their thirties and forties, described similar experiences of periods of ill health—from vague symptoms of exhaustion, persistent headaches or migraines, depression, and back pain to medical diagnoses of lupus and non-Hodgkin's lymphoma—amid recounting the stories of their businesses. In many of these cases, the desire to feel better and "be healed" became intertwined with broader self-reflection about their lifestyle, work rhythms, priorities about work and life more generally, and empathy for many of their business clients whom they saw as sharing similar struggles. Their capacity to connect their own entrepreneurial projects of business, self-treatment, and empathy for their customers also appeared to be central to their vision of success. For women in particular, running businesses, traveling, and managing households, children, and the fabric of extended family life, as one put it, means "life is simply exhausting."

Heather, formerly in human resources for a large private company and now an independent entrepreneur, whose marriage and business story I recount in chapter 2, noted of many of her friends, "Yeah, *women* . . . they're *all exhausted* . . . I recognize the symptoms. The stress is causing women to gain a lot of excess weight they cannot push off and they're battling with illnesses because their bodies are just under too much pressure." The pressures they are under include both the demands for flexibility in the market economy, as adept producers and earners and knowledgeable, up-to-date consumers, and also specific pressures steeped in the gendered culture of Barbadian life that continues to dictate women's responsibility for the lion's share of domestic management and kin work. In this climate in which the affective economy is swelling across personal and market domains, women bear particularly weighty responsibility. The melding of life and work and the saturation of life and work with affect—affective longings, demands, and affective *labor*—are palpable. These generate a new kind of energy that is at once social and individual, motivational and embodied, invigorating and exhausting. While the culture of occupational multiplicity was not new to these women, the awareness, public articulation, and marketing of the affective domain, particularly in the public sphere, were a marked contrast. Equally, the importance of emotional labor is also not new in a country in which domestic service has been a primary sphere of female labor historically and where the national economy has been anchored in tourism for almost a half century. But the nature of the emotions and the expected manner and versatility of expression have expanded, intensified. An emphasis on both an increased emotional reservoir and the customizability of affective exchanges suggests a sea change.

Colleen's wellness center and adventure tour business offers children as well as adults an unprecedented, intimate experience of rugged outdoor exploration, an opportunity to challenge themselves physically through hiking, high ropes courses, and, according to her business website, "a safe and exciting environment, which prompts *learning through self-discovery.*" No doubt, her own illness became bound up with her desire for further education, and in pursuing the new field of sports psychology, she accumulates both knowledge and insight that helps to soothe her own body and mind and also earns her the (respectable) social status and credential that comes with advanced education. Meanwhile, she turns this knowledge toward her business's advantage as it enhances her coaching and leadership training skills and her successful delivery of the kind of caring and attentive service her customers value and she aims to deliver. Her training influences her willingness and interest in engaging in business as a therapeutic encounter.

These affect-laden interactions with clients are also fueled by emotional reserves nourished by her pastoral counsel and her intimate partnership marriage, just as these are heightened by the affects exchanged in her business. Hochschild (1983, 55) made a clear distinction between the emotional labor performed in a commercial setting versus that of the stage, in private or in a therapeutic context, in that "one's face and one's feelings take on the properties of a resource . . . not a resource to be used for the purposes of art, as in drama, or for the purposes of self-discovery, as in therapy, or for the pursuit of fulfillment as in everyday life . . . [but] a resource to be used to make money." However, in Colleen's case, like most of the service-oriented enterprises of the entrepreneurs I interviewed, these exchanges are at one and the same time commercial and therapeutic; they generate capital of both monetary and affective forms and can be experienced as affectively exhausting and/or nourishing.

Colleen invests her time and her emotional energies not only in the running of this business, managing her staff, organizing the marketing and outreach, and the financial and accounting side of the company, but also in the face-to-face, hand-to-hand, and heart-to-heart delivery of comfort, reassurance, and care it takes to instill trust and confidence as well as to safely develop physical strength and agility in her clients. Her website states, "individuals engage in fun and memorable experiences that inspire them to act on new levels of understanding." The promise is that through developing greater physical strength and agility, and the capacity to trust others and work as a team, individuals gain insights that will change their lives—their capacity to work with others, to understand others in all facets of life, and to understand themselves. A recent newspaper feature about her innovative business quotes her personal mission, "For me I feel that the rest of my life is devoted to health and wellness and really helping people to get in touch with themselves and begin searching. I get really concerned when I see people not well, not being able to live fulfilling lives, not being able to go to work, not being able to take care of their kids, and not having basic things such as energy . . . I think . . . many people are searching for something else." She is working to promote the physical and psychological health of her clients, and she is driven by her own parallel journey. In the provision of her services, Colleen offers fearful clients her own calm confidence and trains her staff to offer the same. She says, "People come here and they want to feel comfortable. They don't know you, but you've got to be able to build that trust and rapport in a short space of time. You also have to be able to make them understand it's alright to *feel* the fear, but *go for it*."

To offer these services successfully takes more than the surface acting of a pleasant smile that was expected in her bank job. What she is cultivating in her customers and campers are the precise tools that are increasingly of value in the marketplace as well as in the private realms of life among parents and children, service providers and customers. She is cultivating the capacity to feel and to reflect upon her own and others' emotions: fear, excitement, desire, joy, care, trust, comfort, and so on. In so doing, she is gradually whittling away at the respectable ethic of "grin and bear" and being soothed by and also laboring to foster in herself and her clients a newly expressive therapeutic ethic in which a wider array of affects, in particular, those associated with care and empathy, feelings of trust and comfort, intimacy and concern, are heightened, affirmed, and voiced. Here, the enactment of affective labor, as Michael Hardt (1999, 99) has suggested, signals labor in its highest, most advanced form, and hints at its greatest potential, "not only directly productive of capital but . . . the creation of life precisely in the production and reproduction of affects. . . . Labor works directly on the affects; it produces subjectivity, it produces society, it produces life. Affective labor, in this sense is ontological—it reveals living labor constituting a form of life and thus demonstrates again the potential of biopolitical production." The ontology of affective labor as a form of life lies at the heart of what I am describing as the neoliberal ethic, an ethic of entrepreneurialism and a therapeutic culture whereby business and self, the business of being and the making and feeling of enterprise, become intertwined, mutually reinforcing.

Colleen illustrates this ontology perfectly. Her affective labor defines her, as it does her business; it gives her life meaning, it forms the basis for her livelihood as a means for generating capital. But it also taxes her. "I *found myself* in this. I just want to be out here, it's just important for me," she says. Her business defines her and is equally defined by her; it becomes inextricably connected with every other aspect of her life insofar as the tools with which she navigates each sphere become more and more the same, more and more grounded in states of and exchanges of emotion. As we will see shortly, Colleen's choice of a new, intimate church community in which she can be counseled individually by an accessible pastor, over her husband's family's middle-class Anglican Church, one of the central pillars of respectability, also reflects a shifting set of priorities and desires for emotional connection and personalized care. Through these practices, Colleen and many others like her are actively embracing and redefining an affective landscape that encompasses spheres of work and leisure, intimate, religious, spiritual, and embodied experiences for many middle-class Barbadians.

I see these articulations of selfhood as defined through entrepreneurial means and the neoliberal mandate for entrepreneurial flexibility as expressions of what Foucault (1988, 18) called "technologies of the self" or techniques that "permit individuals to effect by their own means or with the help of others a certain number of operations on their own bodies and souls, thoughts, conduct and way of being, so as to transform themselves in order to attain a certain state of happiness, purity, wisdom, perfection, or immortality." In most of my interviews, especially with entrepreneurs offering new kinds of services in this broadly therapeutic sphere, but also among others in non-service sector businesses which have nonetheless come to emphasize affect-intensive customer service, I found similar resonances. Their narratives suggest individuals who "find themselves" in the course of delivering caring, therapeutic exchanges with clients and customers. They make *themselves* and simultaneously make their *livelihood* in these affectively saturated exchanges. For their customers they create a new climate in which to cultivate themselves, and they meanwhile fuel the capitalist market.

Lilliana, whose story has been woven through the previous chapters, is again of interest here for the manner in which she is drawn to several modes of therapeutic practice, both as a supplemental source of her entrepreneurial livelihood as well as for her own personal benefit. As neoliberalism requires the individual to be constantly adaptable to the whims of the market, its forces are simultaneously fostering an array of services aimed at salving the stresses and disappointments required by these entrepreneurial gymnastics. With agility and gutsy determination, Lilliana has combined part-time teaching in one of the nation's post-secondary institutions, applied for and received a government grant for creative entrepreneurship, and through this program learned elements of business planning, marketing, and development from an entrepreneurial mentor. Her interviews were full of laughter, bold and colorful language, and deep introspection that evoked hope and longing, worry and wisdom. Her resourcefulness spoke to the legacy of West Indian women's capacity for toughness, strength, and economic savvy, while her inclination to articulate her emotional desires about her intimate relationships, motherhood, and her work evoke the newly emerging affective milieu.

She has diversified her work to include both home décor items and designs, alongside producing a documentary film about regional politics and creating a not-for-profit community arts center. All of these activities are launched from Lilliana's simple and picturesque studio, abutting the house she shares with her two children on her family's former plantation grounds. Meanwhile, having practiced yoga for many years, she also advanced her training as an instructor and again, in the West Indian tradition of occupational multiplicity, has been supplementing her design and production business by offering yoga classes on the side. As an independent entrepreneur in her forties from a large and supportive extended family, Lilliana boldly illustrated many of the converging and transforming dimensions of respectability and reputation today. Her business and personal life combine elements of playful, creative, public-sphere reputation with others steeped in traditional feminine respectability. The combination is sometimes a fraught one. With rising inflation and unemployment, retrenchments in the public sector, and the recent promotion and allure of entrepreneurship, there is also a growing unease about competition and risk. Like most of the entrepreneurs today, as with their historical predecessors, Lilliana hedges her bets across multiple sites. She maintains her activities as a business woman, a "public intellectual" and creative producer, mother, sister, daughter, friend, and yoga instructor. However, with money always in short supply, the constant demand to reinvent and market herself, and the desires to expose her children to new educational experiences and travel opportunities that will make them better prepared in the global economy, the pleasures and flexibility of entrepreneurialism are also wrought with anxiety. The notion of a steady paycheck and a stable teaching job hold undeniable appeal. Like several of her friends and relatives, Lilliana was drawn to a variety of newly available therapeutic services for managing the challenges brought about by the new entrepreneurialism.

Among the ailments and struggles I heard others complain of were sleeplessness and back pain, panic attacks, agoraphobia, depression and anxiety, marital tensions, weight gain, and chronic fatigue. Exhilarating but financially precarious, entrepreneurial life requires constant retooling and reassessing in an economy bearing the weight of global recession. For many of these middle-class Barbadians, meditation, yoga, and massage, colonic cleansings, reflexology, iridology, psychological counseling and pastoral care, and the prescription of both herbal treatments and antidepressants have become new sources of support they have sought in efforts to heal themselves and restore a more harmonious rhythm to their lives, conjugal relationships, and families. Together with the search for new, expressive modes of intimacy, they reflect an expanding set of desires and anxieties associated with neoliberal middle-class life. As Nikolas Rose (1992, 152) says, "in transcending despair through counseling or therapy, the self can be restored to its conviction that it is master of its own experience." The manner in which this pursuit of healing also fuels the entrepreneurial ethic, and the broader capitalist system of which it is a part, is both subtle and palpable.

BARBADIAN "GRIN AND BEAR" MEETS THE THERAPEUTIC ETHIC

In Barbadian society, where emotional and psychological life have historically been, as Colleen boldly stated, the preserve of "the priest or the bottle," the contemporary expansion of wide-ranging therapies, counselling services, and treatments geared toward these affective dimensions of life are striking. Neil, a black Barbadian pastor turned entrepreneur, summed up the general antipathy toward therapy, and most things associated with psychology, when describing his friends' reaction to his idea of opening a counselling center. Their caution reflected both the conservative stance I described in chapter 1, anchored in the culture of respectability, which privileged the stable professions and civil service over entrepreneurship, as well as a generalized suspicion toward psychology itself: "In the Barbadian society . . . people don't move from secure to what people see as insecure! This was a venture that nobody [understood]. As a matter of fact, some people told me straight out, friends of mine who were pastors in the church, you know, 'Who are you going to get to come to you? *People don't come for counseling!* You know? Are you *sure* you're moving in that direction?' Because other than persons going to a *psychiatrist . . . reluctantly . . .* counseling was *not* the thing!"

Until recently, the availability of psychiatric and psychological treatment was consigned largely to severe cases of "madness" and/or substance abuse; the locus of treatment was referred to simply as "the mental" (for the mental hospital) or "the madhouse," a walled and imposing structure feared by most who pass its gates. *Madness* according to Fisher (1985, 111) is often attributed to the work of Obeah,[2] or witchcraft, and to speak of either is thought to bring about danger and misfortune. This discomfort and ambivalence toward the psychological is echoed in the scholarly arena of Caribbean studies as well. Outside the domains of religious practice (e.g., spirit possession, vodun), emotional life is minimally engaged in the region's social science. Whereas in literature and the expressive arts there is growing interest in affect, interior psychological life has been relatively unexamined. This absence or avoidance reflects the dominance of economy and material livelihood and support as both the local and regional cultural idiom for well-being and life as well as the dominant tradition of structural functionalism and Marxist political economy in Caribbean social science (Freeman and Murdock 2001). Today, the Barbados phone directory lists an array of such varied psychological services as developmental assessments, autistic spectrum disorders, behavior management, family therapy, marriage counselling and training, and corporate and family counselling. Not unsurprisingly perhaps, one finds more common reference to "depression," "anxiety," "panic attacks," as well as "counseling" and "therapy" in the everyday lexicon of Barbadian life—in the newspapers, radio shows, and in common middle-class parlance. Notably, the ways in which individuals, relationships, and families are conjured in these new arenas are themselves novel in the Barbadian context, for example, classes on parenting geared toward a nuclear family and couples therapy emphasizing intimate and caring communication for the conjugal couple as a social entity. These transformations in understandings of selfhood and kin contrast with a long West Indian tradition in which *the family* referred to an extended kin network and the enduring center of both affective and material support, and where *the couple* has been a more fluid and secondary bond. A further stand of psychological intervention has focused specifically on conquering fears and anxieties in the context of *work* and especially the risks and insecurity of entrepreneurship.

Neil's enterprise was a case in point. A self-described counselor of many specialties (marriage and family, anger management, and executive coaching to name just a few), an author, and ordained minister, he had been married for nearly twenty years and was the father of two teenaged children when we met. Formerly a church pastor full time, his new business combines and extends the kind of "counseling and helping business" he offered through church teachings with his current "change management" focus on entrepreneurship and entrepreneurs. Most of his time is spent giving seminars and workshops to groups in both the public and private sectors. He acknowledged the sudden and growing interest in entrepreneurship and the involvement of churches in promoting and supporting these directions in Barbados,

> that is something . . . new . . . that is happening in the last six, seven, eight years, and churches have seen a need to not only talk to persons about the spiritual but also the temporal, you know, we have a couple of churches here that have moved in that direction in terms of helping their members set up businesses and . . . move toward self-sufficiency. . . . When I was a pastor I had . . . a counseling center and

a feeding program . . . but then I decided I didn't want to serve my pastor only, which I thought was limited, so I felt I was ready to go into counseling, serve a wider constituency. . . . That's what led me to . . . giving up being a pastor and . . . now I'm on the road doing a lot of seminars and workshops. I could touch more people . . . than one on one counseling.

His new business is positioned precisely at the nexus of the entrepreneurial and the therapeutic.

I do a lot of change management . . . I help persons look at the mental and psychological issues in setting up their own businesses. That is a challenge in a Caribbean reality. . . . Sometimes we focus on the financial and the business issues and we don't recognize that if persons are not psychologically prepared . . . and mentally astute in terms of what they're doing or what they *want* to do they're gonna fail, they're not gonna do it well. They have the money and they have the training in terms of business, but you know, unless you focus, unless you *know what you're about* . . . and you can *deal with your fears* . . . then you gonna have some *problems*.

In addition to acknowledging Barbadians' discomfort and lack of familiarity with psychology and counseling, Neil stated plainly that men are "the most reluctant" and hard to reach psychologically. The landscape is changing, however, and with the government sector of roughly 24,000 as his main client, Neil employed seven full-time and eight part-time staff and took out large government-backed loans from the Central Bank in order to underwrite this growth, the purchase of materials and computer equipment, and the expanded payroll. Beyond the Barbados public sector, he now provides workshops and seminars for private companies beyond Barbados, across the eastern Caribbean region.

Other entrepreneurial men expressed a growing interest in selfhood and often focused on the body in particular. They patronized gyms and sports clubs, some were active in the new churches, and a scant few described interest in the psychological. Jimmy, a young entrepreneur in the local fashion industry, was one of them. He said, "if I were to change my career right now I would go and be trained in some type of counseling because I find that men in Barbados have a lot of issues to resolve but there's no outlet for them." The owner of a trendy men's clothing boutique, his business offered a safe space for trying on new styles and new expressions of masculinity more generally. With a comfortable sofa and pleasant earth tones to complement the air-conditioned space, both in soothing contrast to the sharp tropical light and colors outside, he noted, "people come here so often just to sit down and chat, you know . . . unexpectedly. But they're very comfortable in this space and, you know, I'm a good listener . . . without judging or anything . . . sometimes people just want to vent." For Jimmy, as for Colleen and many others, the point of contrast for the sort of "therapeutic encounter" he provides in his shop is the church.

I find that a lot of churches are . . . very judgmental of people, like if you don't fit into what their little box expects of you, whatever the case is. . . . I've had friends, I mean, like young people are having . . . major issues because the church is saying this to them and they're in conflict with themselves and with the church and the church is supposed to *help you* not make you feel . . . *guilty.* . . . This [his business] has been one tremendous experience for me . . . we have these models that we deal with and they're all young men . . . from like eighteen to maybe . . . thirty. . and there's not a place for them. They can't talk to their family, they can't talk to their parents, they can't talk to their girlfriends or whoever they're involved with . . . so it's a challenge! A lot of men have not really addressed their issues they've just grown up and assume this role of being what a man is supposed to be without dealing with themselves and I think that because of that they pile stuff on top of stuff on top of stuff and some day, I mean, it comes to basically haunt you, you know? It's not a society that really encourages counseling. . . . Especially with men, eh? Cause it's supposed to be a sign of weakness and it's really unfortunate. . . . One day a guy came like eleven o'clock in the morning just where I am; he laid down on the couch there and I said to him "what's wrong" and he's like "just let me stay for a few minutes . . . don't talk" and I just left him and then afterward he started to cry and then we went to the bar and we had a drink and then he had like several drinks and that basically encouraged him to be a lot more liberal with his tongue . . . expressing himself . . . he told me . . . stuff that he doesn't necessarily have to be dealing with . . . this assumed role that he has, this assumed responsibility that he must . . . you know . . . he must have because he's *a man* . . . trying to live up to these expectations. . . . And it's very, very sad because I mean like these people who have so much potential are sometimes . . . stifled because of whatever the situation is, there's not an opportunity for them *to express themselves.* When it comes to artistic and creative people, Barbados, I find, is not a very encouraging society and people either become frustrated and give up what they're doing or they leave.

Jimmy's recounting of this man's story highlights many interconnected strands of social convention and social change. On one hand is the explicit illustration of how "unmanly" and unseemly it is to be perceived talking openly, sharing one's feelings, and expressing strong emotion. Related to this is the mandate for a certain kind of masculinity and the prohibitions associated with stepping outside of that (heterosexual) box of masculine reputation. Without any explicit naming of these young men as homosexual, gay, or any other sexual label, it was clear from his story that the oft-cited culture of profound homophobia (Murray 2012) was the stifling referent many of the young men faced. Finally, Jimmy highlights the broader theme of Barbadian cultural conservatism hampering entrepreneurial creativity, echoing the remarks of a government minister in chapter 1 who urged "the liberation of a mindset that restricts us to a sameness and a dullness, . . . a change in attitude. We must believe that we are an innovative people . . . a creative people and we must show support for creativity—we must not stifle it." From Jimmy's vantage point as an entrepreneur and an astute would-be counselor, this creativity and the capacity for individual and social-economic flourishing are diminished by the gendered logics of respectability; homophobia and the fear of emotional expressiveness operate in tandem. Here the emphasis on conformity in gender and sexuality and the "grin and bear" culture of respectability stand in opposition to the neoliberal thrust toward entrepreneurialism, creativity, and self-expression. As Nikolas Rose (1992, 157–58) describes this process,

In the heady days of the 1960s cults of the self promised a liberation of the individual from all mundane social constraints. But today, the therapeutic culture of the self and its experts of subjectivity offer a different freedom, a freedom to realize our potential and our dreams through reshaping the style in which we conduct our secular existence. And correlatively, mentalities of government and technologies of regulation operate in terms of an ethic of the self that stresses not stoicism or self-denial in the service of morality and society, but the maximization of choice and self-fulfillment as the touchstone of political legitimacy and the measure of the worth of nations.

In short, the very essence of the concept of an "enterprise culture" for Rose "is that it embodies a political programme grounded in, and drawing upon, the new regime of the autonomous, choosing self" (162).[3] Jimmy's account of his customers' pain, coupled with similar stories from entrepreneurs like Neil, Colleen, and Lilliana, all highlight the contemporary call for such therapeutic intervention and self-actualization. Indeed, these lie at the heart of what they see, and the market rewards, as the golden ticket to entrepreneurial success in all senses—in the formation of their social status and in the shaping of their own subjectivities.[4] Running through these discourses of faith and therapy are entrepreneurial signs and referents, and they are steeped in the economy of emotion. Spiritual and therapeutic practices are sites in which new middle-class Barbadians are attempting to nourish and calm themselves amid mounting stresses and strains of life under neoliberalism—rising expectations of consumption, intensifying modes of parenting, coupling, and self making, and the demand for flexibility in the labor market together with rising costs of food and fuel. At the same time, all of these represent new loci for the development of new entrepreneurial ventures, new niche markets for emergent or aspirational middle-class actors drawn to the promise of creative and independent self-invention and self-mastery.

NEOLIBERAL RELIGION AND THE NEW SPIRITUALITY

Weber's understanding of the relationship between Protestantism and the entrepreneurial ethic of capitalism was expressed powerfully in one interview I conducted with one of the founders of a newly established congregation, a white businessman who was then travelling in the United States. He said,

> If you look historically at America, their whole spirit comes out of God, very entrepreneurial. The Muslims are much less entrepreneurial; Hindus, less entrepreneurial, less emphasis on freedom, life, hope, on being "possibility thinkers." [My own] gift is with people who are without faith—an evangelistic gift not the pastoral care and counseling—but [I am able] to bring new people in—especially in the business world. I feel there is a great link between faith and business. . . . I didn't know how or when, but I went to [one of the big local companies and the CEO] asked me to take my faith back into the business world . . . my faith has brought a change to this company—true faith translates into tangible change around you. God wants successful businesspeople to be a light—people admire successful business people so they have a platform to speak the message of Christ—*professional people were looked at as the gurus, today it's the businesspeople and athletes—and these are speaking out their faith.*

Entrepreneurs make frequent reference to god as the basis for their business "calling" and perseverance. In even more explicitly instrumental terms, new religious institutions and collectives offer ready client bases as well as communities of support, guidance, and information. One young man I interviewed landed one of his main contracts with the pastor of his new church, when his design sense and multimedia savvy was put to the task of PowerPoint projections for weekly sermons. Another self-described "born-again" woman in the tourism industry geared her market toward "Christian holidays." Madeline, the black single mother and high-ranking civil servant whose story I recounted in chapter 3, also noted the powerful importance of faith in her efforts to hold all of the pieces of life together. Raised Pentecostal but lapsed for much of her life, she has joined a new church and is an active member. As for many of the entrepreneurial women and men I encountered, this is where Madeline finds a sense of belonging. Interestingly, like virtually every woman entrepreneur I interviewed, she made a point of saying that "belonging" and "community" were not to be found in the realm of other professional and business organizations, "I *tried* that but I find they have their set of people they keep in there and don't allow anybody else to come in . . . they don't embrace you." Instead, it is in her church that she finds a network of friends and fellow business people from whom she gets emotional and other forms of support, "It helped me as a single parent, and in my business."

Nadia, a black Barbadian entrepreneur in her forties, whom I introduced in chapter 3, is the single mother of a grown daughter and owner of two successful women's boutiques on the island. When I asked who had been her biggest supporter in the course of starting and running her business, and who she could count on to back her up, she replied,

> I think God basically, I find that I don't have anyone to turn to but God. . . . When I have a problem that's who I kind of pray to, I pray about my problems. . . . I find sometimes when you share your difficulties with people they don't work because I find that there are negatives and positives . . . when you are positive, things happen better for you, when you share things sometimes that are very . . . that are like a challenge and you share with some person that is very negative, they apply so much negativity that you can't even see which direction to go in so why bother talking to people? I talk to God sometimes and he work it out for me, you know and I find even sometimes, before I go before the bank to ask certain things, I would sit down and I would pray about that situation and then I would go and I would say to the

bank exactly what I want . . . because you are so confused with different challenges you know you don't even, can't even think, you know, *and people can't do that for you, you have to do that for yourself because it is only you that know your commitments.*

For Nadia, one could interpret prayer, and her relationship directly with God, as expressive of a heightened independence and reflexivity. She attributes her temperament and inclination toward independence and self-reliance to having traveled abroad and being less insular or "homebodyish" than Bajans can often be. She says:

I try not to get too deep into people . . . and what they're doing, it can distract you. *I focus on me and what I'm about* and that's important and that is why a lot of people in Barbados I find especially women . . . they spend too much energy on the other person. *Spend that time on yourself and you would get so much done and so much within yourself to achieve* . . . if they only could do that little thing . . . because there is so much you can have here. People—foreigners—walk in and just own so much and do so much because they're focused and *they know what they're about* but I find like . . . when [Bajans] stay here, [it] is so small, the only thing they can concentrate on is somebody *else's business*, which is not the thing. You focus and know what you want and go for it and don't envy the other person because you can have that too! But they still haven't grasped that as yet.

Nadia is critiquing what Wilson described as "crab antics," the inclination to pull others down in one's own efforts to climb up, a quality frequently described among women, especially those striving for middle-class status.

The roots of religion run wide and deep in this Caribbean island, as have their creole forms, as Michel-Rolph Trouillot noted (1992, 24), "This is a region where Pentecostalism is as 'indigenous' as Rastafarianism, where some 'Bush Negroes' were Christians long before Texas became 'American,' where some 'East Indians' find peace in 'African' rituals of Shango." Today's growing middle-class Pentecostalism and the growth of new spiritual communities represent part of a long continuum of creolized and syncretic religious forms. What is of interest to our discussion here are the ways in which these new churches, spiritual communities, and forms of religious practice become expressive of many of the signature markers of neoliberalism that I have been examining throughout this work, in particular the injunction for individuals to "take charge" of their own lives, embrace the challenge to invent and reinvent themselves in response to the insecure marketplace, to reflect inward and to examine themselves, and, in effect, become both entrepreneurs in the marketplace and entrepreneurs of themselves in more personal and intimate ways. Further, churches increasingly offer lifestyle advice and counseling rooted not just in the spiritual domain, but in that of enterprise. Indeed, where the island's official Anglican Church has historically expressed precisely the order, hierarchy, and bureaucracy associated with the traditional ethic of *respectability*, I see these new forms of spiritual practice and new models of religious association as expressive of neoliberalism, and in essence, the upward mobility of *reputation*.

Barbados like the rest of the Afro-Caribbean has deep roots in an elaborate complex of churches originating with the mainline Anglicans from colonial days and a wide array of Methodist and Catholic, Seventh Day Adventist, and other churches spawned by missionaries traveling across the region. Where Anglican, Methodist, and Roman Catholic churches have long stood as institutional anchors of respectability for West Indian women and older men (Austin 1984, 103; Wilson 1973), some of the more participatory, charismatic Pentecostal churches have also been central in the lives of lower classes. As Austin (1984, 114) notes of Jamaica, and the West Indies more generally, "the dialogue between born-again and denominational . . . is not always but often a class dialogue between more and less affluent people." These patterns are now being remapped.

Early on in my fieldwork it became plain to me that religion and/or "faith in God" emerged prominently as entrepreneurs reflected upon their journeys, dreams, and challenges. I was introduced to unfamiliar churches, some with charismatic pastors, others more loosely organized in people's homes. Certainly anyone familiar with Caribbean societies would not be surprised to find religion to be prominent in Barbadian life. Indeed, the recent census makes clear that the Anglican Church, though appealing less to many of these middle-class entrepreneurs, still represents the largest single religious group nationally (70,705 of 250,000 or 28 percent) divided relatively evenly between women and men. Pentecostals rank next as a group with 19 percent of the population (7 percent of all men and 11 percent of all women), equaled by the percentage indicating no religious identification (twice as many men than women reported no religious affiliation, 11 percent versus 5 percent).

Notably, some of the new churches are distinctively middle-class congregations that appear to appeal especially to entrepreneurs. Over the past ten years, I have come to see that this appeal has many facets—from the practical and strategic to the spiritual. Entrepreneurialism figures prominently in both aspects. Their styles depart radically from the mainline churches within which many of their parishioners were raised. Many of the new churches reveal a marked shift from the traditional hierarchy, a relationship with the divine as mediated through priests and bishops to one in which individuals express highly reflexive relationships to God. They advocate speaking directly to the almighty, and allowing him to guide their actions in everyday life. Others, eschewing the structure of a church altogether, are increasingly drawn to alternative visions of faith, spirituality, and religious practice.

The explicit convergences in religious and therapeutic dimensions of entrepreneurs' current experiences are striking. For many, the desire to turn attention to the self, to nourish and care for themselves especially in times of trouble (financial difficulty, relationship difficulties, physical illness, and psychological strains) emerges as a part of a new regimen of health that self-consciously consists of both spiritual and physical dimensions. These quests lead many of them toward "faith" and the "spiritual" of a non-mainline sort. For Nadia, Lilliana, Jimmy, and Colleen, an invigorated religious sensibility is gained neither through the churches of their childhoods nor through participation in one of the burgeoning new Pentecostal or evangelical churches, but through a highly personal spirituality, a reflexive faith not mediated by a charismatic preacher, the hierarchical establishment of the mainline churches, or even the primacy of a divine being. Their spiritual sensibility echoes their entrepreneurial sensibility more generally, which begins with a sense of self-reliance, individual determination, and personal responsibility.[5] The notion, as Colleen put it, that "you are the boss over your life," "you take responsibility," lies at the heart of this faith, its integral kinship with an entrepreneurial selfhood, and the belief that God has provided the strength to meet these challenges and achieve success. Maureen, the owner of a popular spa and salon, remarked, "being an entrepreneur is something you are 'called' to do. . . . If you were 'called' to be an entrepreneur, then you were 'called' to serve others. You were 'called' to build a legacy." Spiritual references abound in her description of how she entered the work she does, and also in her interpretation of what draws people to her salon. She notes that just as Barbadians are increasingly looking for new and personal relationships with God through a variety of new churches, so too are the ministers of these churches offering more than just sermons on a pulpit: "People are looking for counseling . . . all kinds of personal counselling, and a lot of the religious people . . . a lot of these ministers . . . are doing that on the side . . . becoming therapists in some ways."

One aspect of the new middle-class churches that is instantly notable is the presence of couples and nuclear families seated together in the congregation. Whereas churches of all denominations are known to attract women of all ages, children, and old men (Wilson's definition of those most invested in respectability), the island's new middle-class churches emphasize and attract couples and nuclear families as central social units. The number of young and middle-aged couples attending all three of the middle-class churches I visited was as striking as the style of dress of those in attendance. Here, a casual neatness prevailed—from trendy "elegantly casual" to pressed T-shirts and "nice" jeans.[6] The pastors and musicians too departed from the robed and formal figures of traditional mainline and Pentecostal churches in their sporty attire and demeanor. A closely fitted polo shirt graced the athletic physique of one pastor, whose energetic sermon and soulful saxophone solo accented his impassioned glow. I heard about his church from an entrepreneur who described it as the "black middle-class version" of another largely white congregation founded by a prominent businessman.

The church was founded in 2001 by an American pastor and his Barbadian wife and combined familiar qualities of charismatic churches described by Harrison (2005)—bold and aggressive messages, vibrant music (his saxophone features powerfully), and appealing visuals projected up onto a large screen. Congregants, especially women, are seized with religious fervour and drop to the floor, hands raised, eyes closed, calling to the almighty; some speak in tongues, as does the pastor. Row by row, members of the congregation rise to make their offerings publicly in baskets at the front of the church. On the morning of my visit, the sermon centered on a story about a leaking house—an analogy of the church whose parishioners were drifting away. A sophisticated website with downloadable podcasts as well as print versions of key points from sermons are readily available, along with links to the many ministries within the church: a "worship team" and special groups for singles, youth, men, and women, a dance group, drama group, marriage or couples therapy, a business alliance, and numerous other specialty seminars.

The underpinnings of entrepreneurship and the neoliberal emphasis on individual self-mastery, self-invention, and flexibility are unmistakable, melding faith and worship to business, individual responsibility, and tithing. Special seminars in business and commands to "*take* it! *take* what is *yours!*" are echoed passionately from the pulpit. The pastor proclaims his pride in being a "prosperity preacher" despite the criticisms some have mounted toward such an approach. Tithing is key and not left to vague understanding. Both the website and PowerPoint slides outline its goals:

> Tithing: Giving the first 10 percent of my income back to God. The reason: "Where your treasure is, there your heart is also" Matt 6:21. "The purpose of tithing is to teach you to always put God first in your life" Deut 14:23. The routine: On the first day of every week, set aside some of what you have earned and give it as an offering. "The amount depends on how much the Lord has helped you earn" I Cor 16:2. "Bring your whole tithe into My storehouse. Test Me in this, says the Lord and see if I won't throw open the floodgates of heaven and pour out so much blessing that you won't have room for it!"

The pastor's wife blogs on the church's website, "Dress for Success—And Keep your Clothes On." Her leadership of "Pillars of the Palace" for women includes a weekly radio broadcast called *The Tiara Show*, marriage and family counselling, and "personality training." She offers a "Personali-Tea Party" to workplaces and women's clubs, "Personality Portraits for Parents" in which the church provides corporate coaching—half- and full-day seminars offered to businesses interested in enhancing "diversity" and "team building" en route to increasing productivity.

The church's Business Alliance holds meetings at local restaurants, and seminars about such themes as "managing cash flow." In his sermon, the charismatic pastor mentions his own ethnic mixture—African American and Chinese—and that he is happily married to a black Barbadian and has three young sons. Interestingly, when I attended this new church its services were held, like that of its predominantly white, middle-class counterpart church, in what used to be a plantation yard—the factory and sugar mill still prominently surrounding the amphitheater in which the congregation gathers. Enlargements of old black-and-white photos of Barbados life—the port, plantations, and Bridgetown street scenes—adorn the walls of the open-air stage and seating area; a large toad hopped over my sandaled feet during the service. I attended the service with Pauline, a Catholic woman in middle age who enjoys visiting different churches and who was eager to see what this new pastor was offering. The drive from town took us through the middle of the country, surrounded by cane fields and through villages and new suburban housing developments. Not the first time we had attended church together, I was struck by the disapproving glance I received when she observed my attire—a floral cotton skirt and sleeveless fitted top, modest-heeled and open-toed sandals.

She, by contrast, was impressively adorned in what I recognized to be traditional church attire: flouncy synthetic dress, tiered with tasteful ruffles, three-quarter length sleeves, high-heeled sandals, and a matching handbag in which she carried her personal leather-bound Bible. She said nothing of my dress, but I was familiar with the fleeting critical glance. Upon our arrival, Pauline was even more dismayed by the appearance of the congregants. She pronounced her disapproval, "showing up like that, and on God's day!" but in time, was moved by the service, shook hands with our neighbors, some of whom she recognized, and in the end she liked the pastor's fervor and style.

Notably, the "faith" message as espoused in many of these new churches is a relational message, as Harrison notes in his study of the African American World of Faith church, formed in direct contrast to that of the mainline denominations. Entrepreneurs frequently described to me the quest for "something different," a spiritual experience that spoke to them outside of the formality of the churches of their childhood. Many of them, especially women, describe a process in which they have "moved around from church to church," listened to one pastor and another, careful consumers in search of a special rapport, an individual relationship with the pastor and a connection to a particular congregation and style of worship.

A prominent Anglican priest I interviewed described in critical and frustrated terms what he saw as the manipulative appeal of popular music and drumming over doctrinal substance and the traditions of the Anglican Church. Indeed, many of the young entrepreneurs I spoke with mentioned the music and participatory aspects of their new churches as a significant part of their attraction. The sophisticated sound systems and high-tech delivery of hymns, biblical passages, and bulleted sermon points projected onto large screens with beautiful and soothing images of the sea, blue skies, a rainbow, not to mention, as was the case in one of the churches, the concert-level performance of the saxophone playing pastor, add dimensions that contrast markedly with the staid and more sombre tone of the mainline churches. The appeal of these new churches is manifold—the music, the message, the casually respectable but comfortable style, the palpable participatory *feeling* of it all, the open and casual physical space, sense of familiarity, and hominess.

These new middle-class churches were appealing to entrepreneurs and others, however, not solely because of their theatrical sermons and popular music. The emphasis on marriage, for example, was not simply presented as a sacred institution endorsed by the church, but an intimate relationship, a partnership, just as I heard over and over again by the entrepreneurs dreaming of or attempting to enact these new forms. Again, this partnership, like a business partnership, was described as a relationship in need of nurturing, care, emotional attunement, all conveyed as hard *work*. An emphasis on the *work* entailed to keep a marriage alive (listening to one's spouse, arranging child care to foster intimacy and time together) and the *work* of being a responsible and caring parent are among the subjects of special pastoral seminars and sermons. The new therapeutic ethic permeated the church service as well as the many associated workshops, seminars, and counseling forums, emphasizing both the project of the self and the labors of self-care and the care of others. The notion that these relationships require work in itself is not new. When one considers the heavy load women and men have born throughout Barbadian history to support their children and households, there is no question of the importance of their labor. On the other hand, the nature of this work, as it is being described and celebrated, includes elements that are distinct, namely the centrality of emotional attunement. Women and men are urged to listen to each other, think of each other's feelings, and value each other for their different roles. Mothers and fathers are entreated not just to "mind" their children, discipline them, and provide for them materially, but also to nurture their spirit of loving kindness and self-esteem. Individuals are prompted to look inside themselves, believe in their self-worth and pursue their hearts' desires.

Over several years, I found myself repeatedly jotting the phrase "born-again" in the margins of my interview notes. Though not a focus I had anticipated, the significance of new forms of faith and religious practice was undeniable. Lisa, a cosmetologist, pronounced with some degree of cynicism, "Haven't you heard? God is a new trend these days!" Among the educated middle-classes in Barbados, "God is cool!" As Queenie, an architect, described it, "when I started the company I had a definite . . . whatever you want to call it, word from God." With striking frequency, many others mention "God's hand" in their entrepreneurial quest—the notion that they were being guided and supported in the risky endeavors by the divine. Queenie described herself as a "born-again" stating boldly that "religion is a huge part" of her. At each stage of her life, she recounted critical junctures that called for faith and spiritual guidance. When she was unhappy in her job, she said God spoke to her and gave her the courage to move on, "I felt it was right to do it because I'd heard from God so I went with it. [I] felt . . . protected." She currently tithes 10 percent of her income to her church. An educated professional woman from a middle-class black Barbadian family, and owner of a successful firm, she noted that while raised in the Methodist Church she has "tried out" many others, both in Barbados and in London when she was studying abroad: "Where ever there is a church that I like I'll go to it." When her work schedule wouldn't permit her to attend services at a Methodist church on Sundays, she joined a home-based church held in the "homes of other educated middle class folks" like herself. This experimentation and fluid participation in a range of spiritual communities and churches was a common practice.

Queenie's faith has several dimensions, both private and collective. On one hand, her individual relationship with God guides her in her life, as a mother, employer, wife, and business owner. On the other, her involvement in a sequence of churches has also connected her closely with other middle-class professionals who have become friends as well as business associates. "I went to Bible Study" she says, "'cause I knew I was going to get work. And I did!" Eric, a dynamic young entrepreneur, also launched his graphics design business through what he described as his "alternative" church. Thirty when I met him, and "very single," as he described himself, he was almost buzzing with entrepreneurial zeal and a palpable confidence. He got into his business as a multimedia designer through the inspiration and support of his pastor in what he described as his "post-Pentecostal" and "post-charismatic" church. When Eric began designing the PowerPoint presentations for his pastor's sermons, he generated a great deal of enthusiasm and business interest among other parishioners and has since won contracts for major government projects and private sector presentations. His involvement in this spiritual orbit and his vision for his businesses are tightly woven into one discourse that bears clear traces of neoliberal and therapeutic culture. He explained the basic orientation of his church by saying, "we look at changing the whole nation . . . we pray for the nation . . . it's about teaching people how to actually live . . . in the workplace, at home, and in families . . . how to be a good business person, and how to actually make your business work." Entrepreneurial networks and the entrepreneurial esprit of new churches and spiritual groups serve to connect people as service providers, clients, and customers and to lend a modern, informal, multimedia feel to religious services and religious communities more generally. These new churches also preach an explicitly entrepreneurial message.

The role of Christian religion as a domain in which Caribbean people, especially women, engage in creative expression as well as conform to order, hierarchy, and hegemonic ideologies has been well noted ethnographically (Austin-Broos 1998). Churches of all denominations offer black and white women of all classes venues for spiritual uplift, social support, charitable voluntarism. Indeed, many of the Barbadian women I have gotten to know over the past twenty years enjoy attending church services not only in their own congregations but also in those of friends and work associates, much as middle-class women elsewhere might try out each other's yoga classes, book groups, or favorite cafes. Exploring other styles of worship, charismatic preachers, as well as the manner of dress, and styles of music, PowerPoint presentations, and congregational modes of participation (public testifying, making offerings, speaking in tongues, singing, etc.) are among the pleasures of these visits. Indeed, it is in the exploration of other churches and modes of worship that many of the entrepreneurs, both black and white, men and women, described for me their recent migrations from the "stiff," hierarchical, and formal qualities of the churches of their upbringing (Catholic, Anglican, etc.) and their new-found pleasure and comfort with a more "modern" style of participation. The entrepreneurial dimensions of such experimentations and explorations are striking—the flexibility in trying out new pastors and new congregations, seeking some forms of reward and benefit from a number of congregations and venues, and tapping into these for advice, inspiration, and potential clients for their own businesses. Entrepreneurs were drawn to new spheres of religions and spiritual practice, and I came to see that these religious and spiritual ventures drew heavily upon themes of entrepreneurship.

During more than a decade of fieldwork, the prominence of religion, faith in God, alternative forms of spirituality, and a variety of new churches, like those mentioned above, became so notable that I found myself attending services along with some of my informants, curious about their appeal and distinction from traditional churches. Immediately striking was the middle-classness of these congregations. Their physical location, the spaces of worship, and the general ambiance of the gatherings all departed dramatically from the formal mainline churches on the island. Far from the "parish church" tradition, in which planters and villagers alike attended the same church (most on foot), today middle-class people with cars travel easily across the island, choosing from a wide array of religious options. Whether in living room churches, large Pentecostal revivals, individual sessions with pastor-counsellors, or in purely personalized prayer, women and men articulate a desire for self-reflection and self-actualization that diverge from what they see as "traditional" religious practice and ritual. The connections between these changing spheres of religious and spiritual life and a surge of new "therapeutic" practices that are burgeoning in

Barbados today illustrate the intensely affective dimensions of contemporary neoliberalism.

For Queenie, the sudden break-up of a long-term romance several years before we met had left her severely depressed, and at the advice of a friend, she sought the help of a psychiatrist.

> Again, it was one of those God decisions, a friend was pushing me and I was saying like "nah" and then I realized that I was praying to God and I realized I had to go and do this, and God was saying, "you know you gotta go and sort it out," so . . . I did and, umm, one of the things that came up was forgiving my ex-boyfriend. He [the psychiatrist] had me in there twice a week, sometimes three times a week cause he said "oh you've got a lot of stuff to deal with" and I tell you it was . . . it was very . . . it was valuable, because not only did I deal with that, *I dealt with myself* and I learnt *who I was*. I learnt where my weaknesses were, where my strengths were, and that helps me with my business. It was actually very good for me, I had some very close friends [in Bible study], one of them was my psychiatrist and he was brilliant, we became very good friends.

The new middle-class churches illustrate the astonishing reach of entrepreneurialism and the neoliberal ethic and the intertwining of spirit and entrepreneurial economy in the contemporary age. One of these churches, founded by a prominent local white businessman, attracts a predominantly white congregation. Set within the same former sugar plantation yard, I visited this church with Justine, a lively and successful thirty-five-year-old entrepreneur, who described herself as having been interested in "finding a spiritual community." She had visited one of the other churches I allude to above and has been approached often by members of this church to come and join. She does a lot of business with one of its founding members and, while curious, has also not wanted to jeopardize her productive business relationship by mixing work and religion. A white Barbadian daughter of a prominent businessman, Justine is attuned to the social and business networks created through church affiliation and pointed out several members of the congregation whom she recognized. Some were "former druggies." The service was set in the open-air amphitheater created out of an old sugar mill structure. The evening was warm, and people were dressed in the familiar casual and trendy clothes. Several men were on their own, others in couples, some looked bored but dutiful. Children had been left in child care rooms close-by, and a few toddlers, babies, and teens remained with their parents in the pews. Justine commented about the striking number of couples—something less evident across other Barbadian churches where congregations are overwhelmingly female and women find companionship and support from each other. Roughly 250 to 300 people filled the pews; they were overwhelmingly white, with the exception of a few interracial couples. A group of young people sang and the congregation joined in the singing and clapping and swaying with eyes closed. Later, the service was projected in PowerPoint on a large screen. The collection basket was passed up and down each row, and twenties and fifties filled it up (I was instructed by Justine in advance to bring at least a twenty-dollar bill for the collection plate).

Over dinner in a seaside café afterward, Justine talked about the service and about the appeal of these churches to growing numbers of people. A witty impersonator, she jokingly repeated many of the ardent phrases and passionate gestures from the evening's sermon. In her comical performance, she expressed a combination of skepticism and desire for some kind of spiritual experience and sense of belonging. Unhappily married and the mother of two school-aged children, Justine's tenacious work habits and unflappable determination were remarkable. Her days typically began before sunrise and entailed hardscrabble negotiating and the management of unskilled laborers and temperamental foreign clients. Over several years I witnessed the tremendous growth of her company alongside the unraveling of her marriage and her health. We discussed the intractability of her marriage, her mother's advice to leave her husband, her father's advice to stay, and the simultaneous booming success of her company. She related a story of her recent visit to a psychiatrist following her second or third panic attack and was visibly worried about her health. After several sessions with this doctor she had begun to feel better. He had prescribed a mild antianxiety medication, and she was responding well to this treatment. At the end of their last session, however, she was shocked by his suggestion that she "find her faith in Jesus." Even more disturbing was his conclusion: that she "would never be cured" until she did so. Justine was furious, saying she had "gone to him as a *medical* doctor and not for religion." However, the intermingling of religion, medicine, therapeutic culture, and entrepreneurialism today is so pervasive that their methods as well as practitioners converge and disentangling them is often difficult. One finds entrepreneurial advice in sermons, clients among fellow congregants, and spiritual guidance in medical offices. Equally, one finds emotional comfort and empathy in commercial services, and self-understanding is fostered and required in all of the above.

The appeal of these new churches has not been lost on the leaders of the mainline congregations. One senior Anglican priest I interviewed described them disdainfully as "yet another cheap import from America," "particularly from hillbillies in the South. People don't want to think," he said, "the Pentecostals give them a simplistic religion . . . the Pentecostals preach an Old Testament religion, and the Old Testament religion is sub-Christian." He conceded that where the Anglican Church has gone wrong, and where the Pentecostal Church has gained in favor, is in the appeal of popular music, especially to young people: "the music, I think, carries them there, whereas we got stuck in this Anglican tradition of Anglican chants and so on. . . ." While his antipathy for these new churches was palpable, he did concede their strong appeal: "People go home feeling better, they all tell you that, they go home feeling better from these [new] churches. I think it has to do with the . . . upbeat music." The entrepreneurial connections, he noted, are not solely to be found in the pews but also in the nature of the religious enterprise of the new churches themselves. "These are big businesses!" he said.

The "business" aspect of these churches held complex and contradictory meanings. For some it marked their illegitimacy as loci of faith and "real" religiosity, for others no such contradiction was clear. The pastor of another recently founded middle-class church recounted the following in an interview:

> Most of us had come through the fun teenage years of partying . . . enjoying life, most were university educated, and had come to a place and wanted more to their spiritual life. . . . You know the term *born-again*? . . . I don't like it, but it is true, revitalized, people finding a real personal relationship with Christ . . . people searching for more meaning in their life. . . . Most came from the Anglican or Catholic Church—most had drifted and were not actively attending. They were not making faith real, relevant. Those forms of worship were not touching the heartstrings of people. The music is part of it, but not alone, something deeper, touching the core of people. Everybody is different but for the majority, the mundane, disenchantment, boredom, there must be more to life. . . . I believe that deep in the heart of every person, is some yearning to find . . . the purpose of life—people are looking for hope, inner strength. This world is changing so fast—maybe a drug problem, maybe others lost their job, or just the happy couple with

kids want to refocus their life—I just know there is a resurgence of interest in faith, with all the trappings of religion aside, and looking for something deeper.

He commented on the close relationship between his church and the mission of many of his entrepreneurial congregants: "The entrepreneurial spirit is . . . in my personal belief, a God-inspired wonderful thing. . . . I feel there is a great link between faith and business. . . . *True faith* translates into tangible change around you. . . . God wants successful business-people to be a light—people *admire* successful business people so they have a platform to speak the message of Christ. [In days gone by] *professional* people were looked at as the gurus; today it's the *business* people and the athletes—and these are speaking out their faith."

I see these new practices and their associated affective dimensions as integrally tied to the neoliberal cultural-economy of flexibility and a changing social order. They reflect a new ethos of living, working, partnering, parenting, and self-definition that for many also bear unmistakable spiritual elements. Weber offered a compelling frame for an older order spirit of capitalist rationality and asceticism (1930). Building upon Weber's exploration, Boltanski and Chiapello (2004:155) suggest that in the mid-twentieth century a new spirit of capitalism hinged upon "responsibility and knowledge" that "places a premium on *activity* without any clear distinction between personal or even leisure activity and professional activity." How might we interpret these new religious and therapeutic discourses and practices that foreground prosperity and individualism and eschew some of the traditional markers of Protestant restraint and respectability that have long been associated with the Barbadian middle class?

Victoria Wolcott (2001) describes the interclass tensions surrounding respectability in the realms of work, home life, and religion in the nineteenth-century premigration American South. In the name of social uplift, and with an emphasis on bourgeois respectability, she says, certain forms and expressions of religion came under scrutiny and attack. She raises an important distinction that is seldom drawn explicitly in the Caribbean context in which the respectability-reputation paradigm has retained such powerful force. For Wolcott, the distinction between African American women in the mainline churches who aspire toward respectability do so as a demonstration of moral worth and purity that holds *public sway*. For the charismatic worshippers engaged in the ecstatic practices of the newer denominations, though their forms of religiosity are frowned upon as unladylike in the wider public domain, their achievement of *self-respect* through individualized spiritual uplift offsets any loss of status they might have endured by those advocating respectability through self-restraint. Indeed, Wolcott argues that one of the dimensions of the Sanctified Church that most attracted African American women was precisely the possibility of attaining status that was otherwise off-limits to them in the established churches. Not only were all members able to achieve the status of "saints" through worship but women could also become preachers within their congregations. Significantly, for these African American women, religious identity was more rooted in *self-respect* than in more middle-class expressions of refined *respectability*. Further demonstrating an intriguing balance of respectability and self-respect was the role of music and drumming within the newer ecstatic churches, since women were able to enjoy and participate in this emerging terrain of blues and jazz without physically entering the tainted and nonrespectable domain of saloons or jook joints (Wolcott 2001, 35). In addition to possession and ecstatic practices, music and drumming were critical dimensions of the newer churches that distinguished them from the more refined and established ones. For both black and white Barbadian women entrepreneurs, the appeal of newer middle-class churches, which meld participatory and more informal means by which to shore up their intimate partnerships, nuclearized families, and themselves as independent, self-reflexive agents, fits squarely into the entrepreneurial landscape of self-improvement, flexibility, and a gradual redefinition of respectability itself.

Weber argued that the Protestant (and especially Calvinist) ethics of asceticism, thrift, and hard work constituted the underlying esprit for the development of capitalism in the West, and both he and Marx characterized "mature capitalism" as coincident with *de*-sacralization, a world of technological rationality, which, as Marx said, "drowned the most heavenly ecstasies of religious fervor, of chivalrous enthusiasm, of philistine sentimentalism in the icy water of egoistic calculation" (qtd. in Giddens 1971, 215). At the same time, the pairing of evangelism with the promise of riches, as bespeaks today's "prosperity gospel," is deeply rooted in American cultural history.[7] While many have since debated the "secularization" thesis of modernity (Meyer 2004), it is worth emphasizing the connections between the shifting spiritual and entrepreneurial tides under the rubric of contemporary neoliberalism, and their culturally particular meanings. Such new articulations of economic, personal, and spiritual self making are integral to the neoliberal esprit as they take shape in the Barbadian milieu. A new sacralizing of economic activity is at play, one that Weber might not have anticipated for the growth of advanced capitalism. The particular expression and form of the sacred has also shifted dramatically. Where once the Anglican Church was a primary arbiter of respectability among middle-class Barbadians, today these alternative churches as well as non-church-based modes of spiritual engagement perform these and a host of other roles. By fostering intimate partnerships, new modes of emotional parenting, and a model of selfhood steeped in a language of affect and reflexive, elastic self-understanding, entrepreneurialism moves out of the oppositional realm of reputation and becomes mobilized not simply for economic livelihood but for every aspect of middle-class life and subjective experience. In so doing, the boundaries of respectability are being loosened and redefined; the therapeutic ethic and the spirit of entrepreneurialism become flexibly aligned to manage both the pleasures and alienation wrought by neoliberalism.

Conclusion

I return to Foucault's (1989, 9) prescient words with which I began. For, just as this book took a direction unknown to me at the outset, so too are the women and men I have briefly introduced charting new and unexpected paths of work, self-exploration and discovery. Their entrepreneurial journeys span the market and the private spheres: they highlight an increasingly ambiguous and intertwining relationship of labor and life, work and subjectivity, as affective labor and affective life become heightened throughout. These trajectories led me into unexpected territory both empirically and theoretically, from traditional businesses to new charismatic churches and venues for leisure and holistic healing, from political economy to affect theory and the anthropology of emotion. In some sense the explorations bring together two strands of inquiry that I have long kept separate in my own thinking—the political economy tradition in which I was trained, and the psychological habitus, in which I was raised. This separation has been comfortably upheld for some twenty years in which I have worked on this small, respectable, conservative island. The theoretical toolkits of Marx, Foucault, and Bourdieu were well suited to interpreting the twists and turns of late capitalism, and I knew to keep any psychological leanings under wraps in a culture more at home with structural relations of power and position than matters of subjectivity and interiority.

For the entrepreneurs whose stories I have collected and lives I have observed, these new paths are not individual quests alone; they are part of a larger social, cultural, and political story. They reflect dramatic structural shifts in a global, regional, and national economy, such that the traditional anchors of employment and growth (sugar for unskilled labor and the civil service for the academically inclined) have yielded to services and related enterprises: tourism and hospitality, financial services, and the mandate for as wide a range of entrepreneurial undertakings as possible. These are familiar signs of neoliberalism. The global financial crisis has hit Barbados hard. Some say the economy has not been this fragile since the Second World War. One radio caller recently noted with alarm that "even white people are taking things *out of their baskets* at the supermarket." With mounting economic insecurity, the entrepreneurial imperative is likely to become even stronger. There are dimensions to these structural transformations that, while equally expressive of a neo-liberal signature, I found harder to interpret, as they fell so far from the traditional frameworks of political economy in Caribbean studies. The co-nundrum is best understood as capitalism's "affective turn," a turn that reminds us that to understand change one must return to history and the rich detail of cultural specificity. To understand economy and structure, one must also look to the emotional registers of social relations and self-understandings. For the crux of neoliberal entrepreneurialism, as I see it, lies in the blurred boundaries between enterprise-as-business and the self (or child, or couple)-as-enterprise, between social relations of business and intimate economies of love and support.

An exploration of entrepreneurship as a means for a new middle-class livelihood led to an equal focus upon kinship, selfhood, and a return to some old chestnuts of Caribbean studies: matrifocality, reputation, and respectability. In so doing, these convergences elucidate not just social and economic transformation via external market forces of neoliberalism—the ways in which the local is transformed by the global—but also a new way of understanding neoliberalism as malleable within specific cultural and geographical contexts. In essence these "local" Caribbean formulations of social practice, labor, and economy—reputation and matrifocality—pro-vide indispensable tools with which to enact life and selfhood in insecure times. Scholars and all people of the Caribbean have long been aware of this fact. What they may not have imagined is that these transformations could become instructive and illuminating for the wider world.

For new entrepreneurs, women and men of all races, whether solidly or anxiously middle class, the converging logics of reputational flexibility and neoliberal flexibility offer tools with which to create new enterprises, form new social and intimate bonds, and envision new selves. Where once entrepreneurship was a mechanism of survival for the poor securely in the orbit of reputation, it has now become both a mandate and an impetus for an alternative form of middle-class respectability. But what is especially fascinating about the "upward mobility" of these long-standing traditions is that the linchpin of these flexible, resourceful practices is found in the growing significance of affect as a site of labor and exchange, whether intimate, inward looking, or public and market based. Again, while it might be tempting to read the growth of this "emotional capitalism" as a Caribbean ripple in the high seas of globalization, such a reading, like that of neoliberal flexibility, would be hasty, partial, and miss what is perhaps most important about neoliberalism's "exceptionalism" (Ong 2006; Freeman 2007).

Under Barbadian neoliberalism, cultural practices that have historically been tools of opposition and resistance to the hegemony of capitalist rationality, bureaucracy, and expansion are now brought squarely into its fold. As they become "upwardly mobile," we see not only how closely they resemble the goals of neoliberal capitalist orthodoxy today but also how they actively redefine the formerly constricting shape of respectability. But the old concepts and formulations of matrifocality and reputation do not go far enough, for they are so embedded within traditional idioms of economy and support that they fail to capture the true *spirit* of these times: the means by which feelings and the exchange of emotion is itself a form of value in both the formal marketplace and outside it. This may be one of the most critical dimensions of neoliberal capitalism today.

A tension between a seemingly "global" discourse and a distinctively Bajan dialect reverberates through this account. For the logics of neoliberalism and those of Caribbean reputation are similar, but their entanglement produces new meanings out of reminiscent forms. What at first glance appear as echos of "global," "middle-class," and "neoliberal" culture and economy must be read otherwise. Discourses of entrepreneurialism permeate space and time: the marketplace and the pulpit, the service counter, schoolroom, living room, massage table, wine-bar date-night, 'quality' family-time, and the therapeutic hour. Meanwhile, for all that sounds and looks familiar, there are accents and permutations that are critically distinct. Indeed, the differences are not simply a matter of concentration or dilution. Neoliberalism takes a Caribbean form, and in turn, the signatures of reputation are reworked and mobilized in its interest.

The rationalization and commodification of affects, as we have seen especially in the realm of services, bring added burdens of labor and at the same time the capacity for defining and asserting the self in pleasurable and meaningful new ways. The contradictoriness is a critical dimension that must be highlighted along with the cultural particularities. As the exchange of affects becomes increasingly required within market relations, these become equally sought and scrutinized within intimate relations. The premium placed upon affects as commodifiable has multiple and contradictory effects.

The new language of affect, and the seductive pull toward emotional experience and expression provides one of the tools by which the neoliberal logic of flexibility achieves its ends. Entrepreneurial flexibility is articulated as a means by which to "be one's own boss," not only controlling work hours, conditions of labor, and other structural dimensions of work but also one's *feelings* about work itself, its reflection of the self, a means by which to actualize and materialize one's personhood. Subjective desires for flexibility become invisibly soldered to objective, extractive forces of neoliberalism through a powerful and subjective discourse of choice and individualism. They are equally embedded within historical and cultural traditions of political economy, labor, *and* affect. So weighty is the affective investment behind these notions of self-mastery and self-realization that the notion that these desires have anything but a personal dimension to them is easily lost. At the same time, as both owner and worker, the entrepreneur readily subjects herself to exploitative conditions of overwork since it is both the enterprise and herself she is always laboring to produce.

The contemporary inducements for individuals to be malleable agents in the marketplace, constantly seizing opportunities to retool and retrain themselves as flexible entrepreneurial subjects, is one of the most striking dimensions of contemporary neoliberalism. At the same time, these very qualities of flexible adaptability (and their expression in not just economic spheres of work but also in other spheres of life, including sexuality, kinship, parenting, leisure and expressive cultural forms of music, story-telling, joking, etc.) lie at the core of Caribbean culture and its highly masculinized value complex of reputation. Throughout this book, my goal has been to signal these convergent logics of flexibility as emblematic of the distinctiveness of Barbadian neoliberalism. But it isn't just the convergence of these two logics that is at stake. They are weighted with different affective resonances that are also gendered. If reputational flexibility (regardless of whether men or women perform it) bears a masculine profile, neoliberal flexibility is, in many ways, decidedly feminine—imbued with a willingness to constantly adapt to change, to "make do," often by mobilizing a reserve of emotions. Flexibility then implies not just occupational multiplicity and the familiar juggling of "productive" and "reproductive" work with the help of extended kin or paid domestic workers. The kinds of flexibility sought by many of these women entrepreneurs entail not only their entrance into the risky public spaces of reputation—the street, the airport, the port, the showroom, conference stage, political platform and so on—but also reconstituting reputational sociability through intimate, emotional recognition and expression. If "maliciousness," gossip, banter, and innuendo mark the discursive tradition of the market and the manner by which upward mobility and the hint of "uppity" superiority have historically been kept in check, the search for intimate understanding and emotional salve turn the tides of affect and trajectories of class in a new direction. Illusory and disappointed as these emotional ideals might be in practice, the very fact that they are actively imagined, articulated, demanded, and nourished in certain new market and popular cultural spheres, hints at a dramatic and risky change in the current cultural milieu. Lilliana's trajectory from the bedrock of plantation respectability to entrepreneurial self making illustrates the profound changes afoot both structurally and emotionally. As she described both her work and her then fragile marriage, she noted, "I guess my expectations are very different from my parents' generation . . . I could not live the life my mother lives . . . and I don't want that for my daughter. I wish her to be financially independent so that she does not have to compromise her dreams, to be educated and hopefully go into a field where she's happy and able to support herself and doesn't have to be dependent on anybody else. I want my marriage to be *everything*, and I think about it in that way; I want it to be spiritual, physical, social, and mental, you know, as parents, as equals, as professionals, on every level. I want to be successful and growing and deepening as a person." The precariousness of life—reflected in rising costs of living and the instability of her business, divorce, parents' ill health, and the struggle to support her children—prompts Lilliana to be flexible and enterprising in seeking out new market niches and new paths of self-reflection and intimacy, as well as physical, spiritual, and professional growth. Each presents novel imaginings, experiences, and risks.

That entrepreneurship entails risk is well understood. Equally universal, it has seemed, women are portrayed as more conservative and "risk-averse" than men. Indeed, among Barbadian entrepreneurs, the cautious manner in which women secured financing and "grew" their enterprises was a self-conscious distinction noted by almost everyone I interviewed. However, the nature of risk today takes new and more diffuse forms. The affective dimensions of entrepreneurialism may thus be among the riskiest aspects of these undertakings. For women, especially, along with stepping into the public domain of the market as independent business people, they are engaging in modes of public and private interaction that have little cultural precedent. The affective layer of entrepreneurial life pushes the boundaries of reputation beyond the social critique of the calypsonian and the savvy erudition of the higgler or street-corner politician into new realms. Perhaps we will start to see its effects in not only new therapeutic enterprises, the new café culture and couple-oriented social spheres, but also in newly creolized cultural forms that blend familiar elements of acerbic humor and social commentary with lyrics of self-reflection, love, and intimacy.

Entrepreneurialism implies observably new structural arrangements of work and life and subtle new subjectivities in formation. The intensity of a new structure of feeling, a neoliberal emphasis on emotion, intimacy, and the introspective self is, I think, a critical marker of these times. These desires are meaningful in both enriching and disciplining ways; they represent both newly sought pleasures and burdens; they can unleash new desires and also become sources of alienation.

How far these intertwining labors seem from Marx's premise of the separation of public and private spheres that was central to his notion of alienation and estranged labor. The entrepreneurial "selves" I have described bear no such separations; seldom do they leave their work behind when they are "at home," and equally, in the course of conducting their businesses they juggle the affective labor of their families, partners, and social networks. For entrepreneurs the language of business is also the language of self-development, the language of family, and of intimacy, each of which is conceived as parts of the entrepreneurial project. These modes of labor become inextricable from their affective skills and subjectivities at work. Such exchanges are not only integral to the conduct of many of their service enterprises in the marketplace—in offering individualized care and concern, insight, personal rapport, and memory—they are also fueled by, and in competition with, affects exchanged outside the market, in life and relationships more broadly. They are the very fabric of the way in which life is being lived, the emotional air being breathed and the quality of interactions, exchanges, and subjective senses of self that are being transformed. Especially intriguing is that the labors performed in service arenas, like the new wine bars and therapeutic salons and clinics, rather than simply depleting or straining the reservoir of emotional energy from the private domestic sphere, are providing recognition of these forms as *valuable*. The value of affects and importance of affective exchange in the marketplace extends to and resounds across private life. While intimacy, care, and support have long been understood in relation to (and in a bargaining exchange for) sex, these may actually be converging with, perhaps even enhancing the importance of, affective desires, experience, and hence, affective labor in private or non-market relations and life.

I have been intent to show that the neoliberal thrust toward entrepreneurship encompasses more than just economy and business in a narrow sense. However, the fact that it *is self-employment* and *business enterprise* that fuel such widespread optimism and expectation among development agencies, officials, and the NGO sector today should not be lost. Where export processing (microcomputer chip assembly, informatics, etc.) was widely seen as the panacea for economic growth and development only twenty years ago, today it is entrepreneurship at all levels that occupies the space of hope. From the euphoria surrounding microenterprise to the growing focus on "small to medium-sized enterprise," or SMES, *business* ownership is being touted from all corners as a neoliberal solution to a precarious global economy. These promises and expectations for self-employment and entrepreneurialism are deemed all the more pronounced for *women*. Kristof and WuDunn's *Half the Sky* (2010) and other such accounts have been wildly successful in the popular domain in part because they offer a seductively simple narrative about women's supposedly inherent altruism and capacity to save, invest, and manage income-generating enterprises alongside their traditionally prescribed domestic duties as mothers and wives. In past centuries when women's labor has been central to particular economic niches (the mills and factories of nineteenth-century textile industries, for example, or the microcomputer chip assembly plants of the late twentieth century), it has been primarily the meticulous physical dexterity and temperamental qualities of patience and calm compliance that have been naturalized as "feminine" and deemed well suited to these forms of low-waged work. Here, the "feminization" of their labor hinged upon the nature of these jobs themselves.

Today, however, in the niches of entrepreneurship and the tremendous growth in microenterprise in particular, the feminine profile attached to this highly profitable sphere of lending rests as much upon these agents' "nonwork" capacities as it does upon their formal industriousness. In other words, women are increasingly portrayed as the de facto and indeed the ideal backbone of the global economy *because they can juggle it all*—the business of the marketplace *and* the social reproduction of their households and families. Many of the contradictions and ironies about the naturalizing of women's suitability in these spheres and their purportedly exceptional promise as panaceas to ailing national economies echo across widely diverse spheres—from the electronically mediated domains of corporations to the hustle-bustle of street market vendors. Across them all, again, *flexibility* and the capacity to combine domestic and market-oriented work, labors of care, nurturance, and love lie at the heart of the story. What is not often made clear, whether deliberately obfuscated or more benignly unexamined, is that these extraordinary capacities for flexibility are neither natural nor reducible to a seemingly liberated individual *choice*. Flexibility is actively cultivated, coerced, and extracted in the interests of many other parties—the state, which might otherwise be faced with provision of some of these supports, and the capitalist market more generally. What has become increasingly complicated about the work-life rhetoric and the neoliberal politics of flexibility is that recently women's self-expressed desires for flexibility, which include not just the practical combinations of paid and unpaid work, formal sector jobs and informal economic activities, family, leisure, self-fulfillment, recognition, and intimacy, have gotten bundled into the same packaging. Subtly at the core of these convergences and bundles is the prominence of affective labor.

This affective turn suggests a sea change in capitalism. Its growth is perhaps most profound among the middle classes—whether in the United States, Europe, China, India, or the small island of Barbados. And as service workers and entrepreneurs are charged with new modes of interior, self-reflexive work, as well as the delivery and exchange of affective labor, these transformations require new analytical tools. For not only are markets and products and services being refashioned and realigned, so too are gender, class, cultural, and racial subjectivities being reconstituted through them. Here I see both intriguing opportunities and troubling foreclosures. For if feminist analyses of the long devalued feminine realm of reproductive labor have provided the groundwork for analyzing immaterial, and in particular, affective labor in the formal market, then it is perplexing to hear that gender is suddenly being unhinged from this work (Mirchandani 2005; Aneesh 2006) at just the moment it is increasingly valuable in the global capitalist system. Are we encountering a rise of "emotional androgyny" (Illouz 2007) at just the moment in which emotional expertise is increasingly recognized as a key skill set, integral to labor processes, a mode of intelligence and form of capital, valuable and exchangeable in the marketplace? What are the implications of this effacement of gender precisely when its traditional expressions are being formally required and thus hailed within the marketplace?

The Barbadian case is instructive here because many of the assumed "traditional" or "naturalized" equations of femininity with soft, nurturing care, and separations between remunerated masculine sphere of productive labor and a nonremunerated private sphere of feminine reproductive labor are historically less pronounced. Nurturance and emotions of care have been a woman's preserve; however, their forms and meanings are under construction: the traditions of "tough love" and "grin and bear" are being actively reimagined and reworked under the new affective regime. Together, the upward mobility of matrifocality and the rise of a new affective economy that reverberate across market and private life in turn create possibilities for enacting new femininities, new masculinities, new intimacies, and new entrepreneurial selves.

Affects are critical ingredients of entrepreneurialism under contemporary neoliberalism. But their forms and meanings are not the same the world over; they are rooted in different cultural logics and expressed in different idioms. Like labor of the material kind, affective labors are also not generic. And when, as modes of labor, these become alienating, the resources people are drawn to for salve and comfort are also not universally the same. In this case neoliberal logics of the self and a new therapeutic culture meld with traditions of matrifocality and reputation, producing both a new mode of entrepreneurial respectability and a new profile of middle-classness. Omnivorous and creolizing, these entangled modes of flexibility may offer new ways of living and feeling and suggest new interpretive frames that reach well beyond Caribbean shores.

NOTES

Entrepreneurial Selves: An Introduction

1. Earlier roots for these observations are found in Foucault (1988).

2. What might have been the final frontier for capitalist rationality, efficiency, and profit-maximization, the mysterious, unpredictable realm of sleep is now also subject to capitalist logic. A new growth industry of sleep science and intervention gears itself not toward the pleasures of sleep as rest, and therefore distinct from work, but instead as integral to productivity, and thus a further sphere for ambition, goals, and improvement (Crary 2013; Fairbanks 2014).

3. The original Zouave uniforms were presented by Queen Victoria to the West India Regiment in 1858, and are still worn today in a weekly ritual before the Garrison clock tower. See Corrie Scott, "Changing of the Guard at the Main Guard," *Caribbean Serendipity* (blog), http://caribbeanserendipity.blogspot.com/2012/03 /changing-of-guard-at-main-guard.html#!/2012/03/changing-of-guard-at-main -guard.html.

4. This creative workshop was held at Columbia University, Mailman School of Public Health, and led to the edited volume by the same title, *Love and Globalization* (Padilla et al. 2007).

5. The hiddenness of same-sex relations was notable in a society in which open and remarkably explicit discussion of sex abounds, and where homophobia is widespread. This is a subject that is finally being addressed widely in the academic literature, legal debates, and popular discourse. I found myself in a difficult ethical position in my interviews with several individuals whom I had understood, through personal networks, to be homosexual, and who made mention in their interviews of "partners" but who kept their sexual identities private. I discuss these cases briefly and the general question of heteronormativity in Barbados in chapter 2.

Chapter 1: Barbadian Neoliberalism and the Rise
of a New Middle-Class Entrepreneurialism

1. See John Clarke's excellent discussion of neoliberalism (2008).

2. See Kipnis (2007, 2008) for critiques of many current anthropological uses of neoliberalism.

3. See Carrie Lane's (2011) ethnography for similar patterns among out of work IT professionals in the United States who absorb and embrace many of the expectations of neoliberal flexibility and their own responsibility to adapt to the market volatility.

4. Trouillot, "The Otherwise Modern," 229.

5. *Visiting union* refers to a fluid romantic union in which partners do not share a permanent residence. Their relationship is recognized, however, and they often have offspring. Flexibility in sexual relationships has been bemoaned but endured by women caught in a sexual double standard that permits men "outside" relations and has led lower-class women to employ their own model of "flexibility" through which they gamble for economic and loving support from different fathers of their children (Barrow 1996; Senior 1991). Marital or union flexibility, and the ability to "shift" or move children to different households for their upbringing, like occupational flexibility, has been a critical dimension of lower-class Caribbean life.

6. Gibson-Graham (1996) would have interpreted the practices and value complex of reputation as part of a continuum of anticapitalist alternatives.

7. See Melanie Newton (2008) for a discussion of the dominant representation of mulatto women as entrepreneurs in late eighteenth-century Barbados.

8. GDP per capita was estimated to be US$23,600 in 2011, one of the highest in the region (U.S. Central Intelligence Agency 2012).

9. Guyana, Suriname, Belize, Jamaica, Trinidad, and Barbados launched the single market in January, with the goal of facilitating the free movement of goods, services, and skilled workers between CSME members.

10. Address by Rt. Hon. Owen S. Arthur, Prime Minister of Barbados, to the Trade Forum of the Private Sector, Kingston, Jamaica, June 26, 2003.

11. The Youth Business Trust was established in 1996 as a development agency to support government efforts toward youth entrepreneurship in Barbados. In 2009 the trust reported supporting over 8,500 new entrepreneurs by offering access to credit, volunteer mentors, and business start-up resources (United Nations Development Programme 2012, 168).

12. The Barbados government provided support to the Enterprise Growth Fund Ltd. in conjunction with contributions from the private sector, such that its capitalization rose from $4.7 million to $10 million in 2003. The fund provides financing and technical assistance to entrepreneurs. Senator Eastmond's speech was delivered Tuesday, November 11, 2003.

13. This shift is marked aesthetically as well in the homes of these new entrepreneurs, who are more likely to display regional art and referents to African diasporic culture, for example, than the traditional glass display cases of Lladro figurines and

the coffee table books about the English royal family that have been a staple of Barbadian middle-class living rooms.

14. As in many other countries in which the public sector has experienced retrenchment (by forced IMF restructuring or otherwise), government jobs offer neither the stability nor the prestige they once did, and therefore the shift in ideology toward the private sector as the reservoir of creativity and success is a growing phenomenon (Birdsall, Graham, and Pettinato 2000).

15. For similar descriptions of the expansion of entrepreneurship in contexts that otherwise have prioritized stability and bureaucratic structure and security, see Dunn (2004), Coughlin and Thomas (2002), Gewertz and Errington (1999), and Thanulingom (2000).

16. China illustrates a compelling case for the importance of cultural and historical particularity in examining middle-classness. Here, the relationship between education, occupation, income, and patterns of consumption have all been in dramatic flux from the pre-communist era through the establishment of the PRC in 1949, and after Deng Xiaoping's reforms, when the term began to appear in local academic work. Zhou and Quin (2010, 98–99) suggest the new Chinese middle class represents a political "rearguard" because the state continues to retain a strong grip on the political structure and, by advancing the market economy, satisfies many of the gains to be sought by these middle classes without their making political demands.

17. Whether or not one agrees with Don Kulick's (2006) analysis of anthropology's masochistic identification with the powerless, as Steven Sangren (2006) put it succinctly, a "self-styled *critique* of power (that) veils an underlying *will to power,*" he has put his finger on a striking (and sensitive) feature of the discipline. Indeed, if we take Kulick's proposal (via Lévi Strauss and Freud) of anthropology as "the *daughter* of this era of violence," and the anthropologist as feminine, and thus predisposed toward masochism, then the explicit turn toward the powerful, or the middle-class for that matter, represents "a real perversion . . . for the anthropologist to explicitly and guiltlessly identify with the power and as the powerful" (Kulick 2006).

18. Beverly Skeggs (1997, 134) uses the singular *working class* and *middle class* (vs. *middle classes*) to make a political point, "that class is about conflict, power, and opposition rather than just sites of differences." By contrast, I find it useful to distinguish among class fractions precisely to highlight these nuances that in turn may lead to particular solidarities and/or their absences.

19. For example, Bonnie Dill (1994), bell hooks (1984), Deborah King (1988), Patricia Hill Collins (1992), and Chandra Mohanty (1991) advocated in the 1980s and 1990s that feminist analysis place the experiences of women of color at its center, not in reference to an assumed normative white middle-class woman.

20. In Pat Mahony and Christine Zmroczek's introduction to Reynolds, they discuss the particularities of race, gender, and class for women entering the middle-class academic world. The playing with accent and the sense of psychic ambivalence, defensiveness, guilt, and so on among those women academics conscious of their

working-class roots and their current middle-class positions helps to illuminate some of the fluid and changing ways in which class is seldom simply transcended but remains a complexly layered identity from which alliances, sensibilities, politics, as well as economic and cultural practices emerge.

21. See Jennifer Freeman Marshall (2008) on Hurston.

22. Although he does not provide a fully developed framework for gender, race, and class analysis, Bourdieu (1984, 107–8) offers an intriguing metaphor of relationship, not that of "intersection" or causation between sex and class but relatedness, when he says that "sexual properties are as inseparable from class properties as the yellowness of a lemon is from its acidity: a class is defined in an essential respect by the place and value it gives to the two sexes and to their socially constituted dispositions" and "the true nature of a class or class fraction is expressed in its distribution by sex or age."

23. A growing literature about black middle classes in the United States (Lacy 2007; Landry 2000; Patillo-McCoy 1999; Wingfield 2008), and the "non-Western" middle classes of India, Nepal, Egypt, Vietnam, Indonesia, Ecuador, Mexico, and Brazil, to name a few recent examples, has much to contribute to demythologizing middle-classness.

24. In this review of Lowenthal and Comitas's anthology, Lewis is nonetheless critical of what he sees as a *de-emphasis* on the fundamental class struggle as the foundation upon which Caribbean societies rest. For recent work that attempts to transcend the bounds of the plantation as synecdoche for Caribbean social and cultural forms by taking up a transnational frame for reinterpreting Creole culture, see Crichlow (2009).

25. More recently, a turn toward middle-class culture and politics in the Caribbean represents an important step in complicating some of the traditional analytical frameworks that have dominated regional scholarship (Thomas 2004; Stafford 2005; Edmondson 2009; Spry Rush 2011). These works tend, however, to take on class *either* as a cultural sphere (e.g., Spry Rush's fascinating discussion of West Indian embrace of British colonial culture that also spawned its own confident articulation of Caribbean respectability; Edmondson's illuminating portrait of Caribbean "middlebrow" leisure culture of reading and performance) *or* as a sphere of (problematic, conservative) political interest.

26. The idea that a woman's class is determined by a male head of household has been widely contested in feminist social science. Marriage as a vehicle for class mobility and as a domain, at times, of class demarcation represents a critical domain in which gender and women's position are debated (Abbott 1987; Goldthorpe and Payne 1986, 535; Roberts 1994).

27. This point is worthy of note, in large part because of the voluminous literature about the entrepreneurial "personality" and the strong streak of independence and risk-taking qualities associated with entrepreneurs. When the pattern began to emerge, I asked each of these alumnae how they interpreted the finding, and they all described being a kind of rebellious "outlier" at school, rebels refusing to conform.

28. The sample included three white men and ten white women out of a total of 107 entrepreneurs; 12 percent were white Barbadians.
29. "UNESCO Institute for Statistics: Date Centre," United Nations Educational, Scientific, and Cultural Organization, September 14, 2007. http://stats.uis.unesco .org/unesco/tableviewer/document.aspx?ReportId=143.

Chapter 2: Entrepreneurial Affects

1. As Jones (1997) notes, divorce rates internationally vary widely over the past fifty years. In the 1960s and 1970s in all Western countries in which divorce has been legal, rates surged dramatically, though they have leveled off in many cases. Yet during the same period, divorce rates in Muslim countries in Southeast Asia declined despite growing industrialization and urbanization. By 1990 rates of divorce in Western countries were roughly four times that of Indonesia, for example.
2. "From an average of 5.4 per 1,000 of the population over the past century, the marriage rate rose to an average of 11.5 between 2000 and 2005. Meanwhile divorce has also climbed steadily. From an average of 192 per year during the 1980s, the number has risen . . . between 1995–2004 from 393 to 507, with the divorce rate per 100 marriages reaching 15.73" (Epstein and Limage 2008, 57).
3. Some have also asserted that marriage was not only the prescription of British colonial tradition but also a traditional form of union brought by African slaves, and that the "dissolution of marriage" is embedded in the ruptures of slavery and the plantation system (Smith 1988, 203).
4. Where the thrust of early Caribbean kinship studies of the 1940s and 1950s was aimed at curing the supposed pathology of the matrifocal family (Frazier 1966; Henriques 1949), today matrifocality is widely understood to be a positively adaptive family form (Barrow 1996; Hodge 2002). And where regional government and aid agencies formerly emphasized male responsibility and the imperative of male employment as the prerequisite for family and national development, more effort has been made in recent decades to address the needs of single mothers and female-headed households. The shift reflects a widespread acknowledgment of matrifocality as an integral dimension of Caribbean social organization and not a temporary aberration based upon economic marginality (Massiah 1983; Morrissey 1998).
5. Citing figures from 2004, the United States ranks highest with 4.95 divorces per 1,000 people. With 1.21 divorces per 1,000 people, Barbados follows directly after Finland, Canada, Australia, New Zealand, Denmark, the United Kingdom, Russia, and Puerto Rico (NationMaster, Ian Graham, staff editor, http://www.nation master.com/country-info/stats/People/Divorce-rate).
6. Deborah Thomas (2009, 97–98) has recently noted that the current context of twenty-first-century neoliberal globalization, with its championing of entrepreneurship, has created an unexpected opportunity with regard to the region's long-standing preoccupation with the nuclear family and "marginal masculinity." However, what I find especially striking in the enormous literature devoted to Caribbean kinship is how little is written about the actual experience of (as opposed

to the form and incidence of) marriage. The powerful symbolic equation between marriage and respectability has weighed so powerfully that its form has subsumed any attention to its variability in content or meaning. We find little exploration of how marriage is enacted, experienced, imagined, or felt. We know little of how marriages unfold over time as relationships and not just structural forms. Belinda Edmondson's (2009, 82) discussion of de Lisser's novel *Jane's Career*, published in 1913, provides an excellent discussion of the model of upward mobility and respectability for women as engendered in the "career" of marriage, motherhood, home ownership, and domesticity.

7. Marcia Inhorn (1994) discusses the emergence of new forms of loving, companionate marriage when infertility deprives couples of one of the key markers of family and social existence. In Egypt, where womanhood is similarly defined in large part via motherhood (albeit within marriage), she found that even where extended families urged men to divorce their wives in cases of infertility, some men and women forged close and protective marriage bonds in the absence of children. In the Caribbean, as Victoria Durant-Gonzalez (1985, 1) notes, systems of emotional support are understood to be the preserve of enduring and extensive networks of female kin and friends.

8. See Collier (1997) for her helpful discussion of individualism and marriage as a project of the self.

9. While uneasy about this naming, I believe it is important to provide a sense of the pluralities not only along the lines of gender, class, and race but also sexuality in a setting that is known for its homophobia. By using the pronoun *she* to refer to their partners, these women were indicating their couple status without giving a specific label to their sexual identification or conjugality.

10. Most of my interviews are permeated by an unconscious but notable heteronormativity in which sexual intimacy and the structure of relationships are framed within heterosexual parameters. This point has been made to me, sometimes critically, by some who have read this work outside the Caribbean region. There are two ways of responding to these queries, an *emic* and *etic* perspective, one derived of internal explanatory terms and the other a more distanced analytic interpretation. Emically, the heteronormative stance rests on a simple assumption of heterosexuality in all respects—in the "respectable" realm of marriage, the practical and more fluid realm of conjugality, as well as the sexual license of "reputation" and its celebration of virility. From an etic perspective, the Caribbean is a region steeped in a highly explicit, seemingly liberated sexual culture, but one that is equally staunchly homophobic. In the Barbadian context the law against *buggery* or male homosexuality is still formally in place (though not enforced), carrying a lifetime sentence. In fact some argue that the political and cultural climate in Barbados, in part related to the rise of fundamentalist churches, has become even more intolerant of "alternative lifestyles" and in particular homosexuality. A series of public town-hall meetings across the country to discuss recommendations to decriminalize homosexuality and commercial sex work was met with stalwart refusal. The sexual landscape is thus paradoxical—on one hand the fluidity of conjugal relations constitutes "vis-

iting unions," for example, as a formally recognized and legitimate "stage" along a continuum of sexual coupling and household formations and, on the other hand, there is a pointed avoidance of (and sometimes opposition to) nonheterosexual unions within public discourse.

11. Today's international press includes frequent reports of "gay bashing" and even murder across the region. See Lacey (2008).

12. Men's reluctance to convey, or lack of reference to, emotional dimensions of their marriages cannot be simply interpreted as an absence of such affect; it may also be an artifact of the interview encounter. With the exception of just a few of the entrepreneurs (four to five), I had only limited interactions with couples together to gauge these relationships in practice and relied primarily upon individual self-reports.

13. Jack Alexander (1984, 1977) and Lisa Douglass (1992) provide rare discussions of love in relation to marriage and conjugal unions in general. Alexander (1978, 11) compares cognatic enduring love with conjugal, suddenly emanating love and concludes that "after marriage, the meaning of love changes from 'being in love,' an inwardly directed feeling of emotion and passion, to practical actions in the public and social arena." Barrow (1996, 265) notes, however, that among the lower class, where marriage is a vehicle for upward mobility, "love is less central to marriage and other criteria such as social status and colour, not altogether absent from the middle class, begin to carry more weight." In essence we know little about the emotional and affective dimensions of these relationships.

14. Like R. T. Smith, Barrow (1996, 172–73) emphasizes the primary affective relationship as that between mothers and their children (sons): "It is a relationship of close emotional and material interdependency, first he on her, then she on him. The relationship survives and he may live at 'home' with her until her death, often a devastating period in the life of the son. The mother-son relationship constitutes the pivot of Caribbean family structure around which the other family relationships revolve." The primacy of men's affective relationships with their mothers has been recently refocused within the lively discussion surrounding "male marginality" (Miller 1991). Barrow, for example, says that male marginality as an argument takes as its premise the expected presence and participation of men as fathers and spouses but precludes their roles as sons, brothers, uncles, and so on. These narrow prescriptions rest upon the normative expectation of a nuclear family and yield a picture of male delinquency and failure, whereas attention to broader kinship roles and activities would generate a different understanding of men's participation in kinship. See also Barry Chevannes (2001).

15. R. T. Smith (1963) notes a number of areas of needed research in the field of kinship studies in the Caribbean. He expresses concern that with the emphasis on large national survey data the in-depth study of family and kinship relationships through case studies are also crucial. Due to inadequate records by clinicians and social agencies, as well as "the inarticulateness of the lower classes, the relative dearth of literary work dealing with lower class life, and the limited number of people who receive any kind of psychotherapy, we know little of a really intimate

nature respecting the personal and family life of Caribbean peoples. Field anthropologists have so far been trying to understand a wide range of behavior and have not had the time for a close study of a limited number of cases . . . that would deepen our understanding of lower class motives, feelings, frustrations, and values" (144).

16. Many of the entrepreneurs (both male and female) expressed that one of the deepest motivations driving their determination to succeed in business was to prove their self-worth to an absent parent (for Myra, her mother; for dozens of others, a father), whose absence and lack of love, support, and involvement had left lasting scars.

17. Yehudi Cohen (1971, 422) was interested in the question of affect and emotion, but argued that in the "Rocky Roads" community of Jamaica he studied, "aside from the motives of sexual gratification, there appear to be few emotions of any significance involved in the formation of sexual friendships. There is no requirement for affection between premarital sexual partners; one may have a sexual relationship with another while still nurturing a dislike for the person."

18. Bradd Shore (2008) also notes the conspicuous lack of love in anthropological works, which historically have favored structures of kinship and marriage over emotion and romance. In the Caribbean social science literature, only discussions of a mother's sense of duty toward her children approximate the notion that *support* is itself an idiom of love.

19. See Smith et al. (2006).

20. *Obeah* refers to practices of witchcraft.

21. The weight of romantic love as conveyed in soap operas was made profoundly clear to me in the course of my early fieldwork in 1989 when tearful and highly emotional discussions among women I knew revolved around the love lives and marriages of the characters of *Days of Our Lives*, then the most popular television show nationally.

22. One of the ironies about the contemporary "gay marriage" debate is the fact that where queer relationships and families, like the matrifocal household, might be seen to offer creative countermodels of intimacy, relatedness, and support vis-à-vis the conventional marriage structure, the effort to gain "marriage equality" shifts attention away from these possibilities in favor of fitting into the traditional marriage mold. See Lynne Huffer's (2013) provocative essay.

23. See Hirsch and Wardlow (2006), especially chapters by Gregg and Erickson.

24. As in many other world areas, as Ong (1995, 52–54) has described in China and Derne (2008) has illustrated for India, the appeal of "modern love" is very much tied to economic affluence. In north India Derne argues that these symbols are especially potent for couples who are already able to support themselves independently. On the other hand, such egalitarian romantic ideals are rejected in favor of traditional gender roles and arranged marriage by nonelite men for whom these symbols of cosmopolitanism create anxiety and unease (Derne 2005, 184; 2008, 129).

25. I am indebted to the work of Gul Ozyegin here for her use of Jessica Benjamin

(1988) in the contemporary Turkish context of youth romance, gender, and sexuality (Ozyegin forthcoming), and her own formulation of "intimacy work" (Ozyegin 2001).

Chapter 3: The Upward Mobility of Matrifocality

1. Edith Clarke (1957) borrowed this evocative phrase, *My Mother Who Fathered Me*, for the title of her path-breaking ethnography of family life in three Jamaican communities.

2. In Mary Patillo-McCoy's recent study of the black middle class in the United States, she notes that marriage has declined for both African Americans and whites in the past several decades. In the 1980s and 1990s, over half of black men and women between twenty-four and twenty-nine had never been married, double the rate in 1950. For whites in the 1980s and 1990s, 40 percent of white men and 26 percent of white women of the same age bracket had never married (Patillo-McCoy 1999, 60).

3. R. T. Smith (1971), in his classic work, *The Negro Family in British Guiana*, and Edith Clarke (1957), in *My Mother Who Fathered Me*, examined these functions among kinship groups or structures in 1950s Guiana and Jamaica, at the time with high levels of male migration and the intensification of a cash economy. Where the early kinship studies of the 1930s and 1940s aimed to unearth the origins of the Afro-Caribbean matrifocal family form as either a survival of African tradition (Herskovits 1958) or the traumatic remnants of plantation slavery (Frazier 1966), following the influential work of R. T. Smith, M. G. Smith, Fernando Henriques (1949) and Edith Clarke (1957), other scholars (Rodman 1971; Safa 1965) attempted to examine matrifocality largely by explaining its prevalence not as culturally unique to the Caribbean but as endemic within systems of economic marginality.

4. Despite the acknowledgment of fluidity, and the option to marry after (rather than as a prerequisite for) children, R. T. Smith also asserts, "marriage as a public act of status affirmation is quite distinct from the (other) . . . almost casual unions." Indeed, what is critical for R. T. Smith is the comparatively weak significance of *all* conjugal unions (including marriage). For Smith, conjugal relations in the West Indies are not centered on "intense affect," as such depth of relationship is concentrated in the mother-child bond. Whereas conjugal ties are fluid and loose, "the relationship which remains strong throughout life is that between mother and child, or between the child and the woman who 'mothered' or 'grew' him" (Smith 1996, 56).

5. Peletz (2005) asserts a similar but inverted argument regarding marriage among the Minangkabau, for whom "entering into (although not necessarily remaining in) a heterosexual marriage, either monogamous or polygynous, is a prerequisite for adult status." One cannot deduce an individual's erotic orientation or sexual or gender identity from his or her participation in this institution. But the sine qua non for social adulthood at issue here does seem important to address in a substantive way when considering Minangkabau normativities and their Others.

By contrast, in the West Indies, it has been motherhood that has far outweighed marriage as the necessary step to adult womanhood.

6. For comparative analyses of matrifocality see Peletz (2005); Nancy Tanner in Rosaldo and Lamphere (1974).

7. As Massiah (1983, 200) observed, roughly half of those households labeled matrifocal have male resident partners who, according to "male marginality" critics, either conceded headship to women or had their own claim to headship taken from them.

8. Lisa Rofel similarly describes the manner in which kinship has served as the ubiquitous trope of Chinese culture in classical anthropology and popular renderings alike. Kinship in China is invoked as an explanatory lens on all aspects of life— "from economic motivation to religious practice. Lurking behind this essentialist trope lies the stereotype that Chinese people are 'group-oriented'—a mentality seen as impeding Chinese peoples' ability to have modern selves because it blocks the expression of individual desire" (Rofel 1999, 226).

9. Recent statistics released by the Pew Research Center (Wang, Parker, and Taylor 2013) about growing numbers of women not only in the formal workforce but also as household breadwinners in families with children under eighteen in the United States (40 percent in 2013 vs. 11 percent in 1960) draws attention to the need to attend not simply to household configurations or conjugal status but also the economic and social continua within categories such as "female-headed households." Those, for instance, in which women out-earn their husbands but where two working adults support the household as a whole, stand on firmer financial ground than those of single mothers whose incomes frequently fall beneath the poverty line.

10. As recent work in the United States indicates, middle-aged women in many parts of the world are finding that "going solo" can foster greater autonomy as well as sociality, and liberation from some of the obligatory aspects typically tied to women's kinship and marriage roles. Klinenberg's *Going Solo* (2012) examines the steady rise in numbers of people living alone in the United States, where 28 percent of the adult population tied with the same proportion of childless couples. The experience of solo living, especially for middle-aged women in the United States, is notable for the purposes of the discussion here, as many cite greater autonomy as well as sociality and pleasure in the capacity to choose and orchestrate social life and experiences outside of the obligatory kin work that characterized the expectations of their previous married lives.

11. bell hooks (1984) notes that the sociological assertion of matriarchy in the black family implies a social and political power that "in no way resembles the condition of black women." She adds that "even in single-parent homes, black mothers may go so far as to delegate the responsibility of being the 'man' to male children. In some single parent homes where no male is present, it is acceptable for a visiting male friend or lover to assume a decision-making role. Few black women, even in homes where no men are present, see themselves as adopting a 'male' role" (370–71).

12. As such, the early kinship studies of Wilson, Alexander, Smith, and Clarke portrayed the black lower classes as the purveyors of creole culture—not only of verbal wit and economic multiplicity but also kinship and union formation—whereas the middle classes were portrayed as the central arbiters of all things respectable.

13. Following the influential works of R. T. Smith (1971), Yehudi Cohen (1964, 1956, 1955), Edith Clarke (1957), Chandra Jayawardena (1963), Sidney Greenfield (1973, 1966), Peter Wilson (1973, 1969, 1964), a new generation of scholarship began to recast the significance and (again) function of the matrifocal family while beginning to note its primacy as a distinctively positive dimension of the region's creole culture (Barrow 1998, 2002; Besson 1993; Bolles 1989; Gonzalez 1984; Morrissey 1998; Senior 1991; Smith 1996).

14. Indeed, by 1970, Nancie Gonzalez (1970) had argued that "neither of these views has much currency today," especially in light of the fact that the matrifocal form of family can be found in such wide-ranging communities as "the Javanese, the Mescalero apache, and the inhabitants of East London."

15. By the 1990s, conventional approaches to "the family," "the conjugal union," and "the household" began to shift toward a range of new feminist approaches and analyses of gender ideologies and identities (including masculinity), sexuality, embodiment, and feminist intersectionalities of race, class, and gender (Barriteau 2003; Mohammed 2002). At the same time there continues to be a tendency to retain the comparative lens of the "normative" patriarchal nuclear family as both an analytical frame of reference for describing difference (matrifocality, visiting relationships, the continuum of conjugality) and as an assumed local yardstick of respectability.

16. Gina Ulysse's (2007) discussion of transnational suitcase traders from Jamaica provides a rich illustration of lower-class black women and their embodiment of gendered, classed, and racialized formulations of strong, independent *womanhood* as opposed to the middle-class respectable *lady* in the manner in which they travel, speak, and navigate the public sphere in their travels.

17. Indeed, if either extreme is rendered more prominently in the historical record, it is undoubtedly that of robust womanhood, physically strong and mentally savvy, embodied in figures of heroism and honor, entrepreneurial ingenuity, and strength: Nanny, the iconic maroon slave leader of Jamaica; Mary Seacole, who traveled independently to nurse the wounded in the Crimean War and posthumously awarded the Jamaican Order of Merit in 1991 and voted in 2004 the greatest black Briton; and Rachel Pringle Polgreen, born a slave around 1753 to an African mother and a Scottish schoolmaster and died at thirty-eight a wealthy woman and one of the island's first hoteliers.

18. Barrow (1996, 166) similarly notes the positive stance by women in visiting unions toward the freedom and flexibility these relationships afford, "safe from the dangers of domestic violence. Less intensive contact between the partners is conducive to greater harmony and, since the relationship is viewed as a prelude to marriage, it does not attract the moral and religious condemnation of common-law living in sin."

19. Douglass (1992) offers an unusual and extremely rich ethnographic portrait of white Jamaican kinship. With the exception of a small number of poor white former indentured servants, or "redlegs," the minority population of white Barbadians have not been primary subjects of ethnographic study. Historical accounts of the white minority in the Caribbean more broadly include Johnson, Watson, and Danowski (1998), Sheppard (1977), and Beckles (1989).
20. This labeling was derived from the informants themselves. However, several of these women noted that while they and others consider themselves to be "white" Barbadians, this is a relative category, and some described being considered "women of color" when they spent time at universities in North America.
21. The discovery that many of the women entrepreneurs had attended Queens College, one of the top secondary schools on the island, and originally an all-girls' school, was striking and unexpected. In order to investigate this pattern, I began to ask these women if they thought there was any particular training or implicit socialization at Queens that prepared them for their entrepreneurial careers. Intriguingly, several women noted that the opposite was true—that they had been "rebels" at Queens, failing their "deportment badges" there and not complying with the more respectable and expected paths of higher education en route to the professions, civil service, or private sector employment.
22. The significance of this distinction is often lost when accounts of "white Barbadians" are made. However, those who hail from indentured labor stock, however affluent they may have become in the professions or trade, remain very much aware of their differential status in relation to the "plantocracy." One such well-regarded white doctor recounted being "black-balled" by a patient when he applied to join the Barbados Yacht Club, as an illustration of how these status distinctions were upheld in his early professional years.
23. See Ozyegin (2013) for a fascinating use of Benjamin's concept of recognition in the changing enactments and sentiments of love, sex, and desire in contemporary Turkey.
24. Patricia Hill Collins (2000, 66; emphasis added) notes, "U.S. black professional women report increasing difficulty in finding middle-class black men interested in marrying them. The smaller number of black men than black women in professional and managerial positions represents one important issue. . . . Given that separated and divorced black women professionals are much less likely to remarry than their white counterparts, higher rates of separation and divorce may become a special problem for married black woman professionals. *When faced with the prospect of never getting married to a professional black man, whether by choice or default, many professional black women simply go it alone.*"
25. Greenfield (1966, 104) noted "it is assumed that a man, especially if moderately successful, will have extramarital affairs." See the following sources, which all make this observation: Sobo (1993), Wilson (1973), Senior (1991), and Barrow (1996).
26. Though seldom acknowledged and socially taboo, the common practice of covert bisexuality would represent yet another dimension of "flexibility" versus stasis in

the private or sexual sphere. Widespread male sexual promiscuity is frequently explained by men to reflect a demographic imbalance of men to women in the Barbadian population, due to the outmigration of male labor and "the need for men to have more than one woman." Interestingly, though this demographic imbalance was the case during the building of the Panama Canal, when many men migrated temporarily, the population has long since stabilized to a roughly equal proportion of males and females. Nonetheless, the rationale persists, and was offered to me on numerous occasions by lower- and middle-class men alike, as a matter of fact.

27. For the manner in which "marriage" has functioned as the singular norm against which all other relationships are (negatively) compared or erased, see Blackwood (2005).

28. The weight of this refusal is hard to overstate, as one of Greenfield's (1966, 127) informants proclaimed, "The owner of a Barbadian house . . . is the boss of everything."

Chapter 4: Neoliberal Work and Life

1. While work-life policies today in the United States attempt to construct flexible arrangements suitable to a diverse labor force, these are most often implicitly aimed toward middle-class, married, working mothers of school-aged children. Clearly, just as different demographic groups have different needs for and ways of conceiving optimal flexibility, different labor niches lend themselves to different degrees and forms of flexibility and cast the relationship between work and non-work differently (Florida 2002). Many of the hotly contested public debates in the United States about work-life balance and gendered work in the current economy have failed to provide careful analysis of class and have often purposely addressed middle-class, dual income families in the United States as the primary subjects, without deliberate study of racial, ethnic, cultural, and class distinctions.

2. The "men's movement" in Barbados has been an interesting phenomenon developing over the past ten years. In the early 1990s I attended what I believe was the first large public forum of its kind, debating "Is the Barbadian Male in Crisis?" Since that time, in 2010, an organization was founded at the University of the West Indies (UWI)–Cave Hill Campus, Males at Cave Hill Operations, better known by its provocative acronym, MACHO. The thrust of this organization is purportedly to correct the "problem" of the disproportionate enrollments of female students over males at the university. However, the larger orbit of the movement, as well as the particular ways of interpreting this educational "problem," have tended to paint the "crisis" as one in which women are "taking over" in Barbados. In essence, these arguments echo generally the "marginal male" position (Miller 1991), in which Caribbean men are painted as actively marginalized and emasculated by women in their societies. Eudine Barriteau (2013), the former director of the Gender and Development Studies at UWI, and the anthropologist Alyssa Trotz (2009) have contributed important critiques of the gender politics of this movement, and several of the women I interviewed also had astute and nuanced critiques of the popular notion that Barbadian women were "taking over men's rightful position in society."

3. I found among the informatics sector workers I studied that their offshore jobs often propelled them into "side" work of a variety of forms (cake baking, needle working, hair braiding, informal commercial importing of clothes and household goods, often for fellow workmates). They might take a class in cake icing or sewing, then turn these new skills to informal economic activity that enhanced their ties to workmates and bosses, providing special-occasion cakes for company parties, beautifully tailored skirt suits for coworkers' wardrobes. These economic and "leisure" activities were often further interconnected on trips subsidized through their employee reward system, allowing them to have fun and explore tourist sites in Miami or a different Caribbean island and also buy goods they could resell back home and subsidize their formal wage (Freeman 2000).

4. Although the formal labor force participation for women in Barbados has historically outpaced that of women in the United States (65 percent compared with 58 percent in 2011), a recent World Bank report titled *Work and Family: Latin American and Caribbean Women in Search of a New Balance* noted as a crucial priority "women's need for greater freedom to choose their identities, which manifests itself as an *unmet demand for flexibility* in the region." On the other hand, the study notes that "subjective well-being" and women's "happiness" have declined in the United States alongside their apparent labor force gains (World Bank 2011, xxii). Just as the ingredients of "happiness" cannot be assumed to be generic across time and place, my argument here is to emphasize the cultural specificity of flexibility. The attempt to attach emotional meanings to such economic and labor force trends is a recent phenomenon in social science surveys. Another recent study of entrepreneurship in the United States argues that entrepreneurs as a group are more "optimistic" than others, and that optimism (in all people, not just entrepreneurs) fosters a more favorable view of work in general. Optimists work longer hours, seldom envision retirement, and in their personal lives are also more flexible and forward looking, more likely to remarry, for example. A fine illustration of a convergence of neoliberal economic agendas and affects is given in Puri and Robinson (2004).

5. A recent study by Yanchus et al. (2010) emphasizes that emotional labor occurs *both* at home and at work, and it attempts to address the gap in the literature that has tended to analyze these separately.

6. Hardt (1999) and others (Leidner 1999; Kang 2010) who focus on affective labor tend to emphasize the kinds of feminine affects central to the flight attendants in Hochschild's study (care, nurturing, well-being, etc.) as opposed to more masculine affects that were central to the bill collectors' work that emphasized the *containment* of compassion and the outward expression of irritation. Others have emphasized the gendered double standards in some service professions, for example, for trial lawyers the masculine affects (aggression and intimidation) required of "Rambo litigators" whose job it is to induce fear, shame, and guilt (Pierce 1996).

7. I have had the benefit of learning from a wide array of excellent scholarship on work-life conditions, and in particular work-family issues, through my involve-

ment in the Alfred P. Sloan Foundation's Myth and Ritual in American Life (MARIAL) Center and its affiliates. My intent here is not a critique of the importance of this work, but more to point out some of the implicit assumptions behind the concept of *balance* and the elements constituting work and life. See Weeks (2011, 2007) and Huffer (2013) for an important queer critique of the dominant heteronormative work-life balance formulation.

8. While planned factory towns such as Fordlandia in the Amazon rainforest, and the industrial company towns in the United States were conceived with the intent of yoking family values and certain kinds of leisure with productive enterprise, and white collar management has long been about the management of emotions (Mills 1951), such a deliberate melding of leisure, labor, and emotional life is a more recent development in Barbados.

9. Here the specificity of time is also important, since the restructuring of the airline industry has changed so profoundly that the kind of nurturing emotional labor that was critical to the flight attendants' jobs during Hochschild's research is now less routine, except perhaps in business-class travel.

10. For discussions of "work's intimacy" (Gregg 2011), the "commercialization of intimate life" (Hochschild 2003), and a particularly interesting challenge to the work-life conundrum analytically and politically, see Kathi Weeks (2007, 2011).

11. The role of paid domestic work as a key to (white) middle-class women's liberation was, as Kathi Weeks (2011, 173) reminds us, a central element of Betty Friedan's platform and a staple of pop culture's representation of middle-class American life (e.g., Morticia Addams of *The Addams Family*, *The Brady Bunch*, *Leave It to Beaver*, etc.).

12. For a helpful discussion of "emotional capital," extending Bourdieu's theory of multiple forms of capital, see Diane Reay (2000).

13. Others have similarly noted particular divisions of labor in the domestic sphere in which mothers, for example, actively choose to retain *certain* roles and jobs such as reading children stories before bedtime, serving husbands or families dinner (though not preparing it), while having more mundane and less emotionally laden domestic and child-care labor performed by paid help (Lan 2006).

14. I first observed these traditions in fieldwork in Grenada in the 1980s, when studying children in a rural district experimenting with computers in their rudimentary primary school. The reticence of children to speak was made plain in classrooms, reinforced through a tradition of rote memorization, and the very real threat of the ruler or paddle that was poised to strike any disruptive, unprepared, or otherwise "naughty" child. The rows of quiet faces contrasted dramatically with their volume and activity outside the grounds of school, especially among the boys. Girls, by contrast, often retained a shy reserve, especially when addressing any adult. Throughout the region, a gendered pattern of early childhood socialization of male aggression and female docility and politeness has been well documented. Today these patterns are being questioned in efforts to examine "aggression as a positive feature of masculinity" and reduce high rates of domestic violence and rape. The Caribbean region is home to "three of the top ten rape rates in the world"

and "48% of adolescents in nine regional islands said sexual initiation was forced" (Doughty 2012).

Chapter 5: The Therapeutic Ethic and the Spirit of Neoliberalism

1. In a psychological study of "The Protestant Work Ethic in Barbados" Adrian Furnham (1991) concludes that, comparatively speaking, Barbadian subjects demonstrated a stronger endorsement of Protestant work ethic beliefs than many other national groups. One explanation he ventures for this is that Protestant work ethic "scores are correlated with conservatism, and because Barbados is a conservative, religious country, the scores reflect its conservatism" (40).

2. Obeah is typically regarded as the "work of enemies," the deliberate intervention and harm most often rooted in jealousy and resentments. Although the actual "working" of Obeah may involve "'duppies,' spirits, . . . and other extrahuman agents," it is generally believed that others' "maliciousness" is at the root of "humbug and murderation" (Fisher 1985, 115).

3. This is not to say that selfhood is devoid of sociality; as Rose (1992, 152) says, "our contemporary regime of the 'self' is not 'anti-social.' It construes the relationships of the self with lovers, family, children, friends, and colleagues as central both to personal happiness and social efficacy. . . . Yet however 'social' this field may be, it can be turned to the account of the enterprising self: for, in recognizing the dynamic nexus of interpersonal relations that it inhabits, selves can place these relations under conscious control and the self can learn the skills to shape its relations with others so that it will best fulfill its own destiny."

4. Valerie Walkerdine (2003, 241) puts the implications of these processes well, drawing upon Foucault, when she says, "the practices of subjectification produce a constantly failing subject who has to understand their position in essentially personal and psychological terms. . . . Psychology has a central role in providing both the discourses through which the psychologized self is understood and the clinical discourses and practices which put that subject together again after the inevitable failure. Equally important are the discourses through which success and failure is understood and therefore the techniques of self-regulation and management which both inscribe the subject and allow him or her to attempt to refashion themselves as a successful subject: the subject of neoliberal choice." Like psychology, religion both offers up explanations for righteousness and failure and becomes a medium through which to enact the self. Others have noted the expanding popularity of Pentecostalism in Africa, Latin America, and other parts of the world, where according to Birgit Meyer (2004), one of the intriguing attractions (in Ghana) relates to a prioritizing of the nuclear family over networks of extended family, therefore fostering a concentration of resources and narrowing of responsibility to immediate kin and residential units, absolving people of duties toward extended networks of relations.

5. Many of these forms of religious and therapeutic practice appear to grow directly from the expanding global outreach of new churches, American televangelists, the World of Faith prosperity doctrine, and a familiar burgeoning of spas, yoga

studios, nail and massage salons, and counseling services in the United States. Within the two largest of these "entrepreneurial" middle-class churches, the links to U.S. evangelical preachers and churches were clear.

6. *Elegantly casual* is a specification often indicated on invitations to designate nice but not formal dress.

7. The rising appeal of the Word of Faith churches in North America and of Pentecostalism across the world is attractive not just to the poor but also among widely diverse groups, including the black and white middle classes globally. One aspect of this burgeoning movement, as expressed by the influential American pastor Creflo Dollar, is the emphasis on *prosperity*.

REFERENCES

Abbott, Pamela. 1987. "Women's Social Class Identification: Does Husband's Occupation Make a Difference?" *Sociology* 21 (1): 91–103.

Abrahams, R. D. 1983. *The Man-of-Words in the West Indies: Performance and the Emergence of Creole Culture.* Baltimore: Johns Hopkins University Press.

Alexander, Jack. 1977. "The Role of the Male in the Middle-Class Jamaican Family: A Comparative Perspective." *Journal of Comparative Family Studies* 8: 369–89.

Alexander, Jack. 1978. "The Cultural Domain of Marriage." *American Ethnologist* 5 (1): 5–14.

Alexander, Jack. 1984. "Love, Race, Slavery, and Sexuality in Jamaican Images of the Family." In *Kinship, Ideology, and Practice in Latin America,* edited by Raymond T. Smith, 147–80. Chapel Hill: University of North Carolina Press.

Appadurai, Arjun. 1986. "Theory in Anthropology: Center and Periphery." *Comparative Studies in Society and History* 28: 356–61.

Appadurai, Arjun. 1991. "Global Ethnoscapes: Notes and Queries for a Transnational Anthropology." In *Recapturing Anthropology: Working in the Present,* edited by Richard Fox, 191–210. Santa Fe, NM: School of American Research Press.

Arthur, Rt. Hon. Owen S., Prime Minister of Barbados, to the Trade Forum of the Private Sector Organization of Jamaica on the Caribbean Single Market and Economy, June 26, 2003, Kingston, Jamaica. Caribbean Community (CARICOM) Press Release 93/2003.

Austin, Diane. 1984. *Urban Life in Kingston, Jamaica: The Culture and Class Ideology of Two Neighborhoods.* New York: Gordon and Breach.

Austin-Broos, Diane J. 1998. "Women and Jamaican Pentecostalism." In *Caribbean Portraits: Essays on Gender Ideologies and Identities,* edited by Christine Barrow, 156–73. Kingston, Jamaica: Ian Randle Publishers.

Barriteau, Eudine. 1998. "Theorizing Gender Systems and the Project of Modernity in the Twentieth Century Caribbean." *Feminist Review* 59: 186–210.

Barriteau, Eudine. 2003. *Confronting Power, Theorizing Gender: Interdisciplinary Perspectives in the Caribbean.* Kingston, Jamaica: University of the West Indies Press.

Barriteau, Eudine, ed. 2013. *Love and Power: Caribbean Discourses on Gender.* Kingston, Jamaica: University of the West Indies Press.

Barrow, Christine. 1986. *Autonomy, Equality, and Women in Barbados.* Caribbean Studies Association.

Barrow, Christine. 1988. "Anthropology, the Family and Women in the Caribbean." In *Gender in Caribbean Development,* edited by Patricia Mohammed and Catherine Shepherd, 156–69. Mona, Jamaica: University of the West Indies Women and Development Studies Project.

Barrow, Christine, ed. 1996. *Family in the Caribbean: Themes and Perspectives.* Kingston, Jamaica: Ian Randle Publishers.

Barrow, Christine. 1998. "Caribbean Masculinity and Family: Revisiting 'Marginality' and Reputation." In *Caribbean Portraits: Essays on Gender Ideologies and Identities,* edited by Christine Barrow, 339–58. Kingston, Jamaica: Ian Randle Publishers.

Barrow, Christine. 2001. "Contesting the Rhetoric of Black Family Breakdown from Barbados." *Journal of Comparative Family Studies* 32 (3): 419–41.

Barrow, Christine. 2010. *Caribbean Childhoods "Outside," "Adopted," or "Left Behind": "Good Enough" Parenting and Moral Families.* Miami: Ian Randle Publishers.

Barrow, Christine, and J. Edward Greene. 1979. *Small Business in Barbados: A Case of Survival.* Cave Hill, Barbados: University of the West Indies, Institute of Social and Economic Research, Eastern Caribbean.

Barthes, Roland. 1972. *Mythologies.* New York: Hill and Wang.

Baviskar, Amita, and Raka Ray. 2011. *Elite and Everyman: The Cultural Politics of the Indian Middle Classes.* New York: Routledge.

Beckles, Hilary. 1989a. *Corporate Power in Barbados: The Mutual Affair.* Bridgetown, Barbados: Caribbean Graphics.

Beckles, Hilary. 1989b. *White Servitude and Black Slavery in Barbados, 1627–1715.* Knoxville: University of Tennessee Press.

Beckles, Hilary. 1989c. *Natural Rebels: A Social History of Enslaved Black Women in Barbados.* New Brunswick, NJ: Rutgers University Press.

Beckles, Hilary. 1990. *A History of Barbados: From Amerindian Settlement to Nation-State.* Cambridge: Cambridge University Press.

Benjamin, Jessica. 1988. *The Bonds of Love: Psychoanalysis, Feminism, and the Problem of Domination.* New York: Pantheon Books.

Berlant, Lauren Gail. 2011. *Cruel Optimism.* Durham, NC: Duke University Press.

Besson, Jean. 1993. "Reputation and Respectability Reconsidered: A New Perspective on Afro-Caribbean Peasant Women." In *Women and Change in the Caribbean,* edited by Janet Henshall Momsen, 15–37. Bloomington: Indiana University Press.

Besson, Jean. 2002. *Martha Brae's Two Histories: European Expansion and Caribbean Culture-building in Jamaica.* Chapel Hill: University of North Carolina Press.

Birdsall, Nancy, Carol Graham, and Stefano Pettinato. 2000. "Stuck in the Tunnel: Is

Globalization Muddling the Middle Class?" Working Paper. http://www.brookings
.org/ES/dynamics/papers/middleclass/.

Birth, Kevin, and Morris Freilich. 1995. "Putting Romance into Systems of Sexuality:
Changing Smart-Rules in a Trinidadian Village." In *Romantic Passion: A Universal
Experience?*, edited by William Jankowiak, 262–76. New York: Columbia Univer-
sity Press.

Blackwood, Evelyn. 2005. "Wedding Bell Blues: Marriage, Missing Men, and Matrifocal Follies." *American Ethnologist* 32: 3–19.

Bledstein, Burton J., and Robert D. Johnston. 2001. *The Middling Sorts: Explorations
in the History of the American Middle Class.* New York: Routledge.

Bolles, A. Lynne, and Deborah D'Amico-Samuels. 1986. "Economic Crisis and
Female-headed Households in Urban Jamaica." In *Women and Change in Latin
America*, edited by June Nash and Helen I. Safa, 65–83. South Hadley, MA: Bergin
and Garvey.

Bolles, A. Lynne, and Deborah D'Amico-Samuels. 1989. "Anthropological Scholarship on Gender in the English-Speaking Caribbean." In *Gender and Anthropology*,
edited by Frances E. Mascia-Lees and Nancy Johnson Black, 171–88. Washington,
DC: American Anthropological Association.

Boserup, Ester. 1970. *Woman's Role in Economic Development.* London: Allen and Unwin.

Bourdieu, Pierre. 1984. *Distinction: A Social Critique of the Judgement of Taste.* Cambridge, MA: Harvard University Press.

Bourdieu, Pierre. 1998. "The Essence of Neo-Liberalism." *Le Monde Diplomatique.*
http://mondediplo.com/1998/12/08bourdieu.

Brodkin, K. 2000. "Global Capitalism: What's Race Got to Do with It?" *American
Ethnologist* 27 (2): 237–56.

Brooks, David. 2005. "Psst! Human Capital." *New York Times*, November 13, A12.

Browne, Katherine. 2004. *Creole Economics: Caribbean Cunning under the French Flag.*
Austin: University of Texas Press.

Bruni, Attila, Silvia Gherardi, and Barbara Poggio. 2005. *Gender and Entrepreneurship: An Ethnographic Approach.* New York: Psychology Press.

Bryce, Jane. 1998. "Young 'Ting Is the Name of the Game': Sexual Dynamics in
a Caribbean Romantic Fiction Series." In *Caribbean Portraits: Essays on Gender
Ideologies and Identities*, edited by Christine Barrow, 320–38. Kingston, Jamaica:
Ian Randle Publishers.

Bush, Barbara. 1981. "White 'Ladies,' Coloured 'Favorites,' Black 'Wenches': Some
Considerations on Sex, Race, and Class Factors in Social Relations in White Creole Society in the British Caribbean." *Slavery and Abolition* 2 (1): 245–62.

Chamberlain, Mary. 1998. *Caribbean Migration: Globalized Identities.* London:
Routledge.

Chaney, Elsa, and Mary Garcia Castro. 1989. *Muchachas No More: Household Workers
in Latin America and the Caribbean.* Philadelphia: Temple University Press.

Chevannes, Barry. 2001. *Learning to Be a Man: Culture, Socialization, and Gender
Identity in Five Caribbean Communities.* Kingston, Jamaica: University of the West
Indies Press.

Clarke, Edith. 1957. *My Mother Who Fathered Me: A Study of the Family in Three Selected Communities in Jamaica*. London: Allen and Unwin.

Clarke, John. 2008. "Living With/in and Without Neo-liberalism." *Focaal* 51 (1): 135–47.

Clough, Patricia Ticineto, and Jean Halley, eds. 2007. *The Affective Turn: Theorizing the Social*. Durham, NC: Duke University Press.

Cohen, Yehudi A. 1955. "Four Categories of Interpersonal Relation-Ships in the Family and Community in a Jamaican Village." *Anthropological Quarterly* 28 (4): 121–47.

Cohen, Yehudi A. 1956. "Structure and Function: Family Organization and Socialization in a Jamaican Community." *American Anthropologist* 58 (4): 664–86.

Cohen, Yehudi A. 1964. "The Establishment of Identity in a Social Nexus: The Special Case of Initiation Ceremonies and Their Relation to Value and Legal Systems." *American Anthropologist* 66 (3): 529–52.

Cohen, Yehudi A. 1971. *Man in Adaptation: The Institutional Framework*. Chicago: Aldine Atherton.

Collier, Jane Fishburne. 1997. *From Duty to Desire: Remaking Families in a Spanish Village*. Princeton, NJ: Princeton University Press.

Collins, Patricia Hill. 1992. "Black Women and Motherhood." In *Rethinking the Family: Some Feminist Questions*, rev. ed., edited by Barrie Thorne and Marilyn Yalom, 215–45. Boston: Northeastern University Press.

Collins, Patricia Hill. 2000. "Gender, Black Feminism, and Black Political Economy." *Annals of the American Academy of Political and Social Science* 568 (1): 41–53.

Comaroff, Jean, and John Comaroff. 2000. "Millennial Capitalism: First Thoughts on a Second Coming." *Public Culture* 12: 291–343.

Coontz, Stephanie. 2005. *Marriage, a History: From Obedience to Intimacy or How Love Conquered Marriage*. New York: Viking.

Coughlin, Jeanne Halliday, and Andrew R. Thomas. 2002. *The Rise of Women Entrepreneurs: People, Processes, and Global Trends*. Westport, CT: Quorum Books.

Crary, Jonathan. 2013. *24/7: Late Capitalism and the Ends of Sleep*. London: Verso.

Crichlow, Michaeline A., and Patricia Northover. 2009. *Globalization and the Post-Creole Imagination: Notes on Fleeing the Plantation*. Durham, NC: Duke University Press.

Crompton, Rosemary. 1989. "Class Theory and Gender." *British Journal of Sociology* 40 (4): 565–87.

Crompton, Rosemary, and Michael Mann. 1986. *Gender and Stratification*. Cambridge: Polity Press.

Dann, Graham. 1987. *The Barbadian Male: Sexual Attitudes and Practice*. London: Macmillan.

Davidoff, Leonore, and Catherine Hall. 1987. *Family Fortunes: Men and Women of the English Middle Class, 1780–1850*. Chicago: University of Chicago Press.

De Caires Narain, Denise. 2002. "Standing in the Place of Love: Sex, Love, and Loss in Jamaica Kincaid's Writing." In *Gendered Realities*, edited by Patricia Mohammed, 334–57. Mona, Jamaica: University of the West Indies Press.

De Caires Narain, Denise. 2012. "Naming Same-Sex Desire in Caribbean Women's Texts: Toward a Creolizing Hermeneutics." *Contemporary Women's Writing* 6 (3): 194–212.

Derne, Steve. 2005. "Globalization and the Making of a Transnational Middle Class: Implications for Class Analysis." In *Critical Globalization Studies*, edited by Richard P. Appelbaum and William I. Robinson, 177–86. New York: Routledge.

Derne, Steve. 2008. *Globalization on the Ground: New Media and the Transformation of Culture, Class, and Gender in India*. London: Sage.

Dill, Bonnie Thornton. 1994. *Across the Boundaries of Race and Class: An Exploration of Work and Family Among Black Female Domestic Servants*. New York: Garland.

Doughty, Melissa. 2012. "UN Official at Aspire Launch: Time to Look at 'MACHO' Men in the Caribbean." *Trinidad Guardian Newspaper*, November 29. http:// m.guardian.co.tt/news/2012-11-29/un-official-aspire-launch-time-look-%E2% 80%98macho%E2%80%99-men-caribbean.

Douglass, Lisa. 1992. *The Power of Sentiment: Love, Hierarchy, and the Jamaican Family Elite*. Boulder, CO: Westview Press.

Dunn, Elizabeth C. 2004. *Privatizing Poland: Baby Food, Big Business, and the Remaking of Labor*. Ithaca, NY: Cornell University Press.

Durant-González, Victoria. 1985. "Higglering: The Rural Women and the Internal Market System in Jamaica." *Rural Development in the Carribbean*, edited by P. I. Gomes, 103–22. London: C. Hurst.

Edmondson, Belinda. 2009. *Caribbean Middlebrow: Leisure Culture and the Middle Class*. Ithaca, NY: Cornell University Press.

Epstein, Irving, and Leslie Limage. 2008. *The Greenwood Encyclopedia of Children's Issues Worldwide*. Westport: Greenwood Press.

Evans, Hyacinth L. 1989. "Perspectives on the Socialization of the Working Class Jamaican Child." *Social and Economic Studies* 38 (3): 177–20.

Fairbanks, Eve. 2014. "Leave Sleep Alone!" *New York Times Magazine*, March 23, 42–43.

Fardon, Richard. 1990. *Localizing Strategies: Regional Traditions of Ethnographic Writing*. Washington, DC: Smithsonian Institution Press.

Fisher, Lawrence E. 1985. *Colonial Madness: Mental Health in the Barbadian Social Order*. New Brunswick, NJ: Rutgers University Press.

Florida, Richard L. 2002. *The Rise of the Creative Class: And How It's Transforming Work, Leisure, Community, and Everyday Life*. New York: Basic Books.

Foucault, Michel. 1980. *The History of Sexuality*. Translated by Robert Hurley. New York: Vintage Books.

Foucault, Michel. 1986. *The Care of the Self*, vol. 3, *The History of Sexuality*. New York: Vintage Books.

Foucault, Michel. 1988. "Technologies of the Self." In *Technologies of the Self: A Seminar with Michel Foucault*, edited by Luther H. Martin, Huck Gutman, and Patrick H. Hutton, 16–49. Amherst: University of Massachusetts Press.

Foucault, Michel. 2008. *The Birth of Biopolitics: Lectures at the Collège de France, 1978–79*. New York: Palgrave Macmillan.

Frazier, E. Franklin. 1962. *Black Bourgeoisie: The Rise of a New Middle Class in the United States*. New York: Collier.

Frazier, E. Franklin. 1966. *The Negro Family in the United States*. Chicago: University of Chicago Press.

Freeman, Carla. 2000. *High Tech and High Heels in the Global Economy: Women, Work, and Pink-Collar Identities in the Caribbean*. Durham, NC: Duke University Press.

Freeman, Carla. 2007. "The 'Reputation' of Neoliberalism." *American Ethnologist* 34 (2): 252–67.

Freeman, Carla, and Donna Murdock. 2001. "Enduring Traditions and New Directions in Feminist Ethnography in the Caribbean and Latin America." *Feminist Studies* 27: 423–58.

Freud, Sigmund. 1966. *Introductory Lectures on Psychoanalysis*. Translated and edited by James Strachey. New York: W. W. Norton.

Fuentes, Marisa J. 2010. "Power and Historical Figuring: Rachael Pringle Polgreen's Troubled Archive." *Gender and History* 22 (3): 564–84.

Furnham, Adrian. 1991. "The Protestant Work Ethic in Barbados." *Journal of Social Psychology* 131 (1): 29–43.

Gewertz, Deborah B., and Frederick K. Errington. 1999. *Emerging Class in Papua New Guinea: The Telling of Difference*. Cambridge: Cambridge University Press.

Gibson-Graham, J. K. 1996. *The End of Capitalism (as We Knew It): A Feminist Critique of Political Economy*. Cambridge: Blackwell.

Giddens, Anthony. 1971. *Capitalism and Modern Social Theory: An Analysis of the Writings of Marx, Durkheim and Max Weber*. Cambridge: Cambridge University Press.

Giddens, Anthony. 1991. *Modernity and Self-Identity: Self and Society in the Late Modern Age*. Palo Alto, CA: Stanford University Press.

Giddens, Anthony. 1992. *The Transformation of Intimacy: Sexuality, Love, and Eroticism in Modern Societies*. Palo Alto, CA: Stanford University Press.

Gill, Rosalind. 2008. "Culture and Subjectivity in Neoliberal and Postfeminist Times." *Subjectivity* 25: 432–45.

Gittens, Marsha. 2013. "Opportunities Still Exist, Despite Recession." *Barbados Advocate*, July 1. http://www.barbadosadvocate.com/newsitem.asp?more=local&NewsID=31328.

Goldthorpe, John H., and Clive Payne. 1986. "On the Class Mobility of Women: Results from Different Approaches to the Analysis of Recent British Data." *Sociology* 20 (4): 531–55.

Gonzalez, Nancie L. 1970. "Toward a Definition of Matrifocality." In *Afro-American Anthropology: Contemporary Perspectives*, edited by Norman E. Whitten Jr. and John F. Szwed, 231–44. New York: Free Press.

Gonzalez, Nancie L. 1984. "An Ancestral Harvest." *Sciences* 24 (1): 52–57.

Government of Barbados. 2000. *Continuous Household Labour Force Survey: Barbados Census*. Government of Barbados.

Government of Barbados. 2005. *National Strategic Plan, 2005–2025*. Research and

Planning Unit, Economic Affairs Division, Ministry of Economic Affairs and
Development. Bridgetown, Barbados.

Government of Barbados. 2006. *Best Practice Guide for Customer Service*. National
Initiative for Service Excellence, Barbados Trade Unions, and Barbados Private
Sector.

Government of Barbados. 2010. *Population and Housing Census, Volume 1*. Barbados
Statistical Service. Government of Barbados.

Greenfield, Sidney. 1966. *English Rustics in Black Skin: A Study of Modern Family
Forms in a Pre-Industrialized Society*. New Haven, CT: New College and University
Press.

Greenfield, Sidney. 1973. "Dominance, Focality, and the Characterization of Domestic Groups: Some Reflections on 'Matrifocality' in the Caribbean." In *The Family in
the Caribbean* (Proceedings of the First Conference on the Family in the Caribbean), edited by Stanford N. Gerber, 31–49. Río Piedras, Puerto Rico: Institute of
Caribbean Studies.

Greenfield, Sidney. 1977. "Patronage, Politics, and the Articulation of Local Community and National Society in Pre-1968 Brazil." *Journal of Interamerican Studies and
World Affairs* 19 (2): 139.

Gregg, Melissa. 2011. *Work's Intimacy*. Cambridge: Polity Press.

Gregson, Nicky, and Michelle Lowe. 1994. *Servicing the Middle Classes: Class, Gender,
and Waged Domestic Labour in Contemporary Britain*. New York: Routledge.

Hall, Catherine. 1992. *White, Male and Middle Class: Explorations in Feminism and
History*. New York: Routledge.

Handler, Jerome. 1981. "Joseph Rachell and Rachael Pringle-Polgreen: Petty Entrepreneurs." In *Struggle and Survival in Colonial America*, edited by David G. Sweet
and Gary B. Nash, 376–90. Berkeley: University of California Press.

Hardt, Michael. 1999. "Affective Labor." *Boundary 2* 26 (2): 89–100.

Hardt, Michael, and Antonio Negri. 2000. *Empire*. Cambridge, MA: Harvard University Press.

Hardt, Michael, and Antonio Negri. 2004. *Multitude: War and Democracy in the Age
of Empire*. New York: Penguin.

Harrison, Milmon F. 2005. *Righteous Riches: The World of Faith Movement in Contemporary African American Religion*. Oxford: Oxford University Press.

Hartmann, Heidi I. 1979. "The Unhappy Marriage of Marxism and Feminism:
Towards a More Progressive Union." *Capital and Class* 3 (2): 1–33.

Harvey, David. 2005. *A Brief History of Neoliberalism*. Oxford: Oxford University
Press.

Heiman, Rachel, Carla Freeman, and Mark Liechty. 2012. *Global Middle Classes: Theorizing Through Ethnography*. Santa Fe: School of American Research Press.

Heinze, Andrew R. 1992. *Adapting to Abundance: Jewish Immigrants, Mass Consumption, and the Search for American Identity*. New York: Columbia University Press.

Henriques, Fernando. 1949. "West Indian Family Organization." *American Journal of
Sociology* 55: 36–37.

Herskovits, Melville. 1958. *The Myth of the Negro Past*. Boston: Beacon Press.

Herskovits, Melville, and Frances Herskovits. 1947. *Trinidad Village*. New York: Alfred A. Knopf.

Hirsch, Jennifer, and Holly Wardlow. 2006. *Modern Loves: The Anthropology of Romantic Courtship and Companionate Marriage*. Ann Arbor: University of Michigan Press.

Hochschild, Arlie. 1983. *The Managed Heart: Commercialization of Human Feeling*. Berkeley: University of California Press.

Hochschild, Arlie. 1997. *The Time Bind: When Work Becomes Home and Home Becomes Work*. New York: Metropolitan Books.

Hochschild, Arlie. 2003. *The Commercialization of Intimate Life: Notes from Home and Work*. Berkeley: University of California Press.

Hodge, Merle. 1981. *Crick Crack, Monkey*. London: Heinemann.

Hodge, Merle. 2002. "We Kind of Family." In *Gendered Realities: Essays in Caribbean Feminist Thought*, edited by Patricia Mohammed, 474–85. Kingston, Jamaica: University of the West Indies Press.

hooks, bell. 1984. *Feminist Theory*. Cambridge, MA: South End Press.

Huffer, Lynne. 2013. *Are the Lips a Grave? Queer Feminist Reflections on the Ethics of Sex*. New York: Columbia University Press.

Hughes, Karen D. 2005. *Female Enterprise in the New Economy*. Toronto: University of Toronto Press.

Hurston, Zora Neale. 1950. "What White Publishers Won't Print." *Negro Digest* 8 (April).

Hurston, Zora Neale. 1990. *Mules and Men*. New York: Perennial Library.

Illouz, Eva. 1997. *Consuming the Romantic Utopia: Love and the Cultural Contradictions of Capitalism*. Berkeley: University of California Press.

Illouz, Eva. 2007. *Cold Intimacies: The Making of Emotional Capitalism*. Cambridge: Polity Press.

Illouz, Eva. 2008. *Saving the Modern Soul: Therapy, Emotions, and the Culture of Self-Help*. Berkeley: University of California Press.

Inhorn, Marcia Claire. 1994. *Quest for Conception: Gender, Infertility, and Egyptian Medical Traditions*. Philadelphia: University of Pennsylvania Press.

Jaffrelot, Christophe, and Peter Van der Veer. 2008. *Patterns of Middle-Class Consumption in India and China*. Los Angeles: Sage.

James, C. L. R. (Cyril Lionel Robert). 1962. *Party Politics in the West Indies*. San Juan, Trinidad: Vedic Enterprises.

Jayawardena, Chandra. 1963. *Conflict and Solidarity in a Guianese Plantation*. London: University of London, Athlone Press.

John-Smith, Marie-Elena. 2007. *Unburnable*. New York: Amistad.

Johnson, Howard, Karl S. Watson, and Raymond Danowski, eds. 1998. *The White Minority in the Caribbean*. Kingston, Jamaica: Ian Randle Publishers.

Jones, Gavin. 1997. "Modernization and Divorce: Contrasting Trends in Islamic Southeast Asia and the West." *Population and Development Review* 23: 95–114.

Kang, Millann. 2010. *The Managed Hand: Race, Gender, and the Body in Beauty Service Work*. Berkeley: University of California Press.

Karch, Cecilia A. 1981. "The Growth of the Corporate Economy in Barbados: Class/Race Factors, 1890–1988." In *Contemporary Caribbean, a Sociological Reader*, 213–41. Maracas, Trinidad and Tobago: College Press.

Karch, Cecilia A. 1985. "Class Formation and Class and Race Relations in the West Indies, 1833–1876." In *Middle Classes in Dependent Countries*, edited by Dale L. Johnson. Beverly Hills, CA: Sage.

Katz, Cindi. 2012. "Just Managing: American Middle Class Parenting in Insecure Times." In *The Global Middle Classes: Theorizing Through Ethnography*, edited by Rachel Heiman, Carla Freeman, and Mark Liechty, 169–87. Santa Fe: SAR Press.

Katzin, Margaret. 1959. "The Jamaican Country Higgler." *Social and Economic Studies* 8 (4): 421–40.

Khan, M. A. 2005. "Internationalization of Services: The Global Impact of US Franchise Restaurants." Special issue. *Journal of Services Research* 5: 187–215.

Kincaid, Jamaica. 1988. *A Small Place*. New York: Farrar, Straus and Giroux.

King, Deborah K. 1988. "Multiple Jeopardy, Multiple Consciousness: The Context of a Black Feminist Ideology." *Signs* 14: 42–72.

Kingfisher, Catherine, and Jeff Maskovsky. 2008. "The Limits of Neoliberalism." *Critique of Anthropology* 28 (2): 115–26.

Kipnis, Andrew. 2007. "Neoliberalism Reified: Suzhi Discourse and Tropes of Neoliberalism in the People's Republic of China." *Journal of the Royal Anthropological Institute* 13 (2): 383–400.

Kipnis, Andrew B. 2008. "Audit Cultures: Neoliberal Governmentality, Socialist Legacy, or Technologies of Governing?" *American Ethnologist* 35 (2): 275–89.

Klinenberg, Eric. 2012. *Going Solo: The Extraordinary Rise and Surprising Appeal of Living Alone*. New York: Penguin Press.

Knowles, William H. 1956. "Social Consequences of Economic Change in Jamaica." *Annals of the American Academy of Political and Social Science* 305: 134–44.

Kristof, Nicholas D., and Sheryl WuDunn. 2010. *Half the Sky: Turning Oppression into Opportunity for Women Worldwide*. New York: Vintage Books.

Kruks, Sonia. 2001. *Retrieving Experience: Subjectivity and Recognition in Feminist Politics*. Ithaca, NY: Cornell University Press.

Kulick, Don. 2006. "Theory in Furs: Masochistic Anthropology." *Cultural Anthropology* 47: 933–52.

Lacey, Marc. 2008. "Attacks Show Easygoing Jamaica Is Dire Place for Gays." *New York Times*, February 24.

Lacy, Karyn. 2007. *Blue-chip Black: Race, Class and Status in the New Black Middle Class*. Berkeley: University of California Press.

Lamming, George. 1954. *In the Castle of My Skin*. New York: McGraw-Hill.

Lamming, George. 1983. *In the Castle of My Skin*. With a new introduction by the author. New York: Schocken Books.

Lamming, George. 2011. *Caribbean Reasonings: The George Lamming Reader*. Kingston, Jamaica: Ian Randle Publishers.

Lan, Pei-Chia. 2006. *Global Cinderellas: Migrant Domestics and Newly Rich Employers in Taiwan*. Durham, NC: Duke University Press.

Landry, Bart. 2000. *Black Working Wives: Pioneers of the American Family Revolution*. Berkeley: University of California Press.

Lane, Carrie M. 2011. *A Company of One: Insecurity, Independence, and the New World of White-Collar Unemployment*. Ithaca, NY: ILR Press.

Lareau, Annette. 2003. *Unequal Childhoods: Class, Race, and Family Life*. Berkeley: University of California Press.

Larkin, Brian. 1997. "Indian Films and Nigerian Lovers: Media and the Creation of Parallel Modernities." *Africa: Journal of the International African Institute* 67 (3): 406.

Lasch, Christopher. 1991. *The Culture of Narcissism: American Life in an Age of Diminishing Expectations*. New York: Norton.

Lash, Scott, and John Urry. 1987. *The End of Organized Capitalism*. Madison: University of Wisconsin Press.

Lazzarato, M. 1996. "Immaterial Labor." In *Radical Thought in Italy: A Potential Politics*, edited by Michael Hardt and Paulo Virno, 133–47. Minneapolis: University of Minnesota Press.

Leidner, Robin. 1999. "Emotional Labor in Service Work." *Annals of the American Academy of Political and Social Science* 561: 81–95.

Lewis, Gordon. 1968. *The Growth of the Modern West Indies*. New York: Monthly Review Press.

Lewis, Gordon. 1974. "On the Dangers of Composing a West Indian Anthology." *Caribbean Studies* 14 (1): 121–32.

Liechty, Mark. 2003. *Suitably Modern: Making Middle-Class Culture in a New Consumer Society*. Princeton, NJ: Princeton University Press.

Lutz, Catherine. 1986. "Emotion, Thought, and Estrangement: Emotion as a Cultural Category." *Cultural Anthropology* 1 (3): 287–309.

Lutz, Catherine, and Jeffrey M. White. 1986. "The Anthropology of Emotions." *Annual Review of Anthropology* 15: 405–36.

Mantz, Jeffrey W. 2007. "How a Huckster Becomes a Custodian of Market Morality: Traditions of Flexibility in Exchange in Dominica." *Identities* 14 (1–2): 19–38.

Marquand, David. 1992. "The Enterprise Culture: Old Wine in New Bottles?" In *The Values of the Enterprise Culture: The Moral Debate*, edited by Paul Heelas and Paul Morris, 61–72. London: Routledge.

Marshall, Jennifer Freeman. 2008. "Constructions of Literary and Ethnographic Authority, Canons, Community and Zora Neale Hurston." PhD dissertation, Emory University.

Marshall, Paule. 1970. *Brown Girl, Brownstones*. New York: Avon.

Martin, Emily. 1994. *Flexible Bodies: Tracking Immunity in American Culture from the Days of Polio to the Age of AIDS*. Boston: Beacon.

Martin, Luther, Huck Gutman, and Patrick Hutton, eds. 1988. "Truth, Power, Self: An Interview with Michel Foucault (October 25, 1982, with Rux Martin)." In *Technologies of the Self: A Seminar with Michel Foucault*, edited by Luther H. Martin, Huck Gutman, and Patrick H. Hutton, 9–15. Amherst: University of Massachusetts Press.

Massiah, Joycelin. 1983. *Women as Heads of Households in the Caribbean: Family Structure and Feminine Status*. Paris: UNESCO.

Mathurin, Lucille. 1975. *The Rebel Woman in the British West Indies during Slavery*. Kingston: Institute of Jamaica.

McMahon, Darrin M. 2005. *Happiness: A History*. New York: Atlantic Monthly Press.

Meyer, Birgit. 2004. "Christianity in Africa: From African Independent to Pentecostal-Charismatic Churches." *Annual Review of Anthropology* 33 (1): 447–74.

Miller, Errol. 1991. *Men at Risk*. Kingston: Jamaica Pub. House.

Mills, C. 1951. *White Collar: The American Middle Classes*. New York: Oxford University Press.

Mintz, Sidney. 1955. "The Jamaican Internal Marketing Pattern: Some Notes and Hypotheses." *Social and Economic Studies* 4: 95–103.

Mintz, Sidney. 1978. "Was the Plantation Slave a Proletarian?" *Review* 2 (1): 81–98.

Mintz, Sidney. 1985. *Sweetness and Power: The Place of Sugar in Modern History*. New York: Viking.

Mirchandani, Kirin. 2005. "Gender Eclipsed? Racial Hierarchies in Transnational Call Center Work." *Social Justice* 32 (4): 105–19.

Mohammed, Patricia. 1988. *The Caribbean Family Revisited*. Kingston, Jamacia: University of West Indies, Women and Development Studies, Project Gender in Caribbean Development.

Mohammed, Patricia, ed. 2002. *Gendered Realities: Essays in Caribbean Feminist Thought*. Kingston, Jamaica: University of the West Indies Press.

Mohanty, Chandra. 1991. *Third World Women and the Politics of Feminism*. Bloomington: Indiana University Press.

Morgan, Paula. 2003. "'Like Bush Fire in My Arms': Interrogating the World of Caribbean Romance." *Journal of Popular Culture* 36 (4): 804.

Morrissey, Marietta. 1998. "Explaining the Caribbean Family." In *Caribbean Portraits: Essays on Gender Ideologies and Identities*, edited by Christine Barrow, 78–92. Kingston, Jamaica: Ian Randle Publishers.

Moses, Yolanda T. 1981. "Female Status, the Family and Male Dominance in a West Indian Community." In *The Black Woman Cross-Culturally*. Cambridge: Schenkman.

Munasinghe, Viranjini. 2001. *Callaloo or Tossed Salad? East Indians and the Cultural Politics of Identity in Trinidad*. Ithaca, NY: Cornell University Press.

Murray, David A. B. 2012. *Flaming Souls: Homosexuality, Homophobia, and Social Change in Barbados*. Toronto: University of Toronto Press.

Nader, Laura. 1972. "Up the Anthropologist—Perspectives Gained from 'Studying Up.'" In *Reinventing Anthropology*, edited by Dell Hymes, 284–311. New York: Pantheon.

Newstead, Clare. 2009. "Regional Governmentality: Neoliberalization and the Caribbean Community Single Market and Economy." *Singapore Journal of Tropical Geography* 30 (2): 158–73.

Newton, Melanie. 2008. *The Children of Africa in the Colonies: Free People of Color in Barbados in the Age of Emancipation*. Baton Rouge: Louisiana State University Press.

Ngai, Sianne. 2013. "On Cruel Optimism." *Periscope, Social Text*. http://www.social textjournal.org/periscope/2013/01/untitled-ngai.php#more.

Ong, Aihwa. 1987. *Spirits of Resistance and Capitalist Discipline: Factory Women in Malaysia*. Albany: State University of New York Press.

Ong, Aihwa. 1999. *Flexible Citizenship: The Cultural Logics of Transnationality*. Durham, NC: Duke University Press.

Ong, Aihwa. 2006. *Neoliberalism as Exception: Mutations in Citizenship and Sovereignty*. Durham, NC: Duke University Press.

Ong, Aihwa. 2007a. "Neoliberalism as a Mobile Technology." *Transactions of the Institute of British Geographers* 32 (1): 3–8.

Ong, Aihwa. 2007b. "Neoliberalism as a Mobile Technology." *Boundary Crossings* 32: 3–8.

Osirim, M. J. 1997. "We Toil All the Livelong Day: Women in the English Speaking Caribbean." In *Daughters of Caliban: Caribbean Women in the Twentieth Century*, edited by Consuelo Lopez Springfield, 41–67. Bloomington: Indiana University Press.

Ozyegin, Gul. 2001. *Untidy Gender: Domestic Service in Turkey*. Philadelphia: Temple University Press.

Ozyegin, Gul. Forthcoming. *Facades for New Desires: Gender, Sex and Self-making among Young Turks*. New York: New York University Press.

Padilla, Mark. 2007. *Love and Globalization: Transformations of Intimacy in the Contemporary World*. Nashville: Vanderbilt University Press.

Pakulski, Jan, and Malcolm Waters. 1996. *The Death of Class*. London: Sage.

Patico, Jennifer. 2008. *Consumption and Social Change in a Post-Soviet Middle Class*. Washington, DC: Woodrow Wilson Center Press.

Patillo-McCoy, Mary. 1999. *Black Picket Fences: Privilege and Peril among the Black Middle Class*. Chicago: University of Chicago Press.

Peiss, Kathy Lee. 1986. *Cheap Amusements: Working Women and Leisure in Turn-of-the-Century New York*. Philadelphia: Temple University Press.

Peletz, Michael G. 2005. "The King Is Dead; Long Live the Queen!" *American Ethnologist* 32 (1): 39–41.

Pierce, Jennifer. 1996. "Rambo Litigators: Emotional Labor in a Male-dominated Occupation." *Research on Men and Masculinities* 9: 1–28.

Potrzeba, Denise Lett. 1998. *In Pursuit of Status: The Making of South Korea's "New" Urban Middle Class*. Cambridge, MA: Harvard University Press.

Puri, Manju, and David T. Robinson. 2004. *Optimism, Work/Life Choices, and Entrepreneurship*. World Bank.

Radhakrishnan, Smitha. 2011. *Appropriately Indian: Gender and Culture in a New Transnational Class*. Durham, NC: Duke University Press.

Rapp, Rayna. 1978. "Family and Class in Contemporary America: Notes Toward an Understanding of Ideology." *Science and Society* 42: 278–300.

Reay, Diane. 2000. "A Useful Extension of Bourdieu's Conceptual Framework? Emotional Capital as a Way of Understanding Mothers' Involvement in Their Children's Education." *Sociological Review* 48 (4): 568–85.

Reber, Dierdra. 2012. "Headless Capitalism: Affect as Free-Market Episteme." *Differences: A Journal of Feminist Cultural Studies* 23 (1): 62–100.

Reynolds, Tracey. 1997. "Class Matters, 'Race' Matters, Gender Matters." In *Class*

Matters: "Working-Class" Women's Perspectives on Social Class, edited by Pat Mahony and Christine Zmroczek, 8–17. London: Taylor and Francis.

Rieff, Philip. 2006. *The Triumph of the Therapeutic: Uses of Faith after Freud*. Wilmington: ISI Books.

Roberts, Bryan. 1994. "Informal Economy and Family Strategies." *International Journal of Urban and Regional Research* 18 (1): 6–23.

Rodman, Hyman. 1971. *Lower-Class Families: The Culture of Poverty in Negro Trinidad*. Oxford: Oxford University Press.

Rofel, Lisa. 1999. *Other Modernities: Gendered Yearnings in China after Socialism*. Berkeley: University of California Press.

Rofel, Lisa. 2007. *Desiring China: Experiments in Neoliberalism, Sexuality, and Public Culture*. Durham, NC: Duke University Press.

Rollins, Judith. 1985. *Between Women: Domestics and Their Employers*. Philadelphia: Temple University Press.

Rosaldo, Michelle Zimbalist, and Michelle Lamphere. 1974. "Woman, Culture and Society: A Theoretical Overview." In *Woman, Culture, and Society*, edited by Michelle Zimbalist Rosaldo, Louise Lamphere, Joan Bamberger, 17–42. Palo Alto, CA: Stanford University Press.

Rose, Nikolas. 1990. *Governing the Soul: The Shaping of the Private Self*. London: Free Association Books.

Rose, Nikolas. 1992. "Governing the Enterprising Self." In *The Values of the Enterprise Culture: The Moral Debate*, edited by Paul Hellas and Paul Morris, 141–64. London: Routledge.

Rowley, Michelle. 2002. "Reconceptualizing Voice: The Role of Matrifocality in Shaping Theories and Caribbean Voices." In *Gendered Realities: Essays in Caribbean Feminist Thought*, edited by Patricia Mohammed, 22–43. Kingston, Jamaica: University of the West Indies Press.

Ryan, Selwyn, and Lou Anne Barclay. 1992. *Sharks and Sardines: Blacks in Business in Trinidad and Tobago*. St. Augustine, Trinidad: Institute of Social and Economic Studies, University of the West Indies.

Sacks, Karen Brodkin. 1989. "Toward a Unified Theory of Class, Race, and Gender." *American Ethnologist* 16 (3): 534–50.

Safa, Helen. 1965. "The Female-Based Household in Public Housing: A Case Study in Puerto Rico." *Human Organization* 24: 135–39.

Sangren, Steven. 2006. "Comment on Theory in Furs: Masochist Anthropology by Don Kulick." *American Ethnologist* 47: 946–47.

Scheper-Hughes, Nancy, and Philippe Bourgois. 2003. Foreword to Donna Goldstein's *Laughter Out of Place: Race, Class, Violence and Sexuality in a Rio Shantytown*, xiii–xvii. Berkeley: University of California Press.

Schreiber, Rita, Phyllis Noerager Stern, and Charmaine Wilson. 2000. "Being Strong: How Black West-Indian Canadian Women Manage Depression and Its Stigma." *Journal of Nursing Scholarship* 32 (1): 39–45.

Schwartz Cowan, Ruth. 1983. *More Work for Mother: The Ironies of Household Technology from the Open Hearth to the Microwave*. New York: Basic Books.

Seager, Joni. 1997. *State of Women in the World Atlas*. London: Penguin.

Senior, Olive. 1991. *Working Miracles: Women's Lives in the English Speaking Caribbean*. Bloomington: Indiana University Press.

Sheppard, Jill. 1977. *The "Redlegs" of Barbados, Their Origins and History*. Millwood, NY: KTO Press.

Shore, Bradd. 2008. "Reading Samoans through Tahitians." *Ethos* 33 (4): 487–92.

Skeggs, Beverly. 1997. *Formations of Class and Gender*. London: Sage.

Smail, John. 1994. *The Origins of Middle-Class Culture: Halifax, Yorkshire, 1660–1780*. Ithaca, NY: Cornell University Press.

Smith, Dan, Jennifer Sue Hirsch, and Holly Wardlow. 2006. *Courting for Love and Marrying for Children*. In *Modern Loves: The Anthropology of Romantic Courtship and Companionate Marriage*. Ann Arbor: University of Michigan Press.

Smith, R. T. 1963. "Culture and Social Structure in the Caribbean: Some Recent Work on Family and Kinship Studies." *Comparative Studies in Society and History* 6 (1): 24–46.

Smith, R. T. 1971. *The Negro Family in British Guiana: Family Structure and Social Status in the Villages*. London: Routledge and Kegan Paul.

Smith, R. T. 1973. "The Matrifocal Family." In *The Character of Kinship*, edited by Jack Goody, 121–44. Cambridge: Cambridge University Press.

Smith, R. T. 1988. *Kinship and Class in the West Indies: A Genealogical Study of Jamaica and Guyana*. Cambridge: Cambridge University Press.

Smith, R. T. 1996. *The Matrifocal Family: Power, Pluralism, and Politics*. New York: Routledge.

Sobo, Elisa. 1993. *One Blood: The Jamaican Body*. Albany: SUNY Press.

Spry Rush, Anne. 2011. *Bonds of Empire: West Indians and Britishness from Victoria to Decolonization*. Oxford: Oxford University Press.

Stafford, Patricia. 2002. "The Star of Hope Is Rising: The Urban Black and Brown Middle Class in Barbados 1838 to 1865." Cave Hill, Barbados: University of the West Indies.

Stafford, Patricia. 2006. *The Growth and Development of the Brown and Black Middle Class, 1838–1988, and Its Role in the Shaping of Modern Barbados*. Cave Hill, Barbados: University of the West Indies.

Steedman, Carolyn. 1986. *Landscape for a Good Woman: A Story of Two Lives*. London: Virago.

Stewart, Kathleen. 2010. "Worlding Refrains." In *The Affect Theory Reader*, edited by Melissa Gregg and Gregory J. Seigworth, 339–54. Durham, NC: Duke University Press.

Stewart, Simon. 2010. *Culture and the Middle Classes*. Farnham, UK: Ashgate.

Swidler, Ann. 2001. *Talk of Love: How Culture Matters*. Chicago: University of Chicago Press.

Thanulingom, N. 2000. "Cultural Dimensions of Modern Entrepreneurship." In *Women Entrepreneurship*, edited by K. Sasikumar, 77–80. Chennai, India: Vikas.

Thomas, Deborah A. 2004. *Modern Blackness: Nationalism, Globalization, and the Politics of Culture in Jamaica*. Durham, NC: Duke University Press.

Thomas, Deborah A. 2009. "The Violence of Diaspora: Governmentality, Class Cultures and Circulations." *Radical History Review* 103: 83–104.

Townsend, Nicholas W. 2002. *The Package Deal: Marriage Work and Fatherhood in Men's Lives*. Philadelphia: Temple University Press.

Trotz, Alyssa. 2009. "MACHO: More Than an Acronym." *Stabroek News*. http://www.stabroeknews.com/2009/features/05/11/macho-more-than-an-acronym/.

Trouillot, Michel-Rolph. 1989. "Discourses of Rule and the Acknowledgment of the Peasantry in Dominica, W.I., 1838–1928." *American Ethnologist* 16 (4): 704–18.

Trouillot, Michel-Rolph. 1992. "The Caribbean Region: An Open Frontier in Anthropological Theory." *Annual Review of Anthropology* 21 (1): 19–42.

Trouillot, Michel-Rolph. 2002. "The Otherwise Modern: Caribbean Lessons from the Savage Slot." In *Critically Modern: Alternatives, Alterities, Anthropologies*, edited by Bruce Knauft, 220–40. Bloomington: Indiana University Press.

Trouillot, Michel-Rolph. 2003. *Global Transformations: Anthropology and the Modern World*. New York: Palgrave Macmillan.

Ulysse, Gina A. 2007. *Downtown Ladies: Informal Commercial Importers, a Haitian Anthropologist, and Self-Making in Jamaica*. Chicago: University of Chicago Press.

United Nations Development Programme. 2012. *Caribbean Human Development Report: The Shift to Better Citizen Security*. Regional Reports: Latin America and the Caribbean. New York: UNDP.

U.S. Central Intelligence Agency. 2012. *The CIA World Factbook 2013*. New York: Skyhorse.

Wacquant, Loic J. D. 1991. "Making Class: The Middle Class(es) in Social Theory and Social Structure." In *Bringing Class Back In*, edited by Rhonda F. Levine and Scott G. McNall, 39–64. Boulder, CO: Westview.

Walkerdine, Valerie. 2003. "Reclassifying Upward Mobility: Femininity and the Neoliberal Subject." *Gender and Education* 15: 237–48.

Wang, Wendy, Kim Parker, and Paul Taylor. 2013. *Breadwinner Moms: Mothers Are the Sole or Primary Provider in Four in Ten Households with Children; Public Conflicted About the Growing Trend*. Pew Research Center. http://www.pewsocialtrends.org/files/2013/05/Breadwinner_moms_final.pdf.

Wardlow, Holly. 1996. "Bobby Teardrops: A Turkish Video in Papua New Guinea: Reflections on Cultural Studies, Feminism, and the Anthropology of Mass Media." *Visual Anthropology Review* 12 (1): 30–46.

Wardlow, Holly. 2006. *Wayward Women: Sexuality and Agency in a New Guinea Society*. Berkeley: University of California Press.

Watters, Ethan. 2010. *Crazy Like Us: The Globalization of the American Psyche*. New York: Free Press.

Weber, Max. [1930] 1998. *The Protestant Ethic and the Spirit of Capitalism*, 2nd ed. Introduction by Randall Collins. Los Angeles: Roxbury.

Weeks, Kathi. 2007. "Life within and against Work: Affective Labor, Feminist Critique and Post-Fordist Politics." *Ephemera: Theory and Politics in Organization* 7 (1): 233–49.

Weeks, Kathi. 2011. *The Problem with Work: Feminism, Marxism, Antiwork Politics, and Postwork Imaginaries*. Durham, NC: Duke University Press.

Williams, Eric Eustace. 1944. *Capitalism and Slavery*. Chapel Hill: University of North Carolina Press.

Williams, Raymond. 1961. *The Long Revolution*. New York: Columbia University Press.

Williams, Raymond. 1977. *Marxism and Literature*. Oxford: Oxford University Press.

Wilson, Peter. 1964. "General and Ethnology: Kinship and Community in Carriacou, M. G. Smith." *American Anthropologist* 66 (1): 172–74.

Wilson, Peter. 1969. "Reputation and Respectability: A Suggestion for Caribbean Ethnology." *Man* 4 (1): 70–84.

Wilson, Peter. 1973. *Crab Antics: The Social Anthropology of English-Speaking Negro Societies of the Caribbean*. New Haven, CT: Yale University Press.

Wingfield, Adia Harvey. 2008. *Doing Business with Beauty: Black Women, Hair Salons, and the Racial Enclave Economy*. Lanham, MD: Rowman and Littlefield.

Wolcott, Victoria. 2001. *Remaking Respectability: African American Women in Interwar Detroit*. Chapel Hill: University of North Caroline Press.

World Bank. 2011. *Work and Family: Latin American and Caribbean Women in Search of a New Balance*. https://openknowledge.worldbank.org/handle/10986/12489.

Yanchus, Nancy J., Lilian T. Eby, Charles E. Lance, and Sabrina Drollinger. 2010. "The Impact of Emotional Labor on Work–Family Outcomes." *Journal of Vocational Behavior* 76 (1): 105–17.

Young, Iris Marion. 2005. *On Female Body Experience: "Throwing like a girl" and Other Essays*. New York: Oxford University Press.

Zhang, Li. 2010. *In Search of Paradise: Middle-Class Living in a Chinese Metropolis*. Ithaca, NY: Cornell University Press.

Zhou, Xiaohong, and Chen Quin. 2010. "Globalization, Social Transformation, and the Construction of China's Middle Class." In *China's Emerging Middle Class: Beyond Economic Transformation*, edited by Cheng Li, 84–103. Washington, DC: Brookings Institution.

Zobel, Joseph. 1980. *Black Shack Alley [La rue Cases-Nègres]*. Washington, DC: Three Continents.

INDEX

Page numbers for figures are followed by f; page numbers for tables are followed by t.

entrepreneurship: calling toward, 49–50, 189–97; gendered dimensions of, 6, 15, 25, 35–36, 46–56, 66–85, 90–94, 102–6, 120, 123–29, 132–34, 139, 145–53, 156, 211–14; as means of economic development, 5, 9, 29–32, 183, 208, 213, 218n12; as means of nation building, 29, 31; reputation and, 10, 23, 34–35, 48t, 109, 205, 209, 215; respectability and, 10, 23–28, 35, 48t, 51, 70, 109, 174, 184, 188, 204, 209, 215; state support for, 13, 31, 32; upward mobility through, 9, 23, 26–27, 34, 46–56, 61, 62, 77, 82, 93, 102, 120

exercise, 50, 84, 131, 164, 172–73. *See also* care: of the self

extractive industries, 27

extramarital affairs, 55, 79, 122, 126, 127, 228n25

family, 30, 60, 61, 71, 72, 73, 159–60, 185; Barbados Family Law Act, 60; nuclear families, 79, 98, 108, 155, 171, 185; structure of in Barbados/Caribbean, 61, 185. *See also* fathers; kinship; matrifocality; mothers; parenting; patriarchy

fashion, 159, 194–96, 199

fathers, 72–73, 76, 79, 81, 98, 119, 121, 129, 152, 158, 162, 163, 165; absence of, 50–52, 68, 74, 117–18, 121, 162–65, 224n16; fatherhood, 88, 128, 158

feelings. *See* emotions

femininity, 15, 22t, 24, 41, 49–55, 69–70, 78, 82, 89, 92, 93, 100t, 102, 103, 107–15, 120, 136, 139, 141, 176, 214

feminism, 115, 171, 227n15; development and, 39; postcolonial, 40, 219n19; race and, 40–41; scholarship on, 39, 137; second-wave, 39, 170, 171

fidelity, 22t, 60, 64, 79, 90, 121, 128, 135

fieldwork, 6, 12–15

flexibility, 10, 16, 28, 30, 35, 58, 59, 70, 97, 106, 108, 134–35, 144, 149, 153, 172, 179, 182, 204, 210–15; matrifocality and, 100, 101, 105, 108, 115, 120, 210; neoliberalism and, 1–4, 9–10, 18–20, 31–33, 48t, 50, 53, 57, 85, 103, 107, 129, 150, 152, 154, 162, 176, 194, 203, 208–10, 214; reputation and, 20–24, 22t, 29, 32, 35, 82, 86, 114, 127, 134, 208

Foucault, Michel, 1–2, 7, 207; on care of the self, 174; on governmentality, 18; on neoliberalism, 18; on technologies of the self, 1–2, 182

Freud, Sigmund, 67, 170, 171

Gates, Bill, 31, 34

gender, 1–2, 6, 9, 13, 16, 24, 35–46, 52–61, 68, 78, 93, 99, 103–5, 126–29, 188, 214–15, 219n20, 220n26, 221n6, 222n9, 224n24, 225n5, 227n15; affect and, 36, 59, 72–73, 141, 230n6; in Caribbean, 69–70, 76–81, 88–92, 105–9, 149, 123–26, 151, 171, 179, 210, 227n16, 231n14; entrepreneurship and, 15, 25, 34–39, 46–56, 66–85, 90–94, 102–6, 120, 123–29, 132–53, 156, 211–14; labor and, 40, 61, 71–74, 115, 151, 229n1; neoliberalism and, 58, 78–82. *See also* femininity; masculinity; social life: sex-segregation of

Giddens, Anthony, 82, 143

globalization, 4, 7, 10, 11, 20, 31, 37, 221n6, 232n5; interactions with locality, 10–12, 21, 89–95, 134–35, 168, 208, 209, 215

God, 49, 189, 190–93, 197–200. *See also* religion

gossip, 24, 55, 69, 133, 211

Hardt, Michael, 181, 230n6

heteronormativity, 69, 217n5, 222n10

higglers, 24, 46, 109, 133

Hochschild, Arlie, 138, 144, 180; "cautionary tales," 63; *The Managed Heart*, 136; surface acting and deep acting, 140–41

Hodge, Merle, 57, 84, 86

homemaking, 157. *See also* domestic work

homophobia, 68–69, 217n5, 222n9, 223n11

homosexuality, 68–70, 138, 188, 217n5, 222n10, 224n22

horizontal mobility, 48, 55

housework. *See* domestic work

Hurston, Zora Neale, 41, 220n21

illness, 145, 178–79, 193. *See also* madness; obesity; psychological services; race: and health; stress; women: health and

Illouz, Eva, 91, 170; therapeutic culture, 6, 170; emotional capitalism, 8, 152

imagination, 2, 3, 20, 32, 156, 171

individualism, 19, 21, 28, 32, 33, 48t, 93, 107, 162, 203, 210, 222n8

informal sector, 22t, 25, 103, 126, 133, 134, 172, 198, 214, 230n3

informatics sector, 12, 125, 155, 230n3

Internet, 9–10

James, C. L. R., 41, 45

Kincaid, Jamaica, 55

kin networks, 43, 53, 54, 75, 76, 117, 118, 121, 126, 155, 177

kinship, 6, 8, 24, 30, 40, 44, 48, 55, 58, 59, 75, 80, 81, 90, 97, 107, 108, 110, 129, 133, 210, 221n4, 221n6, 224n18, 226n8, 226n10; in Caribbean, 42, 44, 61, 62, 65, 75, 76, 79, 80, 85, 86, 88, 90, 91, 93, 95–106, 116, 117, 126–29, 141, 179, 180, 194, 195, 221n4, 223n14, 223n15, 225n3, 227n12, 228n19

labor: affective dimensions of, 3, 6, 14, 36, 74, 79, 82, 94, 95, 132, 135–41, 144, 156, 163, 166–69, 177–81, 197, 207, 212–15; division of, 60, 68, 70–74, 81, 123, 125, 131–68, 231n13; gendered dimensions of, 36, 71, 123, 133, 137, 138, 146; reproductive labor, 40, 71, 95, 133, 134, 137, 138, 151, 210, 214, 215

labor migration, 23, 115, 172, 225n3

labor unions, 27

Lamming, George, 44, 97, 98

leisure, 77, 79, 92, 156, 158–65, 172, 182, 231n8. *See also* quality time; social life

love, 7, 81–82, 91–94, 117, 144, 162, 168, 217n4, 224nn17,18, 228n23; partnership marriage and, 65, 71, 74, 81, 91, 223n13; popular representations of, 84–91, 212; romantic love, 58–62, 82–86, 95, 107, 224n21

madness, 184. *See also* psychological services; stress

Males at Cave Hill Operations (MACHO), 229n2

"marginal male" phenomenon, 79, 81, 99, 126, 221n6, 229n2

marriage, 110t, 225nn4,5; affective dimensions of, 61–66, 69–77, 81, 84, 85, 89–92, 94, 103, 108, 126, 139, 221n6; Caribbean understandings of, 57, 82, 86, 87; companionate/partnership marriage, 57–95, 58t, 107, 108, 196, 211, 221n6; men's narratives on, 70–73; reformulations of, 58, 85, 89, 90, 93, 115; respectability and, 59, 61, 62, 86, 100; spousal abuse, 64, 67, 74, 84; weddings, 83; women's narratives on, 63–70, 201, 211

Martin, Emily, 19

Marx, Karl, 42, 204, 207; on class, 37–38; on labor, 212

masculinity, 10, 15, 22t, 24, 68, 70, 78–82, 127, 128, 186, 188, 215, 221n6, 227n15, 231n14

mass media, 9, 14, 18, 20, 58, 84, 85, 87, 88, 92, 107, 133, 137, 150, 172, 185, 194

matrifocality, 43–45, 58–62, 75–76, 85, 93, 95, 97–129, 100t, 139, 169, 208, 209, 215, 221n4, 225n3, 226n6, 227n15

meditation, 170, 183. *See also* care: of the self

men, 22t, 70, 71, 78; in Barbados, 8, 25, 26, 43, 55, 66, 68, 78, 79, 80, 87, 92, 106, 121, 124, 125, 127, 186–88, 197; emotional expression by, 66, 72, 73, 78, 186, 187, 223n12; marginality of, 79, 81, 99, 126, 221n6, 229n2; masculinity, 10, 15, 22t, 24, 68, 70, 78–82, 127, 128, 186, 188, 215, 221n6, 227n15, 231n14; men's movement, 80, 133, 229n2; relationship with mothers, 76, 80, 127, 223n14, 225n4

Men's Educational Support Association (MESA), 80

middle classes, 8–9, 16–56, 59, 61, 75, 90–95, 107, 182, 189, 219nn19,20; anxieties regarding, 36–47, 158, 160;

middle classes (*continued*)

black middle classes, 27, 41, 153, 194, 220n23, 225n2, 228n24; churches of, 194, 196, 200, 204; culture of, 20, 77, 79, 84, 92, 220n25; pathways to, 9, 14, 62; religion among, 169–205; studies of, 12, 14, 37–39, 219n19. *See also* class; upward mobility

Mills, C. Wright, 136

Mintz, Sidney, 23

mothers, 49, 50, 51, 53, 58, 60, 64, 74, 76, 97, 116, 127, 132, 138, 158, 162, 164; men's relationship to, 76, 80, 127; motherhood, 25, 40, 43, 46, 54, 60, 65, 69, 72, 113, 114, 146–47

music, 63, 85, 210; calypso, 7, 69, 70, 85, 86, 88, 113, 212; in churches, 194, 196, 199, 202, 204; popular music, 61, 88, 92

Nader, Laura, 38

nanny-housekeeper, 51, 54, 147–56. *See also* domestic work

neoliberalism, 1–12, 17–56, 60, 72, 97, 99, 106, 154, 169, 182, 188, 191, 205–15, 218nn1,2; affective dimensions of, 3, 8, 57–58, 95, 135, 169, 177, 189, 200, 209; entrepreneurialism and, 2, 4, 17–20, 24, 48t, 50, 55, 57, 58, 84, 93–94, 99, 102, 111, 131–68, 194, 200, 208; ethic of, 181, 200; flexibility discourses of, 1–4, 9–10, 18–20, 31–33, 48t, 50, 53, 57, 85, 103, 107, 129, 150, 152, 154, 162, 176, 194, 203, 208–10, 214, 218n3; gendered aspects of, 58, 78–82; religion and, 189–205; selfhood and, 1, 94, 135, 191, 192, 232n4; transformations wrought from, 9–12, 17–18, 28–35, 58, 107, 128–29, 144, 155, 166, 167, 171–72, 176, 188, 208

obeah, 84, 86, 184, 224n20, 232n2

obesity, 66, 173

occupational multiplicity, 23, 172, 178, 183, 210

offshore industry, 28, 31, 230n3

Ong, Aihwa, 19, 21

outside women, 64, 122, 126, 127

panic attacks, 178, 183, 185, 201. *See also* counseling; stress; therapy

parenting, 6, 8, 31–33, 58, 63, 72–79, 84, 87, 92, 113, 116–19, 128, 142–48, 157–69, 175–76, 185, 189–97, 203–5, 210–11. *See also* fathers; mothers

partnerships: in business, 14, 28, 74, 77, 111, 148, 161, 197; intimate aspects of, 50, 53, 61, 64–78, 81–82, 91, 94–95, 108, 111, 119, 126, 128, 137, 177, 196, 205; marriage as, 48t, 57–95, 58t, 107, 108, 196, 211, 221n6

pastoral care, 183, 189, 193

pastors, 50, 153, 177, 180, 181, 184, 185, 186, 190, 192, 194, 195, 196, 198, 199, 202

patriarchy, 21, 50, 53, 70, 98, 126, 129, 227n15

personality market, 136

pink collar sector, 46

plantation economy, 8, 23, 34, 42–44, 49, 62, 95, 128, 136, 139, 148, 172, 211

plantation slavery, 6, 11, 23, 25, 42, 44, 46, 86, 87, 98, 101, 105, 139, 140, 172, 225n3

Polgreen, Rachel Pringle, 25, 26f

political economy, 17, 42, 47, 84, 139, 144, 185, 207–8, 210

prosperity churches, 169, 194

psychological services, 184, 185, 200, 201. *See also* counseling; therapy

public sphere, 75f, 77, 92, 106, 203, 211. *See also* social life

quality time, 48t, 71, 75f, 77, 79, 119, 126, 153, 157–58, 160–61

Queens College, 53, 228n21

race, 2, 15, 30, 38, 114, 148, 194–95, 214; in Caribbean, 12–13, 24–27, 35, 41–44, 55, 62, 99–106, 109; and class, 24–26, 34–35, 40–41, 46–49, 110, 115–23, 219n20; and health, 177–78. *See also* Afro-Caribbean; white Barbadians

reflexivity, 4, 6, 30, 143, 193, 204, 205, 214

religion, 30, 63, 169–205, 226n8, 227n18, 232nn4,5; in Caribbean, 42, 84, 86, 97–98, 184, 191–93, 198–99, 224n20,

Made in the USA
Middletown, DE
17 November 2023